Common Innovation

Common Innovation

How We Create the Wealth of Nations

G.M. Peter Swann

Emeritus Professor of Industrial Economics,
Nottingham University Business School, UK

Edward Elgar
Cheltenham, UK • Northampton, MA, USA

Published by
Edward Elgar Publishing Limited
The Lypiatts
15 Lansdown Road
Cheltenham
Glos GL50 2JA
UK

Edward Elgar Publishing, Inc.
William Pratt House
9 Dewey Court
Northampton
Massachusetts 01060
USA

Paperback edition 2016

A catalogue record for this book is available from the British Library

Library of Congress Control Number: 2014950740

This book is available electronically in the **Elgar**online
Economics Subject Collection
DOI 10.4337/9781784714611

ISBN   978 1 84720 050 1 (cased)
         978 1 78643 082 3 (paperback)
         978 1 78471 461 1 (eBook)

Printed and bound in Great Britain by T.J. International Ltd, Padstow

Contents

Figures

Tables

Preface

Those innovations that attract widespread public attention are usually the *aristocracy* of innovation. Some leading examples are these: the Ferrari 458 *Italia*, the Apple *iPad* and the Dyson *Dual Cyclone™*. These stand as a beacon for innovators, showing them how to innovate for business success and for consumer enthusiasm. This aristocracy is usually treated with great reverence. For example, Barthes (1957) wrote of the Citröen *DS*:

> I think that cars today are almost the exact equivalent of the great Gothic cathedrals: I mean the supreme creation of an era, conceived with passion by unknown artists, and consumed in image if not in usage by a whole population which appropriates them as a purely magical object. It is obvious that the new Citröen has fallen from the sky inasmuch as it appears at first sight as a superlative object ...

Those economists who study innovation, however, are also interested in a large number of more modest innovations. These do not usually attract much public attention, but they often play an important role in ensuring the profitability and survival of the innovators and often, though not invariably, in satisfying a large number of customers. The majority of these innovations are made by business, and hence they are usually called *business* innovations. (In some cases, the term, *professional* innovation would be more appropriate, as it encompasses innovation by other organisations and the public sector.)

In this book, however, we are concerned with something more modest still. These are the humble innovations made by individuals, households, clubs and local communities. They are not aristocrats of innovation, nor are they comparable to innovations by business or other professional organisations. I shall call these, *common innovation*. I use the word 'common' here in the same sense as a naturalist might talk of a common flower: it grows everywhere; it is unexceptional, non-proprietary, inexpensive and modest.

Three simple examples illustrate common innovation. The first is depicted on the front cover of this book: building sandcastles has been an essential element of seaside holidays for many generations of children. The second is found in the kitchen: the innovative cook creates a special meal from ordinary ingredients. The third, on a larger scale, is where a community finds a new use for an old industrial site, and thereby creates a valuable amenity. Individually, these examples may seem trivial, but when taken together, they do much to enhance the welfare of family and community.

A typical view amongst business people is that common innovation is simply not an issue for economics. They concede that common innovation may be important for the family and the local community, but they argue that because it happens outside companies, organisations and markets, it plays no role in wealth creation. I believe that argument is plainly wrong.

Any economists familiar with the household production theory of Becker (1965) will recognise that if household production lies within the domain of economics, then so too does common innovation. Put simply, common innovation alters the household production function or the community production function – as the above examples show. Nonetheless, while economists may concede this point, a typical reaction is that common innovation is of minor importance when compared to business innovation. I am not convinced of that. This may be the perspective of people who receive a high salary, and for whom consumption and leisure are expensive activities. But it is not the perspective of those with more modest incomes, who need to use their own intellectual and practical resources to ensure that consumption and leisure are *not* expensive activities. In the same way, the importance of common innovation will vary over the business cycle.

In this book, we shall encounter other reasons why common innovation is likely to grow in importance. Four are worthy of mention here. First, as the distribution of income and material wealth becomes ever more uneven, common innovation will be essential to ever more people. Second, as the focus of business innovation becomes ever more remote from the needs of citizens, common innovation will seem ever more relevant to these citizens. Third, while business innovation remains a 'perennial gale of creative destruction', as Schumpeter (1942) described it, common innovation is, by comparison, a 'gentle and benign breeze'. That sounds like a far more appropriate pattern for sustainable innovation in a finite world. Finally, and most of all, common innovation will become an important counter-balance to the ever increasing power of business innovation, in a world where business was once the *servant* of society, but is now firmly the *master*.

This book draws on work over forty years, and I cannot list all intellectual influences. This book draws in particular on the pioneering work of Eric von Hippel. I am grateful to Hans-Jürgen Engelbrecht and Rui Baptista for very useful comments, which have helped to clarify various parts of the manuscript, but neither is responsible for any errors or idiosyncrasies. I would also like to give warm thanks to colleagues at the University of Nottingham for their support. Above all, my greatest thanks are to my wife, Jenny Swann, for all her encouragement.

PART I

Introduction, Concepts and Frameworks

1. Introduction

> Therefore, to every spirit which Christianity summons to her service, her exhortation is: Do what you can, and confess frankly what you are unable to do; neither let your effort be shortened for fear of failure, nor your confession silenced for fear of shame. And it is, perhaps, the principal admirableness of the Gothic schools of architecture, that they thus receive the results of the labour of inferior minds; and out of fragments full of imperfection, and betraying that imperfection in every touch, indulgently raise up a stately and unaccusable whole.
>
> John Ruskin[1]

This book is concerned with what I shall call *common* innovation. This is not a term in general use, but I think it *should* be, because the concept deserves far more attention from economists and others who study the impact of innovation on the economy.

Common innovation is carried out by 'the common man and woman' for their own benefit. It takes place *quite outside* the domain of business, the professions or government. It could, indeed, be described as *non-business* innovation, to emphasise its essential difference from business innovation. It could also be called *vernacular*, as it is not intended for commercial use,[2] but for the benefit of the innovators and their community.

As such, the concept of common innovation is somewhat unfamiliar to the academic discipline of economics. For the most part, economists who study innovation actually study *business* innovation. And, even more so, common innovation is distinctly 'foreign' to *business itself* – to the extent that some in business, at least, deny there is any such thing as common innovation.

Business innovation and common innovation are fundamentally different. The first is a professional activity carried out by specialists in the business sector. It is often expensive because it involves making unusual, and sometimes exceptional, advances. By contrast, common innovation is non-professional and is carried out by 'the common man and woman' outside business. It often involves quite ordinary and unexceptional activity.

RELATIONSHIP TO OTHER CATEGORIES

I said above that the term, *common innovation*, is not in general use. As there are already so many adjectives added to the noun 'innovation', it is appropriate that we should justify the addition of another adjective.

How does common innovation compare with some other important categories of innovation well known in the literature? The closest are von Hippel's (2005) concepts of *democratic* innovation and *user-centred* innovation. The work in this book builds on these very important concepts, but, arguably, goes one step further. Von Hippel (2005) describes innovation that is designed by the user, and not just by the supplier. Nevertheless, much of what he considers is still *business* innovation, though some of it – especially the more recent work – would count as common innovation.[3] Common innovation also describes innovation that is designed by the user, or by a wide variety of others outside business – but the essential point is that these common innovations are *not* business innovation. Common innovation shares the democratic character of the innovations considered by von Hippel, but the common innovators remove business from the innovation process, or at least, consign it to a marginal role. So while von Hippel's concepts of *democratic* innovation and *user-centred* innovation are obviously quite close to my concept of common innovation, they are not quite the same.

And what of other innovation adjectives that are well known to scholars in the field? Common innovation shares something with Stoneman's (2010) concept of *soft* innovation, in that it examines innovation in areas of activity that were not traditionally considered to be very innovative. Common innovation also overlaps, to some extent, with Chesborough's (2003) concept of *open* innovation. Innovation activities in common innovation are often open, rather than closed. Common innovation is typically 'local', and therefore it also overlaps with the concept of *localised* technological change, discussed by Atkinson and Stiglitz (1969) and developed by Antonelli (1995, 2008). It also overlaps with the popular concept of *frugal* innovation,[4] and again it has a substantial overlap with *social* innovation, which is concerned with those innovations that meet social needs and in doing so help to strengthen society.[5]

The choice of the word 'common' might suggest that common innovation overlaps with the idea of *collective* innovation (Allen, 1983) and that is indeed possible. However, the sense in which we use the word common is different: we are talking of innovation that is frequent, pervasive, non-professional, unexceptional and modest. Certainly, some common innovation activity is *collective*, and it is generally open, non-proprietary and non-rival. But much common innovation is *not* collective.

In short, while *common* innovation may overlap to some extent with all of these other categories of innovation, it is not the same as any of them. Common innovation refers to innovative activities of ordinary people in their everyday life – quite apart from the activities of innovation professionals in the business world. The concept of *common* innovation is *not* made redundant by other innovation adjectives.

ECONOMICS AND COMMON INNOVATION

What do economists have to say about common innovation? The short answer to this question is, 'not very much' – or not yet, anyway. Why not? After all, a standard definition of innovation is this: the successful exploitation of new ideas.[6] And that is a perfectly good definition for common innovation as well as business innovation. Nevertheless, most economists tend to be concerned with various types of business innovation and apply this definition in that context. Moreover, most economists follow the Schumpeterian convention: a new idea is *invention* before it is commercially exploited. It only becomes *innovation* when it is commercially exploited.

In view of that, some might say that common innovation, as I call it, *cannot be innovation* because it does not involve *commercial* exploitation. But I think that is just wrong. Common innovation, which successfully exploits new ideas, also deserves the term *innovation* because it contributes to wealth creation, just as business innovation contributes to wealth creation.

There are three main areas in which common innovation is discussed in economics though not by that name. The first is in the context of household production theory (Becker 1965). Becker's theory sees the household as a production unit. Just as a business innovation may enhance the productivity of a production unit in business, so a common innovation can enhance the productivity of the household production unit. The second is in some of the work of von Hippel's (2005) on democratic innovation. His work has been uniquely important in getting us past the idea that innovation is (and should be) monopolised by business, but as I said above, it is slightly different. The third is the area of social innovation. Much work on social innovation originated outside economics, but it has been embraced by the economics discipline too – see Moulaert et al. (2013) and Mulgan (2007) for summaries.

AS IMPORTANT AS BUSINESS INNOVATION?

One explanation for the relatively small literature on common innovation could be that it is of secondary importance compared to business innovation. I am certainly not convinced of that. I believe that common innovation as a whole could in some contexts be as important as, or even more important than business innovation. This has to remain a conjecture at this stage as we simply don't have the evidence on wealth creation by common innovation.

How could this be true? Suppose that innovations of economic size x are found with frequency $f(x)$. By economic size, I mean the overall contribution of that innovation to wealth creation. Now suppose, for simplicity, that $f(x)$ follows a power law:

$$f(x) = ax^{-k} \tag{1.1}$$

(where $k \geq 0$). Then the total value of innovations of value x is:

$$v(x) = xf(x) = ax^{1-k} \tag{1.2}$$

From this it is clear that:

If $k > 1$, then $v(x)$ is a decreasing function of x
If $k < 1$, then $v(x)$ is an increasing function of x
If $k = 1$, then $v(x)$ is constant, regardless of x

Crudely speaking, then, we can compare the contributions made by common and business innovation to wealth creation:

If $k > 1$, then common innovation is more important
If $k = 1$, then they are equally important
If $k < 1$, then business innovation is more important

It seems probable that in some economies and some particular economic circumstances, k would indeed be above 1. This would mean that common innovation as a whole could be even more important than business innovation.

We should add that it would be most unlikely that the function $f(.)$ is constant, and independent of economic circumstances. In particular, it seems very likely that, in a recession, demand for many large-scale commercial innovations will decline. But some people, at least, will attempt to support their standard of living by a higher level of common innovation. In the language of Equation (1.1), it means this: k may be less than 1 in normal economic circumstances, but there is good reason to expect k to increase in a recession. I shall revisit this last idea in Part IV of the book. In particular, I think there are good reasons to expect that the austerity policies adopted by many governments will indeed lead to an increase in common innovation.

STRUCTURE OF THE BOOK

In the rest of this chapter, I shall give a brief sketch of how the book is organised. I start with a one-paragraph summary of the book as a whole. It is in four Parts. Part I is concerned with some of the key concepts and frameworks that are needed to understand the different roles of business innovation and common innovation. In Part II, we revisit the Schumpeterian idea of business innovation as *creative destruction*; we examine seven brief case studies of business innovation and in particular the 'destructive' side of these. In Part III we give a brief introduction to some examples of common innovation, especially as they relate to consumption, the arts, science, education, health, the natural environment and the socio-economic environment. Part IV concludes by answering the 'so what?' question. We explain why common innovation is already important and may become ever more important in future.

The reader may also find it helpful if I give a slightly longer summary of each part of the book. In Chapters 2, 3 and 4, we explain three essential distinctions which play a large part in what follows. The first is the difference between what I shall call M-wealth and R-wealth. (Roughly speaking, this is the difference between material wealth and welfare). The second is the distinction between business innovation and common innovation. And the third is the difference between *oikonomia* (the ancient Greek word from which economy is derived) and the modern concept of the economy.

Then, in Chapter 5, we turn to an essential point that is well understood by economists but is often overlooked in business and policy circles. It is not straightforward to assess the value of a business innovation or its contribution to wealth. The value to the innovator, the value to the user and the value to society as a whole are three rather different calculations and need bear little relationship to each other.

In Chapter 6 we describe the frameworks we shall use to analyse the role of innovation in wealth creation. To understand the role of business innovation in creating M-wealth requires a relatively simply framework. But to understand the role of common innovation in creating R-wealth, we need a more complex framework.

Part II contains a series of seven brief case studies which illustrate some of the destructive side-effects of innovation. These are a fairly random selection, chosen for interest and not as a carefully structured sample to represent the population as a whole. But all of them, in their different ways, illustrate that the destructive side of business innovation is for real, and can be devastating. Two are historical examples: Chapter 7 on wide frames and the Luddites, and Chapter 8 on the division of labour. The rest are contemporary: Chapter 9 is about online and local booksellers, Chapter 10 concerns software innovation and e-waste, and Chapter 11 examines what we call, Parkinson's Law of traffic. Chapter 12 examines how innovation may damage the consumer as a person and Chapter 13 examines the destructive side of a particular financial innovation (high frequency trading). To help the reader form a concise overview, Chapter 14 offers a brief summary of the destructive effects found in these cases.

Part III follows on from the discussion in Chapter 3. There we argued that if business innovation is a 'perennial gale of creative destruction', then common innovation is usually closer to a 'gentle and benign breeze'. Part III describes some examples of how common innovation can create R-wealth by its effects on: consumption and the home (16), the natural environment (17), the socio-economic environment (18), education (19), arts (20), sciences (21) and health (22). Then in Chapter 23, we look at some of the innovation activities in business and the marketplace that are closer to common innovation than business innovation. We also see that common innovation and business innovation can sometimes act in an informal joint venture – but only if business innovators keep the good will of their consumers, their employees and the citizens in neighbourhoods where they operate.

Finally, in Part IV, we summarise the implications of common innovation and advance several hypotheses which suggest that common innovation may become more important in the future.

The first two chapters spell out some important implications. In Chapter 24, one implication is that some common assertions about business, innovation and wealth creation are really just myths. Our analysis implies that business has no monopoly of wealth creation, nor a monopoly of useful innovation. It also implies that it would be quite wrong to assume that M-wealth is more important than R-wealth. In Chapter 25, we discuss a second implication: that there are many paths to R-wealth creation and business is not necessarily the main channel to R-wealth creation.

The final chapter (26) states some hypotheses about C-innovation, and why it may become more important in future. We note that that standard methods of national accounting cannot capture the role of common innovation in wealth creation, and we suggest how such a role might be measured in future. We suggest that C-innovation is better suited than B-innovation to the pressing need for sustainability in a finite world. And we conclude that C-innovation is likely to become *more* important in future, that B-innovation may become *less* important in future, and C-innovation may become an important counter-balance to business innovation in a world where business was once, perhaps, the servant of society, but is now firmly the master.

NOTES

[1] Ruskin (1904/1996, vol. 10, p. 190).

[2] Ilich (1982) made some essential observations about the social role of the vernacular.

[3] After this manuscript was finished and the book was in production, Rui Baptista drew my attention to some recent work by von Hippel and colleagues on *patient innovation* (see Stock et al., 2013). This is undoubtedly a powerful example of common innovation, as I use that term, in the particular context of health care.

[4] See Guardian (2012a) and Radjou et al. (2012).

[5] See Moulaert et al. (2013) and Mulgan (2007).

[6] A popular definition, used in the UK, is the 'DTI Definition of innovation' – after the government department (formerly DTI, now BIS) responsible for promoting innovation. This can be summarised thus: 'the successful exploitation of new ideas'. On the face of it, this does not limit attention to commercial exploitation, but as a government department for business and industry, it is unsurprising that their main focus is on business innovation.

2. M-Wealth and R-Wealth

The sub-title of this book is 'how *we* create the wealth of nations'. We are concerned, above all, with how innovation creates wealth for the nation. To understand the arguments in this book, the reader needs to understand the distinction between two concepts of wealth. For the sake of brevity, we shall refer to these as M-wealth and R-wealth. Some of the ideas that follow were developed in a very introductory way in Swann (2009a, Chapter 19), and some readers may find it helpful to read that before embarking on this book.

ETYMOLOGY OF WEALTH

The reader may be surprised that we start with a brief excursion into etymology. But this is very helpful to understand the distinction we make in this chapter.

The modern English word, *wealth*, derives from the Old English words *weal* or *wela*.[1] But today, there is a difference between *wealth* and *weal*. The older words were most commonly used to describe welfare, well-being, happiness and prosperity, rather than material wealth – although the expression, *worldly weal*,[2] was sometimes used to describe an abundance of riches and possessions.

The new word grew out of the Middle English words *welth* or *welthe*.[3] Originally it was used in both senses: welfare and riches. But gradually, the new word *wealth* was used to mean the second sense: material wealth, an abundance of possessions, 'worldly goods', riches and affluence. The use of the word *wealth* to describe welfare became less common. Indeed, in literature, some authors revived the word *weal* to describe welfare, well-being, happiness and prosperity.

In what follows, M-wealth refers to the modern sense of *wealth*, while R-wealth refers to the old sense of *weal*.

RUSKIN AND J.S. MILL

An even easier way to grasp this distinction is offered by the ideas of John

Ruskin. Again, it may surprise the reader that I refer to this source. Most economists think of Ruskin as a critic and historian of art – if, indeed, they think of him at all! But Ruskin himself claimed that his critique of political economy, *Unto this Last* (Ruskin, 1904/1996, vol. 17), was his greatest work, and with hindsight he was probably right. The paradox about Ruskin is that although his thinking underpins the twentieth century welfare state, and his thinking about environmental matters was equally prophetic, his work is little known and rarely read by modern economists.

In the *Principles of Political Economy*, J.S. Mill (1848/1923, p.1) had asserted:

> Every one has a notion, sufficiently correct for common purposes, of what is meant by wealth.

Many economists would probably agree with that. But Ruskin took exception to this apparently innocuous claim:[4]

> There is not one person in ten thousand who has a notion sufficiently correct, even for the commonest purposes, of 'what is meant' by wealth; still less of what wealth everlastingly is.

Ruskin developed a critical distinction between what he called mercantile wealth and real wealth. This is essentially the same distinction that we make between M-wealth (mercantile or material) and R-wealth (real wealth or Ruskin wealth).

If Mill had said, 'Every one has a notion, sufficiently correct for common purposes, of what is meant by *mercantile* wealth', then Ruskin would probably not have disagreed. But Ruskin was determined to establish that true wealth means much more than mercantile wealth alone. I share that determination and that is why I insist on talking about 'R-wealth'.

Mercantile wealth is made up of the valuable items traded by merchants and bought by consumers. Ruskin argued that all items of mercantile wealth had 'intrinsic value', or a 'life-giving power'. But to Ruskin, possession of mercantile wealth was no guarantee of real wealth. In his terms, this intrinsic value is only translated into 'effectual value' (real or Ruskin wealth) if there is 'acceptant capacity' (the capacity to use it):[5]

> Where the intrinsic value and acceptant capacity come together there is Effectual value, or wealth; where there is either no intrinsic value, or no acceptant capacity, there is no effectual value; that is to say, no wealth. A horse is no wealth to us if we cannot ride, nor a picture if we cannot see ....

From this Ruskin drew out one of his key assertions:[6]

Wealth, therefore, is the possession of the valuable by the valiant.

Ruskin distilled this into his most memorable and justly famous maxim:[7]

There is no wealth but life.

This book is about wealth in this sense. Hereafter, we shall use the abbreviations, M-wealth and R-wealth.[8] The letter 'M' reminds us that this was the sense of wealth discussed by Mill, and that it is money, material and mercantile wealth. In contrast, the letter 'R' reminds us that this was the sense of wealth discussed by Ruskin, and that it is something real as opposed to monetary. We can also think of M-wealth as the *means* and R-wealth as the *result*.

With this dual focus, it makes no sense to ignore the role of common innovation in wealth creation. If our focus were just on M-wealth, then it would be understandable perhaps if we were primarily concerned with business innovation. But when we also consider R-wealth, then we find that common innovation plays an essential role.

WHY NOT USE THE WORD 'HAPPINESS'?

Some readers may be wondering why I do not simply use the word 'happiness' instead of the more cumbersome, R-wealth. After all, since the work of Easterlin (1973, 1995), and others, research into the connection (or lack of connection) between M-wealth and happiness has become an important part of the research agenda in economics.

There are two reasons why I prefer to use the term R-wealth. The first is simple: there is so much more to R-wealth than happiness alone. Ruskin's maxim, 'no wealth but life' indicates that what he has in mind is much closer to Aristotle's concept of εὐδαιμονία (*eudaimonia*). Although this is sometimes translated as 'happiness', there is general agreement that is not an adequate term.[9] *Eudaimonia* refers to the highest human good, or: 'the good composed of all goods'.[10] It refers to happiness, certainly, but also living well and virtuously, individual development, flourishing as a person, achieving fulfilment of our potential, and having sufficient resources to achieve these human goods.

The second reason is that I want to reclaim the word 'wealth' and the term 'wealth creation' from the monopoly of business. If we only allow the word wealth to mean 'M-wealth', and if the only form of wealth creation we acknowledge is M-wealth creation, then business appears to hold a monopoly. Business has not been slow to exploit that monopoly and to lobby politicians to place business interests above most other interests in society. That is unhealthy. By accepting the term R-wealth we remove that monopoly, and we give due recognition to the role other parts of society play in the creation of R-wealth. It is essential that we do that.

In focussing on R-wealth, indeed, I am taking a similar route to Sen (1999), and Nussbaum and Sen (1993), who developed the 'capabilities approach' to development. By capabilities, they mean 'substantial freedoms', such as life expectancy and political freedom. From this perspective, development is defined as an abundance of capabilities, while poverty is defined as the deprivation of capabilities. This is clearly different from a traditional economic perspective that defines development by economic growth, and poverty by the deprivation of income.[11]

SHOULD ECONOMICS STUDY R-WEALTH?

Some critics have suggested that economics should really limit itself to the analysis of M-wealth, because many of the factors that contribute to the creation of R-wealth lie outside the boundaries of economics.

I don't agree with this argument. As we have already seen, the analysis of *happiness*, and in particular, the question of whether growth increases happiness, is now a widely recognised field within economics.[12] Happiness is not the same as R-wealth, but what they have in common is that they are both attempts to go beyond M-wealth alone and consider the effects of that M-wealth on the human condition. Many of the factors that contribute to the creation of happiness lie outside the boundaries of economics, but this has not stopped the analysis of happiness from becoming an accepted branch of economics. In the same way, the fact that many of the factors contributing to the R-wealth lie outside economics is no reason for excluding R-wealth from economics.

Some critics have suggested another reason why R-wealth is not a proper subject of study for economists. I paraphrase their objection as follows: 'Surely I accept that we cannot measure R-wealth? And if we can't measure it, then what is the point of studying it?' True, we can't measure R-wealth now – but we can describe it. And description is usually an essential step on the path to measurement. As to the second question, 'what is the point of studying it', part of the answer is, 'so that we can measure it at some point in the future!'

In my view, indeed, these objections betray a hopeless attitude to economic research, because they lead to the principle that what cannot be measured properly should be omitted from analysis. But we know perfectly well this can lead to all kinds of problems with omitted variable bias. And if we don't start to analyse a concept, but ignore it because we have no measure for it, then we shall never develop a measure for it. We have to start somewhere! Granted, Lord Kelvin was probably right when he said:[13]

> I often say that when you can measure what you are speaking about, and express it in numbers, you know something about it; but when you cannot measure it, when you cannot express it in numbers, your knowledge is meagre and of unsatisfactory kind; it may be the beginning of knowledge, but you have scarcely in your thoughts advanced to the stage of science, whatever the matter may be.

But the reaction to that should *definitely not* be, 'we have no decent measures in this field, so let's study something else instead'. That may be a pragmatic approach for a PhD student, but it is a hopeless attitude for a senior academic. The right response to Kelvin's observation is this: we may not have advanced very far yet along this path, but let's try to advance a little further, because it is important to do so.

NOTES

[1] *Oxford English Dictionary* (2013).
[2] *Oxford English Dictionary* (2013).
[3] *Oxford English Dictionary* (2013).
[4] Ruskin (1904/1996, vol. 17, pp. 131–2).
[5] Ruskin (1904/1996, vol. 17, p. 154). Another good example would be if a rich but non-musical collector lends his Stradivarius violin to an outstanding violinist. Aggregate M-wealth may be unchanged by this transfer, but R-wealth is much increased.
[6] Ruskin (1904/1996, vol. 17, p. 88).
[7] Ruskin (1904/1996, vol. 17, p. 105).
[8] Swann (2001b) discusses Ruskin's concept of wealth in some detail.
[9] For example, Nussbaum (1986, pp. 1–6).
[10] Wikipedia (2013c). In several of the innovation examples that follow, I have made use of Wikipedia entries as a very useful and up-to-date reference on the specific innovation. Not so long ago, many academics would be reluctant to admit that they used Wikipedia: it would be considered a sign of shallow research unworthy of a proper scholar. Today, happily, attitudes have changed, and academics researching the most recent economic events see Wikipedia for what it is: a valuable, easily accessible and very up-to-date source, which is sometimes of uneven quality, but is almost always a very useful starting point. Indeed, this change of attitudes is proof of the sheer power of 'crowd-sourced' social innovations such as Wikipedia.
[11] See also Chick (2013).
[12] Easterlin (1973, 1995), Scitovsky (1976), Layard (2005).
[13] Here quoted from the *Oxford Dictionary of Phrase, Saying and Quotation* (1997, p. 377).

3. B-Innovation and C-Innovation

This chapter compares common innovation (*C-innovation*) to business innovation (*B-innovation*). We shall see that one important difference between the two types of innovation is the objective of the innovator in each case. In business innovation, there may be a separation between those who devise the innovations and those who are the ultimate users. Business innovators are concerned with the performance of their business, and only indirectly concerned with the welfare of those who use the innovations. In short, the interests of the innovator and the interests of the user are not the same. In common innovation, on the other hand, that separation is much less pronounced, and often the users and the innovators are the same people. In that latter case, the interests of the innovator and the user are naturally the same.

And there is another important difference between business innovation and common innovation. If the former can be described as Schumpeter's 'perennial gale of creative destruction', the latter is usually much more like a 'gentle and benign breeze'. Indeed, we shall see in Part II of the book, that some business innovations have substantial 'destructive' power which can cause dysfunctional side-effects. This happens because the innovator accounts for the benefits to his business, but does not account for the damage done to other interests. In Part III of the book, we study common innovation, and there such destructive power is unusual. The interests of the innovator and the user are close, and the innovator is unlikely to pursue projects that are against the interests of the user.

The first two sections below describe business innovation and common innovation, while the third section reflects on the implications of our new perspective for government policy towards innovation. Then we re-examine Schumpeter's concept of 'the perennial gale of creative destruction'. In the light of that, we propose a two-dimensional scale for describing creative destruction, and we consider two illustrative examples of the application of this scale. We conclude by asserting that economics must not ignore C-innovation.

BUSINESS INNOVATION

Business innovation describes those innovations undertaken by companies to increase their profits or revenues, their market share or some other strategic goal. Although business innovation in the round is undoubtedly an important contributor to M-wealth creation, and although business people are in the habit of calling themselves 'wealth creators', we need to be clear that maximising the M-wealth of the economy, as such, is not the explicit goal of business innovation.

Am I 'splitting hairs' here? No I am not. As we show in detail in Chapter 5, some business innovators are very successful at increasing revenues and profits by 'grabbing' business from a rival. They do this by offering a slightly cheaper or slightly better product or service than the rival, or, more generally, a product or service that is slightly better value for money. In doing so, the innovators make a small increase in the M-wealth of the economy, but that effect may be small compared to the large increase in the innovator's revenues and profits.

Indeed, the 'paradox' is that the business innovations that do most to increase profits and revenues may be relatively minor innovations from a technological or innovation point of view. For the business aiming to increase profits or revenues will often seek out well developed markets and 'grab' some of that business, rather than face the challenge of building a market for more radical innovations. By contrast, the business that pursues a radical innovation may make a greater contribution to national M-wealth creation, but may not enjoy such profits or revenues because the market for that radical innovation does not exist and has to be created. Once again, the reader is referred to Chapter 5 for more detail.

Although I described this difference as a 'paradox', it can be interpreted as an example of a well known idea in the economics of innovation. When we analyse the market failures caused by externalities, there is a clear difference between the implications of positive externalities and the implications of negative externalities. In the first case, there is underinvestment in innovation, because some socially profitable innovations are not privately profitable for the innovator. By contrast, in the second case, there is overinvestment in innovation, because some privately profitable innovations are not socially profitable. Radical innovations that occupy a part of product space that is currently empty will typically create positive externalities to followers. But minor innovations that grab market share from rivals in a densely populated product space will typically create negative externalities.

And this offers a (partial) explanation of the 'paradox'. There is under-investment in radical innovations because some are privately unprofitable even when socially profitable. And there is over-investment in minor innovations because some are privately profitable, even when they are socially unprofitable.

As the reader will know, the literature on the economics of innovation recognises many species of innovation: product innovations, service innovations, process innovations, organisational innovations, marketing innovations, architectural innovations, and so on. The differences between these are economically important in many contexts.

In the present setting, however, these considerations are secondary. The distinction between business innovation and common innovation remains broadly the same, regardless of the species of innovation we are looking at. We shall see that in Parts II and III, where we consider examples of several species of innovation in the two different contexts: business innovation and common innovation.

COMMON INNOVATION

As described in the Preface, we use the word common here in the same sense as a naturalist might talk of the 'common flower'. That is, common innovation is widespread, ordinary, unexceptional, vernacular, usually non-proprietary, inexpensive, dispersed and modest. This is in clear distinction to business innovation, which is less widespread, often exceptional, professional, often proprietary, expensive, concentrated and less modest.

Moreover, in contrast to business innovation, common innovation is generally directed explicitly at R-wealth creation. In common innovation, innovators and users are close together, and not separated by a market. Indeed, the users and the innovators are often the same people, and when that is the case, the interests of the innovator and the user are naturally the same. This is in clear contrast to business innovation, where the interests of the innovator and the interests of the user are simply not the same.

The simplest possible example of common innovation illustrates the point. Consider an innovation affecting the household production function: for example, this could be the household cook's new recipe for creating a good meal from simple and cheap ingredients. The explicit and direct objective here is creating R-wealth for the family. Or, alternatively, consider the example of a community that devises an environmental innovation to turn a derelict site into a community resource. Once again, this can be seen as an innovation in a 'community production function', and here again, the explicit and direct objective here is to create R-wealth for the community.

In summary, with business innovation, the innovator and the user are not close together, and their interests are not close either. For that reason, the link from business innovation to M-wealth creation for the user is not a simple and direct one. By contrast, with common innovation, the innovator and the user are very close together, and their interests are very close too. For that reason, the link from common innovation to R-wealth creation is simple and direct.[1]

Does this last fact mean that common innovation is more efficient at creating R-wealth for the user? It is tempting to give a simple answer, 'yes', but in reality the answer is not necessarily so simple.

Simple considerations might suggest that if you wish to devise innovations to maximise some social objective, it is best to give the innovation task to those whose own objectives are as close as possible to the social objective. This proposition has something in common with Hayek's (1945) argument that professional knowledge is not the only knowledge of value, but there is also a large body of 'very important but unorganized knowledge' – which could be called the local knowledge 'of time and place'. Indeed, Hayek considered that almost everyone, 'possesses unique information of which beneficial use might be made' (Hayek, 1945, p. 521). Hayek put these observations at the centre of his thesis that decentralisation is superior to central planning, because local economic efficiency requires the use of specific local knowledge which in not known by a central planner. But we could also use these observations to argue that, in the absence of strong economies of scale, localized innovation is a superior route to wealth creation (whether M-wealth or R-wealth) than centralized innovation.

However, Kay's (2010) general theory of obliquity is relevant here. He argues that many goals are more likely to be achieved when pursued indirectly. For example, Kay argues that the most profitable companies are not the most aggressive in chasing profits. As Kay explains, this argument is especially relevant when we are analysing complex evolving systems:[2]

> Obliquity is the best approach whenever complex systems evolve in an uncertain environment and whenever the effect of our actions depends on the ways in which others respond to them. There is a role for carrots and sticks, but to rely on carrots and sticks alone is effective only when we employ donkeys and we are sure exactly what we want the donkeys to do. Directness is appropriate when the environment is stable, and objectives are one-dimensional and transparent, and it is then possible to determine when and whether goals have been achieved. And only then.

The penultimate sentence of the above quotation tells us why directness may be quite satisfactory in the most common innovation of all: common innovation in the household. For many lucky people in the UK, at least, the household is a stable environment, objectives are of limited dimension (if not exactly one-dimensional) and usually transparent, and it is usually possible to determine if the family members have done the tasks set for them.

GOVERNMENT POLICY TOWARDS INNOVATION

Government policy towards innovation is not a central concern of this book, though it arises as an issue in some chapters. But I mention it here, because the various analytical frameworks introduced in Chapter 6 offer some very interesting insights into how policy should be designed.

Innovation policies are often rationalised as promoting business innovation to create M-wealth. For two reasons, I don't think that is the right focus. Firstly, I agree with the sentiments of Sir Keith Joseph,[3] who doubted that it made sense to tax ordinary people to pay business to do what business would have done anyway. Rather, the role of policy is to get things to happen that *wouldn't* otherwise happen. What does that mean in practice? Here we have a different answer according to our school of economics. The neoclassical and mainstream view is that policy innovations are driven by a desire to correct market failures. The standard evolutionary view is that policy innovations are driven by a desire to correct system failures or system weaknesses. Rodrik (2004) argues that policy innovations should emerge from an iterative process where business and government identify newly emerging market failures and system failures, and devise policies to adjust for these.

Secondly, I don't think that business and M-wealth should be the sole focus of policy. Often, policy needs to focus instead on the creation of R-wealth through the application of common innovation. Indeed, I believe that there are just as many system failures that get in the way of creating R-wealth, and policy needs to be directed at these. Once again, the aim should be to make things happen that wouldn't otherwise happen, but in this case, to develop and disseminate our capacity for common innovation, and our ability to make R-wealth from M-wealth. As we shall see in the analytical frameworks of Chapter 6, policy directed at R-wealth and common innovation operates through quite different channels from policy directed at M-wealth and business innovation, and is usually quite different in character.

A PERENNIAL GALE OF CREATIVE DESTRUCTION

Explicit objectives are not the only distinction between business innovation and common innovation. There is another very important difference. As all students of the economics of innovation know, Joseph Schumpeter (1942) likened innovation to a 'perennial gale of creative destruction'. But that metaphor certainly does not describe common innovation; a better metaphor would be a, 'gentle and benign breeze of creativity'.

Schumpeter was not the first to use this concept. Although Marx did not use the expression 'creative destruction', as such, it is implicit in Marx's analysis of the accumulation and destruction of wealth in capitalism (Marx and Engels, 1848; Marx, 1857). Reinert and Reinert (2006) argue that the concept entered the social sciences through the work of Nietzsche and Werner Sombart. Indeed, even if he did not articulate a concept of 'creative destruction', Adam Smith clearly saw how innovation could be both creative and destructive – as we shall see in Chapter 8. But Schumpeter was the first to put this concept at the heart of his analysis.

However, the expression, 'perennial gale of creative destruction' deserves some etymological analysis, because the word 'perennial' carries an ambiguity. The oldest use of the word is botanical: a perennial plant remains alive through the years – as opposed to an annual plant which dies at the end of its first season. In modern use, the word today still implies persistence and endurance, but there are two different senses:

- Constant or perpetual (i.e. continuing without interruption).
- Recurrent (i.e. regularly repeated or renewed).

Which of these did Schumpeter mean? I'm not sure that we know,[4] so I shall make an informed guess. When people in the USA speak of 'perennial hurricanes', they don't mean that hurricanes continue without interruption, every hour of every day, throughout the year. Thankfully, hurricanes are not perpetual like that and, if they were, it would be nigh impossible to live in such conditions. What they mean is that the hurricanes regularly recur every year – mostly between June and November, and with a peak period from mid-August to mid-October.

In the same way, it is unlikely that Schumpeter meant that innovation was a 'constant, perpetual and unrelenting gale'. It seems much more likely that he meant a 'regularly recurring gale' which would come, relent, and then recur some weeks or months later. Indeed, business innovation, as described in this book, is much more like a regularly recurring gale than an unrelenting gale.

In Schumpeter's eyes, business innovation deploys powerful tools which can be an aid to many, but it achieves its effects by upheaval and turbulence. Much writing about innovation, from the perspective of business strategy, uses 'battle' or 'war' as a metaphor. For example: Foster (1986) writes of, 'the attackers advantage'; Braun (1997) writes of 'the innovation war'; Gagliardi (2006) writes of the 'business warrior'; and Jones et al. (2012) write of the, 'the battle for sustained innovation leadership'. The destructive side is clearly acknowledged, and yet relatively few economists in the Schumpeterian tradition give as much attention to destruction as they should.

Common innovation is simply not like this. An appropriate metaphor would instead be a 'gentle and benign breeze of creativity'. Common innovation is not about 'business grabbing', creative destruction or turbulence. It does not involve a battle between products of rival companies. Instead, common innovation is about a very large number of small, local initiatives to create R-wealth. It works by creating where there is nothing, and not by undermining and destroying what is there. I hope the examples in Part III will illustrate that this is indeed the reality of common innovation.[5]

A 'BEAUFORT SCALE' OF CREATIVE DESTRUCTION

As Schumpeter used the word 'gale' to describe innovation, it is tempting to pursue that metaphor and define a scale of creative destruction. Superficially, at least, this scale would have something in common with the 'Beaufort Scale', which describes wind speed, the condition of the sea, and the implications for damage on land – or indeed, the 'Saffir-Simpson Scale' which describes wind-speed and the damage done by hurricanes.[6] These wind scales are one-dimensional: that is, for any wind speed implied by a particular point on the scale, there is a 1:1 mapping to a level of damage.

The scale for creative destruction, however, would need to be two-dimensional: the first dimension describes the creative energy of the innovation and the second describes its destructive power. The relationship between these two dimensions need not be a 1:1 mapping. The reading for creative destruction would be written C:D, where C and D describe (respectively) the creative and destructive effects of the innovation. The elements of this argument have been advanced already. In common innovation, the incentive of the innovator is directly to create R-wealth, and often (though not invariably) this will involve little destruction of others' R-wealth. In business innovation, by contrast, the incentive of the innovator is to create revenues and profits from sales to customers. Often (though again not invariably) this is best done best by siphoning off the market shares of competitors, which implies a marked reduction in others' M-wealth.

Figure 3.1 illustrates this modified 'Beaufort Scale'. (The units on the graph are purely notional.) A group of business innovations are drawn in the middle of Figure 3.1, while a group of common innovations are drawn on the lower left-hand side of Figure 3.1. What is the rationale for that? It follows from the arguments in preceding paragraphs. But we shall also consider, in more detail, the effects of a business innovation and a common innovation, and see that these provide a further rationale for what has been drawn.

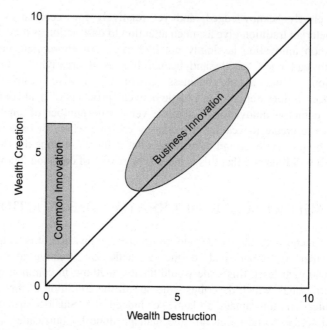

Figure 3.1 The 'Beaufort Scale' of Creative Destruction

Business Innovation

Suppose there are two producers, A and B, and that producer B is about to introduce an innovation. Before that innovation (by B), producer A has a competitive advantage over B (whether by superior product and service or by lower price) and enjoys a higher profit as a result ($\Pi_1 > \Pi_0$). Now producer B makes an innovation which means that its product or service offers a slightly higher surplus to consumers than A's product or service, and as a result, many consumers switch to B's product/service. Because of this, B now enjoys a higher profit than A ($\Pi_1 > \Pi_0$).

Table 3.1 Profit / Surplus before and after a Business Innovation

	Producer A	Producer B	Consumers	Aggregate
Before	Π_1	Π_0	Σ	$\Pi_0 + \Pi_1 + \Sigma$
After	Π_0	Π_1	$\Sigma + \varepsilon$	$\Pi_0 + \Pi_1 + \Sigma + \varepsilon$
Change	$\Pi_0 - \Pi_1$	$\Pi_1 - \Pi_0$	ε	ε

Table 3.1 shows the net effects of the innovation. (I assume, purely for

simplicity, that the values of Π_1 in column 2, row 2 and in column 3, row 3 are the same as each other; and likewise, I assume that the values of Π_1 in column 2, row 3 and in column 3, row 2 are the same as each other.)

The table shows the profit or surplus enjoyed by each producer, the consumers, and the aggregate of these three, before and after an innovation by producer B. The implications of the innovation are as follows. There is a transfer of profit from producer A to producer B: A suffers a loss in profit of $\Pi_0-\Pi_1$ while B enjoys a gain in profit of $\Pi_1-\Pi_0$. Consumers gain a small amount of surplus ε. The net picture is a small net gain in social surplus (ε), but mostly a large transfer from A to B. This is a clear case of creative destruction – mainly creation of profit for B and destruction of A's profit, with a small gain to consumers. This is consistent with the representation of business innovation in Figure 3.1.

Chapter 5 takes a more detailed look at this question. It uses a simple model to explore the assertion that the returns to the innovator from business innovation may be well in excess of the contribution to national M-wealth creation. This can happen when the main effect of the innovation is to take market share away from an incumbent. But we also show that in the case of a radical innovation that opens up a new market, it is probable that the contribution to consumer surplus exceeds the profit to the innovator.

Common Innovation

By contrast, a pure example of common innovation shows a very different pattern. Here we consider a case where a village (or other small community) makes an innovation to improve a community resource (a local park, a village hall, or something similar). Here we can produce an equivalent table, but this time describing the implications for a different set of three groups.

Table 3.2 Profit / Surplus before and after a Common Innovation

	Builder A	Rivals B	Citizens	Aggregate
Before	Π_0	Π_2	Σ_0	$\Pi_0+\Pi_2+\Sigma_0$
After	Π_0+d	$\Pi_2-\varepsilon$	Σ_0+x	$\Pi_0+\Pi_2+\Sigma_0+d+x-\varepsilon$
Change	d	$-\varepsilon$	x	$d+x-\varepsilon$

The community employs a local builder to do the necessary work, and that firm makes a small increase in profit (d). The citizens make a more substantial gain in surplus from their community innovation (x). And the only loser(s) are rival attractions (B) that lose some business ($-\varepsilon$) when the community uses the new improved community resource rather than the rival attraction. However, in this simple example, use of the community resource is very inelastic, so that loss is small.

In this case, $x \gg d \gg \varepsilon$. So the main effects are R-wealth creation for the community, and destruction is very minor. This is consistent with the representation of common innovation in Figure 3.1.

SHOULD ECONOMICS STUDY C-INNOVATION?

We noted in the preface that some consider that common innovation is not really a proper subject of study for economists. I completely disagree. As most readers will know, the idea of business production has been borrowed and applied in other areas of human activity.[7] We also apply the concept of a production function in the public sector, the health service, the third sector and even in the household – the household production function (Becker, 1965). If it makes sense to talk of a production function in these contexts, it also makes sense to talk of innovation. And in the context of household production, innovation is indeed common innovation. For that reason, it makes no sense to exclude common innovation from economics when the idea of a household production function is an accepted part of the landscape.

We shall see in Part III of the book that some common innovation can be seen as an attempt to improve the household production process to generate a higher level of R-wealth from given material inputs. We could describe this as an improvement in the art of consumption. This is by no means a new idea. A hundred years ago, Mitchell (1912) considered it a priority for economic analysis to pay attention to the art of consumption: he argued that that the art of consumption was less well developed than the art of production, and that there was a pressing need to improve the former. For, if the art of consumption is underdeveloped, we will find it hard to create R-wealth from M-wealth. Indeed, this observation is not very far from Ruskin's point above that, 'a horse is no wealth to us if we cannot ride'.[8]

Other critics have suggested that even if we accept that common innovation is a part of economics, it would be better if economists treat business innovation as a self-contained category in its own right, and treat it separately from common innovation. This idea may be appealing, but we shall see that it doesn't really make sense. We can use the analysis of separability[9] to tell us the conditions in which it is reasonable to isolate one economic decision from others, so that it can be treated as a self-contained problem in its own right.

Suppose we study the effects of business innovations on the quality and prices of business products (X). Now, consider the consumer's consumption of different business products and services (X) and his own common innovations (Y). Suppose the consumer's utility function is defined over these two vectors (X and Y), and additionally, assume the function is weakly separable as follows:

$$u = u\left\{\theta_X(X_1,....,X_n), \theta_Y(Y_1,....,Y_m)\right\}$$ (3.1)

In this case, as is well known, optimisation of the different elements of X can be done separately from optimisation of the different elements of Y. In other words, optimisation of X can be treated as a self-contained problem, treated apart from the optimisation of Y.

This is very convenient, as it allows us to treat demand for business innovations as a self-contained and separable problem in its own right, and it allows us to ignore common innovation, if we wish to. *But is it realistic?*

In practice, it is very unlikely indeed that such a separability assumption is justified. Let us examine the special case where m = n, and where X represents the goods and services bought, while Y represents the capacity for common innovation from these material goods. In that case, the utility function could not possibly look like Equation (3.1). Instead, if any separability assumption at all is valid, it is more likely to look like this:

$$u = u\left\{\psi_1(X_1,Y_1),....,\psi_n(X_n,Y_n)\right\}$$ (3.2)

This is the case where products (X_i) are grouped together with the consumer's common innovation activities (Y_i) using those products. For simplicity, consider the special case of Equation (3.2) where:

$$u = u\left\{\psi_1(X_1 * Y_1),....,\psi_n(X_n * Y_n)\right\}$$ (3.3)

where the $\psi_i(.)$ are increasing functions. In that case, it is clear that optimisation of X_i is intimately related to optimisation of Y_i.

To illustrate this take a simple practical example. Suppose I have a talent for woodwork (item 1) but no talent for cooking (item 2). In that case, I can produce some valuable common innovations in woodwork, but none of value in cooking. In that case, it make sense for me to do my own DIY woodwork, but does not make sense for me to do my own cooking. Consumption decisions about material items are inextricably linked to talent for different areas of common innovation.

I hope the reader is persuaded why economics must take proper account of C-innovation. I shall argue in Chapter 26 that if economics ignores common innovation, it may make serious errors in national accounting.

NOTES

[1] For those who favour a mathematical definition of C-Innovation, it can be described thus. If I is the set of all innovation, B is the set of all business innovation, and C is the set of all C-innovation, then $C = I - B$. That is, C is the complement to B within the set I.

[2] Kay (2010, p. 179).

[3] Sir Keith Joseph, later Lord Joseph, was perhaps the most thoughtful minister in Margaret Thatcher's government.

[4] We cannot resolve the puzzle by looking at the German version of the book, because Schumpeter wrote the original version of *Capitalism Socialism and Democracy* in English. However, it is interesting that in the first German version (1946), Susanne Preiswerk translated this phrase into 'ewigen Sturm der schöpferischen Zerstörung'. Ewigen ('eternal') carries the same sense of endurance, but once again does not distinguish between constancy and recurrence.

[5] Common Innovation could be described as innovation for the *Harmonious Society* – as described in Chinese economic thought from Confucius onwards (Hu Jichuang, 2009). This same term was also been used in policy announcements by former Chinese leader Hu Jintao (see Zheng and Tok, 2007).

[6] The Beaufort Scale runs from 0 (calm) to 12 (hurricane), while the Saffir-Simpson scale runs from category 1 to category 5.

[7] Some critics might say that the idea of a production function has perhaps been applied to an excessively wide range of human activities, some of which are not properly part of economics. Be that as it may, I don't see any sense in arguing that the art of consumption should be considered to lie outside economics.

[8] Ruskin (1904/1996, vol. 17, p. 154).

[9] The concept is due to Leontief (1947), Strotz (1957) and Gorman (1959).

4. *Oikonomia* and the Outer Economy

I am sure most readers need no reminder that the English noun, 'economy' ultimately derives from the ancient Greek, οἰκονομία (hereafter, *oikonomia*). The word came into English from French, into French from Latin, and into Latin from Greek.[1] However, there is a substantial difference between the meaning of *oikonomia* in ancient Greek and the meaning of 'economy' in modern English.

In ancient Greek, *oikonomia* stands for, 'management of a household or family, husbandry, thrift'.[2] In essence, *oikonomia* refers to a very small-scale, or micro-economic unit – the household. By contrast, 'economy' refers to a very large-scale, or macro-economic unit – the economy as a whole.

A very basic assertion by Adam Smith (1776/1904b, p. 159), places *oikonomia* at the centre of the economy:

> Consumption is the sole end and purpose of all production; and the interest of the producer ought to be attended to only so far as it may be necessary for promoting that of the consumer. The maxim is so perfectly self-evident that it would be absurd to attempt to prove it.

However, most discussion of economics and the economy today is very remote from *oikonomia*. Instead, most discussion refers to what we shall call the 'outer economy' – drawing an obvious analogy to astronomy where the Earth is surrounded by its atmosphere and beyond that lies 'outer space'. These elements of the 'outer economy', such as financial markets, corporate performance, trade, business innovation, and so on, are important in influencing how well capitalist business can create M-wealth and hence supply consumer needs. But these concepts are remote from *oikonomia* and remote from the understanding and experience of many ordinary people.

Nevertheless, there are good reasons why economists think mainly about the outer economy. While household management is not trivial, the co-ordination challenges faced in this outer economy are far more complex than those found in *oikonomia*. Indeed, *oikonomia* is really closer to 'home economics',[3] and some economists would prefer to distance themselves from that subject, and argue that they are concerned with higher things.

Nonetheless, it is not good if economics as a discipline forgets that *oikonomia* lies at its heart. And however we measure the performance of an economy, we must not rely only on measures from the outer economy, but must also focus on how well this outer economy serves the core *oikonomia*. That is why this book is concerned with how well innovation serves *oikonomia* and how well it helps to create R-wealth.

A MAP OF *OIKONOMIA* AND THE OUTER ECONOMY

The simple supply chain diagram below illustrates what we mean when we speak of *oikonomia* contrasted to the outer economy. It is a stylised supply chain that would be relevant for consumer electronics and personal computers, amongst other things.

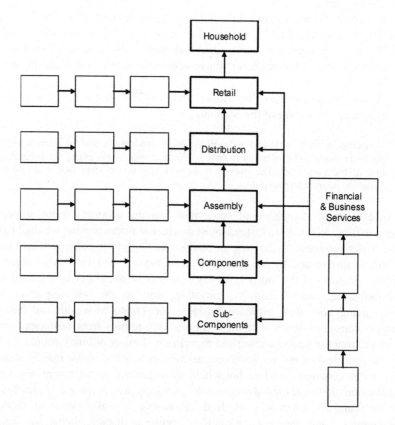

Figure 4.1   Supply Chain

The household is the final consumer, and *oikonomia* is concerned with what happens in the household. The outer economy refers to the long and complex supply chains that feed the main chain from sub-components and components to the household.

HYPOTHESIS

One important hypothesis, which we shall revisit in Part IV of the book, is that innovations in the outer economy generally have a smaller impact on the end consumer than innovations close to the household. Take for example a cost-reducing innovation that reduces the cost of an input that will ultimately contribute to one unit of final output. The closer that innovation is to *oikonomia*, the greater the proportion of the cost saving that is passed on to the final consumer, while the further out into the outer economy, the smaller the proportion of any cost saving is passed on.

The accuracy of this hypothesis is ultimately an empirical matter, not a theoretical matter. But the following sketch provides a rough justification for the hypothesis. Assume that at each stage of the supply chain, production is described by a Cournot oligopoly model. Assume that the (inverse) demand function is:

$$P = a - b\sum_{i=1}^{N} X_i \tag{4.1}$$

where X_i is production by firm i. If, as usual in the Cournot context, firm i has zero conjectural variations, then its total revenue (*TR*) and marginal revenue (*MR*) are given by:

$$TR_i = PX_i = aX_i - bX_i \sum_{j=1}^{N} X_j \tag{4.2}$$

$$MR_i = a - 2bX_i - b\sum_{\substack{j=1 \\ j \neq i}}^{N} X_j \tag{4.3}$$

Suppose that this stage of the supply chain enjoys a cost-reducing innovation, which reduces marginal cost by ΔMC, and suppose this innovation is available to all producers. Suppose indeed that all producers are identical, so that equations (4.1), (4.2) and (4.3) apply for all i = 1, ..., N, and $X_i = X$ for all i = 1, ..., N. Then for profit-maximising firms, we can solve

(4.1) and (4.3) as follows:

$$\Delta P = bN\Delta X \tag{4.4}$$

$$\Delta MC = b(N+1)\Delta X \tag{4.5}$$

From which we obtain:

$$\frac{\Delta P}{\Delta MC} = \frac{N}{N+1} \tag{4.6}$$

In short, at each stage, the share of the reduction in marginal cost passed on to the next customer as a reduction in price is N/(N+1). In the case of monopoly, this is 50 percent, in the case of oligopoly it is between 50 percent and 100 percent, and in the case of a very large number of firms (perfect competition), it approaches 100 percent.

Finally, suppose that we work out the net cost saving from this innovation as passed all the way down the K links in the supply chain. In the simple case where market structure is the same at each stage, this is:

$$\frac{\Delta P_0}{\Delta MC} = \left(\frac{N}{N+1}\right)^K \tag{4.7}$$

Except in the case of very large N (perfect competition), this is consistent with the hypothesis that that innovations in the outer economy generally have a smaller impact on the end consumer than innovations close to the household. Table 4.1 gives some illustrative calculations for different values of N and K. From these illustrative calculations, it is clear that in a concentrated oligopoly ($N \leq 4$, say), innovations in the outer economy have little net effect on prices to the final consumer in the household.

What happens to the cost savings that are not passed on to the final consumer? They are absorbed by intermediate corporate customers in the supply chain and show up as increased profits for these various customers. Note, moreover, that this is a Cournot model in which each oligopolist has zero conjectural variations. Contrast this with the theory of the kinked demand curve, where conjectural variations are not zero. In that latter case, no reduction is passed on, because oligopolists reason that any reduction in price will be followed by rivals.

Table 4.1 Solution to Equation (4.7) for Different N *and* K

		K				
		1	2	4	8	16
N	1	50%	25%	6%	0%	0%
	2	67%	44%	20%	4%	0%
	3	75%	56%	32%	10%	1%
	4	80%	64%	41%	17%	3%
	6	86%	73%	54%	29%	8%
	9	90%	81%	66%	43%	19%
	19	95%	90%	81%	66%	44%
	∞	100%	100%	100%	100%	100%

CONCLUSION

We shall revisit this hypothesis in Chapter 26 where we speculate on diminishing returns to B-innovation in the outer economy. But the essential message is an important one – if also an obvious one. In most cases, the returns to *oikonomia* from innovations in the outer-reaches of the economy are small compared to the returns from innovations close to *oikonomia*. This is often forgotten in those analyses that use innovation, with no attempt to assess whereabouts these innovations are located in the wider economy.

I have concluded the previous two chapters with a discussion of the whether economics should be concerned with R-wealth and C-innovation, respectively. In view of Adam Smith's assertion, quoted at the start of this short chapter, I think it is self-evident that there is no need to justify our discussion of *oikonomia* in this book.

NOTES

1 *Oxford English Dictionary* (2013).
2 *Oxford English Dictionary* (2013).
3 The Wikipedia (2013d) entry for home economics refers to, 'consumer education, institutional management, interior design, home furnishing, cleaning, handicrafts, sewing, clothing and textiles, commercial cooking, cooking, nutrition, food preservation, hygiene, child development, managing money, and family relationships.'

5. The Values of Innovation

The object of this chapter is to clarify what is meant by the 'value of an innovation'. There are at least three 'values' in common use. The first is the value of an innovation to the innovator. The second is the value of an innovation to the customer. And the third is the overall social value. When we are talking of business innovation (B-innovation), certainly, it is unlikely that these three values are all the same. But when we are talking of common innovation (C-innovation), it is quite possible that the three values are the same or similar.

Let us start with B-innovation. Recall Schumpeter's concept of innovation as creative destruction. Part of the value of innovation to the innovator is that it increases the size of the market, but much of the value to the innovator may be that it takes market share away from a rival. How does it do this? By offering the customer a better deal – perhaps only a slightly better deal – than the rival can offer.

In this case, therefore, we have a big positive value for the innovator, a more modest positive value for the customer, and a big negative value for the rival. The social value of the innovation is the sum of these three – assuming that we can neglect any influence on third parties. In the special case where the value to the innovator is exactly offset by the cost to the rival, then social value would equal customer value.[1] But when part of the value to the innovator is the increase in market size, then this special case does not apply. In general, therefore, innovator value, customer value and social value are all different from each other.

Now let us turn to common innovation. In this case, by contrast, the values of common innovation to innovator and customer are often the same or similar. Why so? There are two possible reasons. In many cases, the C-innovator is the same person as the customer. Or even if the innovator and the user are different people, the innovator has a direct objective to create R-wealth for the end user. Moreover, as we discussed above in Chapter 3, C-innovation is a 'gentle and benign breeze' compared to the 'perennial gale' of creative destruction entailed in B-innovation. This means that the negative externalities from C-innovation are typically small. That means innovator value, customer value and social value are all quite close to each other.

In the rest of this chapter, we shall explore the relationship between innovator value, customer value and social value in two contrasting cases of business innovation. The first is an incremental cost-saving innovation, and the second is a radical product innovation.

INCREMENTAL COST-REDUCING INNOVATION

In this context, we shall see that the value of a business innovation to the innovator is often well in excess of the value to the customer. But this is not invariably the case, and it depends on particular assumptions about parameter values.

Let us start by considering the incumbent (firm 0) in an existing market, who supplies volume X_0 at price P_0 and unit cost C_0 with revenues equal to R_0 $(= X_0 P_0)$ and profits equal to $\Pi_0 = X_0(P_0 - C_0)$. Let ψ_0 represent the incumbent's mark-up on costs – i.e. $P_0 = (1 + \psi_0)C_0$.

Suppose that an innovative entrant (firm 1) has *sole* use of a cost-reducing innovation that allows it to produce an almost identical product at a unit cost r percent below the incumbent – i.e. $C_1 = (1-r)C_0$. For simplicity we assume that the entrant takes advantage of its cost saving innovation to undercut the incumbent, selling at a lower price P_1 which passes the whole of the cost saving onto the consumer. Hence:

$$P_1 - C_1 = P_0 - C_0. \tag{5.1}$$

and

$$P_0 - P_1 = C_0 - C_1 = rC_0 \tag{5.2}$$

At this lower price, the innovator can take some (m percent) of the existing market. But in addition, because it is selling at a lower price than the incumbent, the innovator enjoys some new sales to new customers, who did not buy at P_0. These new sales are an additional n percent (by volume) on top of the original X_0.

What are the implications of this innovation for the profits of the innovative entrant and incumbent, and for consumer surplus? The innovative entrant will make profits in two ways: first by taking market share from the incumbent, and second from sales to new consumers. The value of profit raised in the first way is:

$$mX_0(P_1 - C_1) \tag{5.3}$$

while the value of profits from sales to new consumers is:

$$nX_0(P_1 - C_1) \tag{5.4}$$

Using equation 5.1, the total profit for the innovative entrant can be rewritten:

$$\Pi_1 = (m+n)X_0(P_1 - C_1) = (m+n)X_0(P_0 - C_0) = (m+n)\Pi_0 \tag{5.5}$$

The incumbent loses m percent of sales to the innovative entrant, and hence suffers a loss in profit of:

$$-mX_0(P_0 - C_0) = -m\Pi_0 \tag{5.6}$$

The effect on consumer surplus is in two parts: first, m percent of existing consumers benefit from a lower price by buying from the innovative entrant rather than the incumbent, and second, the new consumers enjoy some consumer surplus. The value of the first part is:

$$mX_0(P_0 - P_1) = mX_0 rC_0 \tag{5.7}$$

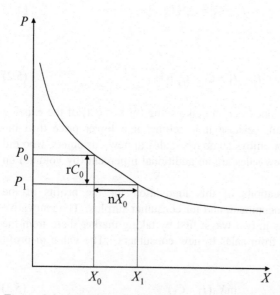

Figure 5.1 Aggregate Demand Curve: Incremental Innovation

To assess the value of the second part, we need to know something about the aggregate demand curve. Suppose this is as illustrated in Figure 5.1, and that the demand curve is linear between (P_0, X_0) and (P_1, X_1). Then the additional consumer surplus from the new sales (nX_0) is given by:

$$\frac{nX_0(P_0 - P_1)}{2} = \frac{nX_0.rC_0}{2} \tag{5.8}$$

Hence the total increase in consumer surplus can be rewritten:

$$rX_0C_0(m + n/2) \tag{5.9}$$

The implications of this innovation for the profits and consumer surplus are shown in Table 5.1. The expressions in this table describe the changes in profit and surplus caused by this innovation.

Table 5.1 Effects of Innovation on Profits, Consumer Surplus and Net Social Surplus

Innovator Profit (Π_1)	Incumbent Profit	Consumer Surplus	Net Social Surplus (Σ)
$+ (m+n)\Pi_0$	$- m\Pi_0$	$+ rX_0C_0(m + n/2)$	$+ n\Pi_0 + rX_0C_0(m + n/2)$

Using the results in Table 5.1, the ratio of innovator profit to net social surplus can be rearranged as follows:

$$
\begin{aligned}
\Pi_1/\Sigma &= (m+n)\Pi_0/(n\Pi_0 + rX_0C_0(m+n/2)) \\
&= (m+n)\psi_0X_0C_0/(n\psi_0X_0C_0 + rX_0C_0(m+n/2)) \\
&= (m+n)\psi_0/(n\psi_0 + r(m+n/2))
\end{aligned} \tag{5.10}
$$

In general, it is hard to say whether this ratio is greater than or less than one. It all depends on the parameter values. But it is worth considering two specific scenarios where it is easier to generalise about the size of this ratio.

No New Demand (n = 0)

In a wide variety of consumption decisions, demand for one brand of good rather than another brand is quite price elastic, while total demand for the good is not very price elastic. Let us start with an extreme version of this case where n = 0. In short, the extra profit to the innovator is simply the profit denied to the incumbent – nothing more than that. That is a simple transfer from one producer. However, there is a gain in consumer surplus as the innovator passes on its cost saving. In this case, Equation 5.10 simplifies to:

$$\Pi_1/\Sigma = \psi_0/r \qquad (5.11)$$

If ψ_0 (the incumbent's mark-up on costs) is greater than r (the percentage cost reduction available to the innovator) then innovator profit *exceeds* net social surplus. But if ψ_0 (the incumbent's mark-up on costs) is less than r (the percentage cost reduction available to the innovator) then innovator profit *is less than* net social surplus.

What does this mean in economic terms? If the incumbent is highly profitable (e.g. if the incumbent is a monopoly), and a small reduction in cost is sufficient to switch market share from the incumbent to the innovator, then the value of the innovation to the innovator is greater than the value of the innovation in terms of net social surplus. In Schumpeterian language, this means that when creative destruction is very strong, the value of the innovation to the innovator is larger than the value of the innovation to society as a whole. But if the incumbent is not profitable (e.g. operates in a highly competitive market), then the value of the innovation to the innovator is less than the value of the innovation to society as a whole.

So for example, if the incumbent has a profit margin of 50 percent on costs – that is, price is 50 percent above costs – and the innovator's cost reduction is 10 percent, then the ratio of innovator profit to net social surplus gained is 5. In that case, the innovator's profit overstates the value of the innovation from a social point of view, by a factor of five.

No Market Share Loss by Incumbent (m = 0)

The opposite extreme to the last case is where m = 0 but n > 0. In that case, Equation 5.11 simplifies to:

$$\begin{aligned} \Pi_1/\Sigma &= n\psi_0/(n\psi_0 + rn/2) \\ &= \psi_0/(\psi_0 + r/2) \end{aligned} \qquad (5.12)$$

If r > 0, then the denominator is greater than the numerator, and hence the innovator's profit is less than net social surplus. This makes sense, because there is no loss to the incumbent, but there is some gain in consumer surplus.

RADICAL INNOVATION

Finally, we consider the case of a completely new radical innovation, produced for the first time by the innovative entrant. In this context, we shall see that the value of a business innovation to the customer is often well in excess of the value to the innovator.

Up to a point, we can treat this within the above framework, using the parameter value m=0 (no market share loss by incumbent). However, that doesn't fully capture the substantial gains in consumer surplus that can follow from radical innovations. Assume that the radical innovation is produced by the innovative entrant at cost C_1, and sold at price P_1, where:

$$P_1 = (1 + \psi_1)C_1 \qquad (5.13)$$

where ψ_1 is the innovator's mark-up on costs. Now consider the simplified demand curve shown in Figure 5.2, and assume this demand curve is linear in the range $(P_{max},0)$ and (P_1,X_1).

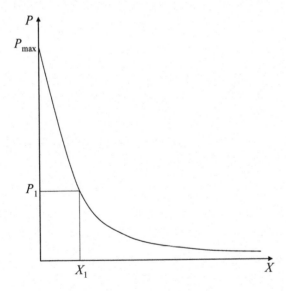

Figure 5.2 Aggregate Demand Curve: Radical Innovation

Then the innovator profit is $\psi_1 C_1 X_1$ and consumer surplus is $(P_{max} - P_1) X_1/2$. As there is no loss of sales for the incumbent, the net social surplus is made up of two components: the innovator's profit plus the consumer surplus. The net social surplus must therefore exceed the innovator's profit by the extent of the consumer surplus. The latter must be positive, and may be relatively large when $P_{max} \gg P_1$.

In summary, for the case of a radical innovation, the innovator's profit is an underestimate of the role of innovation in M-wealth creation – and may be a substantial underestimate.

NOTE

[1] The Schumpeterian rhetoric argues that innovation plays a valuable economic role when it drives inefficient firms out of business. The arguments in this chapter would tend to cast doubt on whether this is really such a valuable role. The social value of this result may be far less than it appears at first sight, because it only takes a modest cost-saving innovation to displace firms that do not adopt that innovation. Moreover, the death of firms hastens the unwelcome era of monopoly, which may swallow any benefit accruing from the death of inefficient firms.

6. Analytical Framework

This chapter illustrates the rough analytical framework we use to answer the question: how do different types of innovation create wealth?

By the word 'framework' we do not imply anything of great precision. It is simply a simply a collection of inter-connected categories describing areas or activities in the economy and society, plus two concepts of wealth. The categories are: business, marketplace, socio-economic environment, natural environment, science, art, education, health and consumption, and the two concepts of wealth are M-wealth and R-wealth. The framework is a more detailed development of that in Swann (2009a, Chapter 19), and some readers may find it helpful to read that in addition to this chapter. I would also recommend that they read the very interesting paper by Engelbrecht (2014) based on a similar framework.

As we shall see, the framework used differs according to which type of innovation we are discussing (business innovation or common innovation) and which perspective we are taking (the view of business or the view of society at large). The model we use to analyse the business view of how business innovation creates M-wealth is much simpler than the model required to understand the role of common innovation in creating R-wealth.

CATEGORIES AND CONCEPTS

Let us start with the categories and concepts that will be used in this framework. Most of these are quite obvious, but it is as well to be clear about where we draw the boundaries between some of these categories.

Business and the Workplace

This could be any type of business, from sole traders right up to large multinationals. The key characteristic of all of them is that they aim to make profits, or at least revenues, by selling outputs (which could be products or services) to customers. Business, especially large business, is obviously an important locus for innovation   In this framework, 'business' also incorporates the 'workplace'.   This is very important, because in what follows we shall consider both the impact of a 'workplace' on a worker's health, R-wealth, and other variables, and also the impact of business in general on all our other categories.

Marketplace

While many physical services are by definition delivered to the customer at the point of production (e.g. a haircut), this need not be so for products. Many businesses do not sell their products direct to the customer at the point of production, but through a marketplace. The marketplace can be a local market, a supermarket, a high street filled with retail outlets, or a virtual (online) market. Some of these marketplaces are also businesses in their own right (e.g. supermarkets) but some are public goods (e.g. local markets). The marketplace is also a venue for innovation, much of it business innovation, some of it government innovation and some common innovation.

Socio-Economic Environment

This broad category includes anything about the socioeconomy that might impact on or be impacted by the other variables in our frameworks. This could include geographical distribution of economic activity, unemployment, distribution of income, condition of the welfare state, property rights, etc. In particular, we shall be interested in how business innovations affect the socio-economic environment, and how innovations in the socio-economic environment affect R-wealth. We shall not attempt to provide a comprehensive list of what is included in this category, but a clear picture will emerge as we use this category in later parts of the book.

Natural Environment

This is another broad category that includes anything about the natural environment that might impact on or be impacted by the other variables in our frameworks. This could include the quality of the natural environment, the quality of the housing and building stock, the physical and environmental condition of cities and towns, pollution, congestion, etc. We shall be interested in how business innovations affect the natural environment, and how innovations in the natural environment affect R-wealth.

Science

By 'science', I mean scientific knowledge held in universities, research laboratories and government laboratories, and its use and dissemination. A large part of this is held in the public sector, and its creation is often funded by governments, though it can attract substantial supplementary funding from business. We shall be interested to explore how science impacts on many of the other categories in our framework, and not just on business.

Arts

This category includes all the arts (painting, architecture, music, pottery, weaving, sculpture, etc.) and also covers the whole spectrum from the fine arts to applied and industrial arts. It is likely that the fine arts and applied arts contribute to wealth creation in different ways, and in principle it could be useful to sub-divide this category. But for two reasons we have not done so. Firstly, for ease of exposition, I did not want to create more categories than we have here. Secondly, as Glaser (1989) has argued, it is not necessarily easy to define the boundary between fine art and applied art.

Education

While 'science' is the formal knowledge residing in scientific specialists, education – in our framework – refers to the human capital of all citizens. Much education is funded by government, some by customers (or their parents) and some by business directly (e.g. executive education). A part of the role of education is to prepare students for work, but it is quite wrong to focus on that to the exclusion of all else. Good education is a 'good thing' in its own right, to be used to broaden the minds and capabilities of citizens, and to enhance their ability to create R-wealth from their M-wealth.

Health

The health and wellbeing of citizens is, of course, a vitally important influence on their productivity in the workplace, but even more so, is one of the most important factors influencing R-wealth. In our framework, several of our categories can impact (positively or negatively) on health.

Consumption

By consumption we mean use of products and services by final consumers to create R-wealth. However, it is well recognised that there are many types of consumer behaviour. Elsewhere (Swann, 2009a, Chapter 15), I have called these: the economic consumer, the Galbraith consumer, the Marshall consumer, the Douglas consumer, the Bourdieu consumer, the Veblen consumer, the Green consumer, the Ethical consumer and the Routine consumer.   Some of these consumers assert their autonomy to create R-wealth, while others show very little autonomy.   These differences have important implications for the extent to which consumption of M-wealth is capable of creating R-wealth. We will revisit these issues in Chapter 12.

Those are the nine categories in our framework, to which we add the two measures of wealth, M-wealth and R-wealth, as defined in Chapter 2. In the next sections, I present a framework to illustrate the workings of business innovation and common innovation. The precise details of these diagrams are open to debate, and some researchers may wish to re-draw them. But the most important point to note is that Figure 6.1 is simpler than Figure 6.2, which in turn is simpler than Figure 6.4. The remainder of the chapter considers the implications of these frameworks for innovation policy, and the Leontief models that can be used to formalise these frameworks.

BUSINESS INNOVATION AS SEEN BY BUSINESS

We start with a framework to describe business innovation – as seen by business. The core of this framework is based on the so-called 'linear model' of science, business and wealth creation. That linear model is based on two strong assumptions:

a) business innovation *only* contributes to wealth creation through its effects on the workplace, the marketplace and consumption;
b) the flow is strictly from left to right – i.e. from science to innovation in business, to the marketplace, and so on.

Within innovation studies, assumption (b) is considered especially inappropriate, because it neglects many feedback mechanisms.   For that reason, the framework in Figure 6.1 is somewhat more general than the linear model, as it does allow for some forms of feedback from right to left. Nonetheless, it is still based on assumption (a).

Indeed, the model is consistent with the way that many (most?) macroeconomists see business innovation: as a factor that increases productivity.   For example, HM Treasury (2000) describes the economic effects of innovation as follows:

> Innovation and technological progress are important factors in determining economic growth. Productivity growth relies on a continual stream of inventions and innovations of both new technologies and improved working practices. New ways of working provide a source of efficiency gains, enabling workers to operate more effectively and providing firms with greater opportunities to use labour and capital inputs in ways which maximise their productive potential.

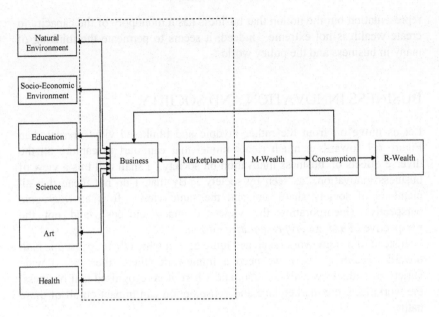

Figure 6.1 Business Innovation as seen by Business

This perspective is not wrong: business innovation does indeed have these effects on the economy. But this perspective is incomplete: these are definitely not the only effects of innovation on the economy.

In Figure 6.1, the locus of business innovation is within the rectangle marked with the dotted line. By that, we mean that business innovation can influence any of the categories or linkages in that area. For example, business can take outputs from any of the categories on the left hand side, and use these as part of an innovation strategy to enhance the performance of the business model. That leads to more/better/cheaper products and services being offered in the market place, which increases M-wealth and, in turn, increases R-wealth.

We could treat the categories on the left hand side as exogenous to this model. However, as drawn, business can (by financial incentives) direct the focus of some scientific work and some education (e.g. executive education) and can (perhaps by buying private health care plans for its executives) work to improve the health of its workforce and thus enhance productivity.

While some may wish to debate some of the details of the model as drawn, assumption (a) remains one of the essential features. The only route to wealth creation is through business production sold in the marketplace and consumed to create R-wealth. That may perhaps seem a rather extreme representation but the notion that business has a monopoly of the capacity to create wealth is not extreme. Indeed, it seems to permeate the thinking of many in business and the policy world.

BUSINESS INNOVATION AND SOCIETY

Let us move on from the rather myopic and blinkered view presented in Figure 6.1 towards a much richer model that can start to capture all the diverse effects on business innovation on society. I shall call this a view of business innovation, 'as seen by society'. By that, I do not mean that all members of society share one and the same view. It is an *aggregate* perspective (incorporating the views of many citizens), and not the perspective of a single, *representative* citizen.

Instead of a framework (such as Figure 6.1) in which there is just *one* path towards wealth creation, we need a framework where, there are a wide variety of paths to wealth creation, and where it is recognised that business, the workplace, the marketplace and consumption can impact on all of these paths.

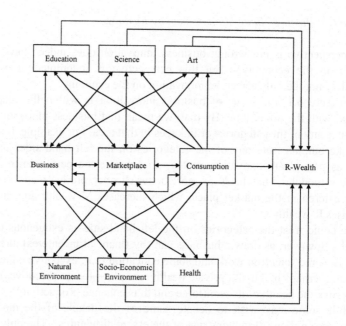

Figure 6.2 Business Innovation as seen by Society

Figure 6.2 shows the essential linkages. This diagram contains all the linkages of Figure 6.1. But, in addition, it is recognised that business (and the workplace), the marketplace and consumption can impact on all other categories (education, science, art, natural environment, socio-economic environment and health), and in turn, that all of these latter categories have an impact on R-wealth. (To conserve space in the diagram, I have omitted the box named M-wealth that was found in Figure 6.1.)

This structure can capture a variety of wealth-creating and wealth-eroding mechanisms. In the same way as Figure 6.1, it captures the role of consumption in creating R-wealth. But it can also capture 'procedural' sources of utility (Frey et al., 2004) – for example, the beneficial and malign effects of the workplace and the marketplace on the worker's R-wealth (perhaps via health or education). It also captures the environmental sources of R-wealth (emanating from the natural and socio-economic environment), and the human side of R-wealth (health, education, arts, science). Business, the workplace, the marketplace and consumption impact on all of these, and each linkage could, in principle, be composed of positive and negative effects.

As such, Figure 6.2 is far better suited than Figure 6.1 to capture the wide variety of creative and destructive effects that may follow from business innovation. Indeed, this structure can capture most or all of the destructive effects of business innovation discussed in Part II of the book. But as I said before, the diagram is rather 'busy', and may be quite hard to follow. Many readers will find it easier to work with a matrix representation of this diagram.

In Figure 6.3 below, the 10*10 matrix can be used to describe the connections from one category to another. In this matrix, an entry of A_{ij} in row i and column j describes the effect of a change in category j on category i. In this matrix, we have shaded some of the cells in grey to indicate that there will not necessarily be any linkage of that type in our model. But where the cells are white, it is an essential feature of the model that there will be a connection (perhaps positive or perhaps negative) from the column variable to the row variable.

The reader may be wondering: do we really need to embrace such complexity as in Figure 6.2? My answer is that even if some of the linkages shown are not relevant in certain cases, it is possible to find examples of all (or almost all) of these potential linkages. Therefore we need a completely general framework. Moreover, we shall see that when we use Figure 6.2 (or Figure 6.3) to calculate the overall effects of innovation on wealth creation, we usually obtain much larger effects than by using Figure 6.1.

The essential difference between this framework and that in Figure 6.1 is that the different categories of our model can impact on the creation of R-wealth through *many* different channels, and not just through business. So, while Figure 6.1 effectively gives business a monopoly of R-wealth creation, that is emphatically not the case here. This difference is of considerable policy significance – a point we shall return to below.

		Effect Of:								
Effect On:		Education	Science	Art	Business	Marketplace	Socio-Econ. Environment	Natural Environment	Consumption	Health	R-Wealth
	Education	■	■		■		■	■		■	■
	Science	■	■		■		■				■
	Art	■			■		■				■
	Business	■	■	■	■		■	■	■	■	■
	Marketplace					■					
	Socio-Econ. Envt.	■	■	■	■		■	■			■
	Natural Envt.	■	■		■		■	■		■	■
	Consumption	■	■	■	■		■	■	■		■
	Health	■	■		■		■	■		■	■
	R-Wealth	■			■	■	■	■	■	■	■

Figure 6.3 Business Innovation as seen by Society (Matrix Form)

A simple example brings out the fundamental difference between Figures 6.1 and 6.2. In Figure 6.1, health improvements contribute to R-wealth creation only inasmuch as they reduce days lost through illness and thus increase productivity. Now, for sure, that is a real and significant effect. But it does seem to reflect the cynical calculus of the mill owner, who only cares for the wellbeing of his workers because without that, productivity and profitability are reduced. In Figure 6.2, by contrast, improved health can also contribute directly to R-wealth. We have adopted Ruskin's famous dictum, 'There is no wealth but life' as the implicit definition of R-wealth, and life is better when healthy! Figure 6.2 has the humanity that is so sadly lacking from Figure 6.1.

A final example develops this point *ad absurdum*. I recall a presentation where the researcher had examined the effects of early musical education on the child's subsequent numerical and mathematical ability. These effects were apparently quite strong (and statistically significant). But surely we don't suggest that parents encourage their child's musical education with the express and sole objective of enhancing career prospects in accountancy!

Figure 6.1 is a major over-simplification of the way that business innovation can create or erode R-wealth. Figure 6.2 is a substantial step forward, as we shall see in Part II. But even Figure 6.2 does not do justice to the sheer variety of ways in which common innovation creates R-wealth.

COMMON INNOVATION

To create a framework capable of understanding common innovation, we need a framework where, at least in principle, 'everything is connected to everything else'. Common innovation uses of one of our categories to enhance another category. In principle, common innovation may create a linkage from any of the categories to any of the others.

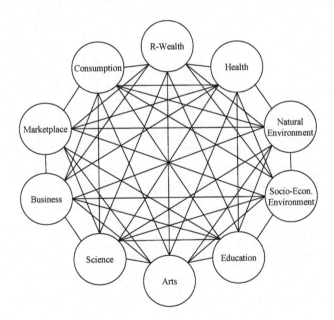

Figure 6.4 Common Innovation

This framework has all the linkages of Figure 6.2, but also has a bank of other linkages connecting the non-business categories in our framework – notably science, arts, education, socio-economic environment, natural environment and health. It also recognises that all of these last can impact on the 'art of consumption' – that is, how intelligent consumption increases the R-wealth created from a given volume of M-wealth.

As before, it is probably easier for the reader to follow the diagram in matrix format. Once again, the reader may be wondering: do we really need such complexity as this? My answer is that, even if some of the linkages shown are not relevant in certain cases, we shall see in Part III of the book that it is possible to find examples of almost all of these potential linkages. Therefore we need a completely general framework. Moreover, we shall see that when we use Figures 6.4–6.5 to calculate the overall effects of common innovation on R-wealth creation, we usually obtain much larger effects than by using Figures 6.1 or Figures 6.2–6.3.

		Effect Of:								
		Education	Science	Art	Business	Marketplace	Socio-Econ. Environment	Natural Environment	Consumption	Health	R-Wealth
Effect On:	Education										
	Science										
	Art										
	Business										
	Marketplace										
	Socio-Econ. Envt.										
	Natural Envt.										
	Consumption										
	Health										
	R-Wealth										

Figure 6.5 Common Innovation (Matrix Form)

As before, the reader may wish to debate the exact structure of these diagrams. Swann (2009a) and Engelbrecht (2014) present slightly different approaches to the model framework, and both of these work well in their specific contexts. I have devoted a lot of thought to how we should capture these ideas in diagrams like Figures 6.1, 6.2 and 6.4, and have learned three main lessons:

a) There is no single 'right' way to construct the diagram, and there is quite a bit of leeway for personal preference.
b) The 'right' way generally depends on the objective for which the diagram is being used. I reckoned that the framework illustrated above works best in this particular context.
c) The most important things are the differences between Figures 6.1, 6.2 and 6.4. These comprise: the simplicity of Figure 6.1, the greater complexity of Figure 6.2, and the, 'everything is connected to everything else', character of Figure 6.4.

POLICY TOWARDS INNOVATION

Although innovation policy is not the main theme of this book, it is worth considering the implications of these different perspectives for the design of policy. Let us start with Figure 6.1. This seems to describe the way in which some (many?) in government appear to think that policy should work in support of innovation and business. There is an alarming implication of this perspective. It can be taken to imply that the natural environment, the socio-economic environment, science, arts, education and health are only important to society to the extent that they provide useful material to enhance business innovation and business productivity.

So, from this perspective, a project to improve the natural environment in a run-down area is only important to the extent that it improves business innovation or business productivity. Certainly, the economic analysis of clusters tells us that natural environment is one of the 'attractors' that pull in exceptional start-up companies, and hence improves innovation and productivity in the cluster. But the frightening implication seems to be that in the absence of such economic effects, there is no place for schemes to improve the local environment in run down areas, because there is no prospect of these impacting on the innovative economy. The framework of Figure 6.1 would seem to justify such a policy.

And indeed, this is no fiction! British government files released under the '30-year rule' late in 2011, demonstrated that senior Conservative ministers tried to persuade Mrs Thatcher to, 'consider abandoning Liverpool to a fate of "managed decline"' (BBC, 2011d). She was advised that it would be a waste to spend public money on the 'stony ground' of Liverpool and Merseyside, as this would be like, 'trying to make water flow uphill'. Clearly the politicians were aware that this would be political dynamite, but nonetheless they advanced such ideas in writing.

The ultimate implication of this attitude to policy is that there may be no point in repairing the desecration in some northern towns in England, because there is little chance that the international business which politicians want to attract to the UK (by low tax, subsidies and other privileges) would wish to locate in these northern cities. Instead, to the bewilderment of many in the North, government policy based on Figure 6.1 would rate it a greater priority to concentrate our resources in improving the infrastructure of London and the South-East of England.   To people in the North, this is utterly bizarre: what is the sense in taxing poorer people in the North of England to subsidise richer people in London? The framework of Figure 6.1 could appear to offer a rationale for such a very strange and very divisive policy.

It seems to me that we urgently need a more sensible framework to analyse policy design. If business innovation remains the priority for policy, then the framework we need is described by Figures 6.2 and 6.3. But if policy thinking were to advance beyond the promotion of business innovation, and also to give attention to common innovation, then the required framework is described in Figures 6.4 and 6.5.

In general, it seems to me that the appropriate framework is that of Figures 6.4–6.5. Policy measures could focus on any of the columns in the matrix of Figure 6.5. This framework recognises that policy to promote innovation is relevant in many areas of society and economy, and not just in business. And, while some policy innovations may do nothing to increase M-wealth, they could have an important role in increasing R-wealth. Moreover, some of these policy measures may need be directed at correcting some of the dysfunctional side-effects of business innovation.

Chapter 8 below examines a striking example of this. Although Adam Smith was often sceptical about government interventions, there was at least one case in which he felt it was essential. In Book I of his *Wealth of Nations*, he illustrated the enormous power of the division of labour – arguably the most important organisational innovation *of all time* – in enhancing labour productivity. But in Book V, he also acknowledged in graphic detail how the division of labour contributed to the debasement of human capital.   To compensate for this, Smith argued it was essential for England to follow the example of Scotland, and provide public funding for basic education of those who were most likely to suffer from the division of labour in their later lives.

Chapter 8 goes into this in much more detail. In terms of the frameworks and concepts of this book, we can see this as a policy measure to sustain the

R-wealth of ordinary people, which would otherwise suffer from the most damaging consequences of the division of labour. While this book is not about policy, as such, this example shows how enlightened policy can contribute to R-wealth – just as common innovation contributes to R-wealth.

LEONTIEF MODELS

I have sought to keep the use of mathematics to a minimum in this book, but here is one more context in which a little mathematics will deliver massive dividends in our understanding of common innovation. All of the variants in this analytical framework can be seen as special cases of a *Leontief Model* (Leontief, 1953):

$$X = C + AX \tag{6.1}$$

Here, X is a ten-element vector containing the ten categories described above:

$$X = \begin{bmatrix} X_0 \ (\text{Education}) \\ X_1 \ (\text{Science}) \\ X_2 \ (\text{Arts}) \\ X_3 \ (\text{Socio-Economic Environment}) \\ X_4 \ (\text{Natural Environment}) \\ X_5 \ (\text{Health}) \\ X_6 \ (\text{Business}) \\ X_7 \ (\text{Marketplace}) \\ X_8 \ (\text{Consumption}) \\ X_9 \ (\text{R-Wealth}) \end{bmatrix} \tag{6.2}$$

C gives the initial values of each element of X. The matrix A describes the linkages that exist between one category and another: each element A_{ij} describes the *short-run* effect of variable j on variable i. In the Appendix, we show that the *long-run* effect of variable j on variable i (where $i \neq j$) can be written:

$$dX_i / dX_j \;=\; A_{ij} + \sum_{g=0}^{9} A_{ig}A_{gj} + \sum_{g=0}^{9}\sum_{f=0}^{9} A_{ig}A_{gf}A_{fj}$$

$$+ \sum_{g=0}^{9}\sum_{f=0}^{9}\sum_{e=0}^{9} A_{ig}A_{gf}A_{fe}A_{ej} + \ldots$$

(6.3)

In the case where variable i = 9 (R-wealth), this result reinforces Figure 6.2 in giving a very clear illustration of the multiplicity of routes that lead to wealth creation. The first term describes the direct effect of j on R-wealth. The second term describes the ten 'two-step' effects of j on R-wealth (via g). The third term describes the hundred 'three-step' effects of j on R-wealth (via f and g). And the fourth term describes the thousand 'four-step' effects of j on R-wealth (via e, f and g). In principle, we could add in 'five-step' effects, 'six-step' effects, and so on, but these will typically be quite small. We shall revisit this model in Chapter 25.

The frameworks illustrated in Figures 6.4 and 6.5, where anything can influence anything else, are the most general forms of the Leontief Model. Some of the other frameworks above are much more restrictive, with many zero parameters. The Appendix discusses some other special cases.

FIGURES 6.1, 6.2, 6.4 AND FOOTBALL

As I compare Figures 6.1, 6.2 and 6.4, I cannot help but draw an analogy with two deeply contrasting approaches to playing football ('soccer'). In Figure 6.1, we have something akin to the 'Route One' approach adopted by many English Clubs – including some in the Premier League. In Figures 6.2 and 6.4, by contrast, we have something much closer to the 'Tiki-Taka' passing game, associated with FC Barcelona and the Spanish National team (Wikipedia, 2014t).

The 'Route One' approach used in the English game is where a goalkeeper, defender or midfield player boots the ball up-field towards a centre forward, or another tall and strong player, who tries to win it in the air, and then a serious attack can start. 'Route One' is the main channel from defence to attack – and what we see in Figure 6.1 is just that: one main channel. This approach may lack refinement and sophistication, perhaps, but it has stood the test of time in the English game.

The 'Tiki-Taka' approach is entirely different. It involves a rapid passing game between a large number of players – defenders, midfielders and attackers. There is no single channel from defence to attack, but a multiplicity of different routes. In Figure 6.2, every player is, in principle, *equally* involved in the 'Tiki-Taka', and perhaps even FC Barcelona would not be able to live up to that ideal.[1] But the analogy is otherwise a very close one. The economic model of Figure 6.2 offers a 'Tiki-Taka' approach to the creation of R-wealth: there are many possible routes, and we are definitely not limited to a 'Route One' monopoly!

Some clubs in the English game (notably, Arsenal FC) developed a more modest variant of this widespread passing game, to give a 'passing' route from defence to attack. Interestingly, the key player for this purpose, within the Arsenal team of a few years ago, was an ex-Barcelona man, Fábregas.[2] But interestingly, also, it subsequently became clear that Spanish footballers who had come to play in the English Premier League were possibly 'too English' to be satisfactorily re-integrated into the Spanish national side.[3]

'Tiki-Taka' has been a successful strategy in the Spanish context. Before it, the Spanish national team was not one of the leading international teams. But since the adoption of 'Tiki-Taka', the Spanish national team won the UEFA Euro 2008, the 2010 FIFA World Cup and the UEFA Euro 2012.[4]

To provide an adequate representation of 'Tiki-Taka', within a Leontief model, could require an expansion of the Leontief Inverse to 10 or more terms. Contrary to the view of business innovation described in Figure 6.1, very long and complex routes to wealth creation (or goal scoring) may ultimately be very successful!

NOTES

[1]   'Tiki-Taka' requires exceptional accuracy in passing, and a few players manage to achieve a 100 percent success rate in individual games (*Daily Telegraph*, 2013).
[2]   Fábregas famously said (*Guardian*, 2008a), 'At Arsenal there is only one channel between the defence and attack and that is me, so I'm involved in practically all of the attacks, but here with Spain there are more variations, more ways of attacking'.
[3]   *Daily Mail* (2008).
[4]   This chapter was written well in advance of the Football World Cup, 2014. While the book was in production, the Spanish National Team – prime exponents of 'Tiki-Taka' were heavily beaten (5–1) by the Netherlands. Some popular newspapers in the UK proclaimed, with relish, that 'Tiki-Taka is dead'. We shall see.

PART II

The Destructive Side of B-Innovation

7. Wide Frames and the Luddites

A huge amount has been written about the *creative* power of business innovation. Rather less, however, has been written about its *destructive* power. This is surprising since Schumpeter made it so clear that innovation is a perennial gale of creative destruction: the destruction goes hand in hand with the creation.

It is not my purpose here to cast any doubt on the *creative* power of business innovation. Nor is it my purpose to add any new evidence of this. It seems to me that it is well understood, well documented, and needs no further elaboration.[1] And, in any case, I have nothing of much novelty to add here on the subject.

Rather, my purpose in this part of the book is to study the *destructive* side of the 'perennial gale'. I don't do this because I believe it is larger than the creative side – in general, I believe it is not. But I do this because it seems to me that relatively few of those who research the economics of innovation give any attention to its *destructive* side.

We need to give proper attention to the *destructive* side of innovation, for two reasons. First, we need to know more about it and the form it takes. Second, it will help us to investigate the hypothesis I advanced in Chapter 3 about the essential difference between business innovation and common innovation. Is it true that the former is a 'gale' where great creative power is accompanied by destructive power? And is it also true that the latter is a 'gentle and benign breeze' where creative power is more modest, but destructive side-effects are less important?

In my original plan for this book, Part II was to contain a larger number of longer case studies. But when these were finished, Part II was starting to overwhelm the rest of the book – and, indeed, to obscure the main message of the book. Accordingly, I have reduced the number of cases and shortened them.

A CASE STUDY OF THE LUDDITES

The obvious example with which to introduce a discussion of creative destruction is an episode of mechanisation, so damaging to the interests of some that they, in turn, chose to damage these machines. I refer to the Luddite movement of 1811–1816, where impoverished weavers reacted against the indiscriminate use of wide frames, which destroyed their livelihood.[2]

However, I must start this chapter with a caveat: I am certainly no scholar of the Luddite movement, nor indeed of this period of economic history, nor of the textile industry. The Luddite story is one that seems to get more confusing the more sources one consults. Accordingly, I urge the reader to take this short chapter as a motivating example of creative destruction at work, and certainly not to rely on its historical accuracy or completeness.

MACHINE-BREAKING AND GOVERNMENT POLICY

Machine breaking had been known before the Luddite movement. But the Luddite movement attracts attention because of the sheer intensity of machine breaking at its peak, and the punitive measures government introduced to prevent it.

In some earlier episodes, governments were well aware of the likely resistance of traditional workers to machinery that would destroy their livelihood, and they sometimes tried to prevent the application of such machinery.

In 1589, William Lee, a curate at Calverton in Nottinghamshire, invented the stocking frame, a machine for knitting fabric. In due course (and after some further development), this would become one of the most sophisticated textile machines in use, and play a central role in the development of the hosiery industry, and the textile industry more generally (Lewis, 1986).

One version of his story is that a young woman whom he was courting was always preoccupied with knitting when he visited her, and out of his frustration he developed the machine so that she would instead give him her attention. Now, that might sound like a case of common innovation, but in fact Lee had greater ambitions for his invention (Victorian Web, 2005).

After he had successfully developed this machine, and knowing that Queen Elizabeth I was fond of knitted silk stockings, he sought a patent from her. But she did not give him the encouragement that he had expected. She is said to have opposed the invention on the ground that it would surely deprive a large number of poor people of their employment of hand knitting (Victorian Web, 2005).

In 'The Strife between Workman and Machine', Marx (1867/1974, pp. 403–4) describes several earlier episodes of the destructive power of technological change and the reaction to it:

In the 17th century nearly all Europe experienced revolts of the workpeople against the ribbon-loom, a machine for weaving ribbons and trimmings, called in Germany *Bandmühle*, *Schnurmühle*, and *Mühlenstuhl*. These machines were invented in Germany. Abbé Lancellotti, in a work that appeared in Venice in 1636, but which was written in 1579, says as follows:

'Anthony Müller of Danzig saw about 50 years ago in that town, a very ingenious machine, which weaves 4 to 6 pieces at once. But the Mayor being apprehensive that this invention might throw a large number of workmen on the streets, caused the inventor to be secretly strangled or drowned.'

In Leyden, this machine was not used till 1629; there the riots of the ribbon-weavers at length compelled the Town Council to prohibit it.

'In hac urbe,' says Boxhorn ... referring to the introduction of this machine into Leyden, 'ante hos viginti circiter annos instrumentum quidam invenerunt textorium, quo solus plus panni et facilius conficere poterat, quan plures aequali tempore. Hinc turbae ortae et querulae textorum, tandemque usus hujus instrumenti a magistratu prohibitus est.'[3]

After making various decrees more or less prohibitive against this loom in 1632, 1639, &c., the States General of Holland at length permitted it to be used, under certain conditions, by the decree of the 15th December, 1661. It was also prohibited in Cologne in 1676, at the same time that its introduction into England was causing disturbances among the workpeople. By an imperial Edict of 19th Feb., 1685, its use was forbidden throughout all Germany. In Hamburg it was burnt in public by order of the Senate. The Emperor Charles VI., on 9th Feb., 1719, renewed the edict of 1685, and not till 1765 was its use openly allowed in the Electorate of Saxony. This machine, which shook Europe to its foundations, was in fact the precursor of the mule and the power-loom, and of the industrial revolution of the 18th century. It enabled a totally inexperienced boy, to set the whole loom with all its shuttles in motion, by simply moving a rod backwards and forwards, and in its improved form produced from 40 to 50 pieces at once.

Marx, however, singles out, 'the enormous destruction of machinery that occurred in the English manufacturing districts during the first 15 years of this century, chiefly caused by the employment of the power-loom', for particular attention.

THE GRIEVANCES OF THE LUDDITES

The first incident of the Luddite revolution was on 11 March 1811, when workers attacked a shop in Arnold, then a village in Nottinghamshire and now a suburb of Nottingham City, and smashed 63 wide frames installed there, 'belonging to those hosiers who had rendered themselves the most obnoxious to the workmen' (Beckett, 2012). No other damage was done and no violence was reported. After this large number of similar incidents took place in Nottingham and Nottinghamshire, and in due course the Luddite movement spread to other counties.

What were the grievances of the machine-breakers? A good answer is provided by Binfield (2004, p. 15):

> The grievances consisted, first, of the use of wide stocking frames to produce large amounts of cheap, shoddy stocking material that was cut and sown rather than completely fashioned and, second, of the employment of 'colts', workers who had not completed the seven-year apprenticeship required by law.

In his survey of historical documents relating to the Luddite movement, Thomis (1972) draws our attention to a letter from Thomas Hayne, a lace manufacturer of Nottingham, to the Home Secretary (12th February, 1812). Hayne (1812) elaborates on these grievances:

> The alleged cause of breaking these frames, was their making stockings upon wide frames, two at once, and were also 'cut-ups'. It may be proper to observe here, that these wide frames were originally constructed for the purpose of making pantaloons, which required wider frames than were then in use, and for the making of fancy stockings called 'Twills', which were made the length way of the frame. This description of stocking, is now out of use, and pantaloons not being wanted for the Continent, these frames were not employed in the work they were originally intended for, but being applicable to make two stockings at once, many of them were put to work in that way. The men can gain as much or more by their labour on this work — as in frames of other descriptions.

Another source emphasises that the 'cut-ups', and those who produced them, were the real target (Crich, 2012):

> These goods were known as 'cut-ups' and were very bad pieces of work; they represented the real target of the Luddites. Only wide frames could produce these cut-ups, because a large piece of cloth was needed to be cut up and sewn together. The cut-up was then passed off as having been knitted in one piece (what is known even today as fully fashioned). Only those owners who were engaged in 'cut-up' work should have been the targets and only those who had wide frames could do the shoddy work. So, it was not only the new technology that the Luddite attacked, but also the unscrupulous undermining of the reputation and quality of their trade.

The Historian, John Beckett (2012), takes a slightly different line. He argues that the weavers were not opposed to the wide frames or the colts, as such, but objected when employers continued to rely on these wide frames and colts during a trade depression, and thus undermine the skilled workers operating the old narrow frames.

The Luddites knew that the use of wide frames and colts would mean that stockings would no longer be 'completely fashioned' but would instead be made from cheap shoddy stocking material that was cut and roughly sewn into a stocking. They feared, correctly, that these shoddy goods would undermine the market for superior work produced on traditional frames by skilled workers, especially in a recession. They also feared, again correctly, that this trend would do long term damage to the stocking industry in Nottingham.

On this last point, it is interesting to read Babbage's (1835) account. Writing of the difficulties in the lace trade, he observed:

> all the witnesses attribute the decay of the trade more to the making of fraudulent and bad articles, than to the war, or to any other cause ... no orders are now sent for any sort of Nottingham lace, the credit being totally ruined.

And Babbage continued:

> In the stocking trade similar frauds have been practised. It appeared in evidence, that stockings were made of uniform width from the knee down to the ankle, and being wetted and stretched on frames at the calf, they retained their shape when dry, but that the purchaser could not discover the fraud until, after the first washing, the stockings hung like bags about his ankles.

A CONTEMPORARY ECONOMIC PERSPECTIVE

Thomis (1972) draws our attention to a remarkable analysis of these issues provided by Rev. J.T. Becher. Becher was a clergyman and writer on social economy, and later the founder if the Southwell Workhouse. In his letter of 11th February 1812 to the Home Secretary, Becher (1812) provides quite a sophisticated economic analysis of the problem. He notes that until a short while beforehand, there was no problem of over-production:

> Until the commencement of the present war the demand for the Nottinghamshire manufacture exceeded the produce of the machinery & labour in the market. The frames were regarded by every workman as the tutelary guardians of his house: To these the family was indebted for food and raiment, so that they became the objects of their attentive care & most vigilant protection.

He made some important observations about the ownership and hire of frames (Becher, 1812):

> The Frames, upon which Lace & Stockings are woven, are hired by the workmen at stipulated weekly rents, seldom amounting to less than 12 percent, & occasionally to 20 percent, upon the original cost. The prices of these frames vary from £16 to £50, without including additional machinery; and the interest arising from capital so vested has induced Farmers, Servants, Labourers, & others, totally unacquainted with the interests & management of the trade, to become frame owners & to embark their money in this speculation, which was artfully recommended by those hosiers who were desirous of engaging in the lace or hosiery business or of extending their concerns without possessing sufficient pecuniary resources. The frames thus introduced are denominated 'Independents'.

His analysis of the problems proceeds as follows (Becher, 1812):

> The check imposed upon the trade of Nottinghamshire was, at first, but partially felt, because the stock on hand was comparatively of little value; but, as the practice of multiplying Frames & Artificers was continued with unabated zeal, long after the demand for them had ceased, the period arrived, when the warehouses were crowded with goods for which no vent could be found: and the Hosiers, sensible of their difficulties, began to devise arrangements for preventing their increase.
>
> In this emergency, if the Hosiers had acquainted the Workmen with the true situation of the trade; if they had retained those who by long services or large families possessed the best title to protection, the young men would have engaged in other employments or would have entered into the army or navy; and none of our present disturbances would have occurred. But the workmen had, in the season of prosperity, dictated with insolence to their Masters; and an opportunity for retaliation now appeared, of which the latter indiscreetly & unfeelingly availed themselves.
>
> The first attempt to abate the prices of labour originated, as I have been informed, with Mr. Nun the lace manufacturer above seven years ago. As the proposal was novel to the workmen they could not reconcile their minds to a reduction upon the compensation allowed for work; but, after many conferences, they tendered an increased rent for their frames to which the agent of Mr. Nun acceded & all parties were perfectly satisfied. This agreement however was erroneous in its principle & injurious in its operation, since it assisted in concealing the redundancy of labour in the market, while it encouraged the introduction of independent frames with which the trade was then overstocked, and facilitated the projects of needy adventurers who carried on their business by means of the 'Independents'.

And he also comments on the deterioration in quality of production (Becher, 1812):

> The quality of the manufactured goods was progressively deteriorated; and the Workmen found their utmost industry incapable of securing a livelihood. Some Masters in addition to these arrangements delivered out only half the usual weekly work to the Artificers, while they claimed the full rent of their frames while the means of employing them was denied.

He concludes with a policy proposal (Becher, 1812):

> But if tranquillity is to be permanently established it will be necessary to adopt some plan for preventing the frequent renewal of such alarming conflicts. I am aware of the delicacy attaching to any interference with regulations of trade, yet I beg leave most respectfully to submit for your consideration the expediency of passing an act to prescribe by a regulated table, what could be easily drawn, the rent to be paid for every species of frame used in the lace or stocking trade, which might be so estimated, as not to exceed 7½ percent upon the prime cost, and to prohibit any person not supplying a frame with full work from demanding more than half the rent.

DISTRESS OF DISPLACED WEAVERS

Whatever the reader may think of the methods employed by the Luddites, it is essential to understand the sheer distress of the displaced weavers. Marx (1867/1974, p. 404) estimates that, 'in England the power-loom threw 800,000 weavers on the streets'. And he concluded (Marx, 1867/1974, p. 406):

> When machinery seizes on an industry by degrees, it produces chronic misery among the operatives who compete with it. Where the transition is rapid, the effect is acute and felt by great masses. History discloses no tragedy more horrible than the gradual extinction of the English hand-loom weavers, an extinction that was spread over several decades, and finally sealed in 1838. Many of them died of starvation, many with families vegetated for a long time on 2½ pence a day.

Lord Byron's 'maiden' speech to the House of Lords (Byron, 1812) also dwelt on this at length:

> But whilst these outrages must be admitted to exist to an alarming extent, it cannot be denied that they have arisen from circumstances of the most unparalleled distress. The perseverance of these miserable men in their proceedings, tends to prove that nothing but absolute want could have driven a large and once honest and industrious body of the people into the commission of excesses so hazardous to themselves, their families, and the community ... The rejected workmen, in the blindness of their ignorance, instead of rejoicing at these improvements in arts so beneficial to mankind, conceived themselves to be sacrificed to improvements in mechanism. In the foolishness of their hearts, they imagined that the maintenance and well doing of the industrious poor, were objects of greater consequence than the enrichment of a few individuals by any improvement in the implements of trade which threw the workmen out of employment, and rendered the labourer unworthy of his hire ... And, it must be confessed, that although the adoption of the enlarged machinery, in that state of our commerce which the country once boasted, might have been beneficial to the master without being detrimental to the servant; yet, in the present situation of our manufactures, rotting in warehouses without a prospect of exportation, with the demand for work and workmen equally diminished, frames of this construction tend materially to aggravate the distresses and discontents of the disappointed sufferers.

And Thomas Carlyle, writing some years later, delivered a memorable attack on the 'captains of industry', who he considered responsible for this state of over-production (Carlyle, 1843/1899, p. 171):

> My lords and gentlemen, why, it was you that were appointed, by the fact and by the theory of your position on the Earth, to 'make and administer Laws'– that is to say, in a world such as ours, to guard against 'gluts'; against honest operatives, who had done their work, remaining unfed! I say, you were appointed to preside over the Distribution and Apportionment of the Wages of Work done; and to see

well that there went no labourer without his hire, were it of money-coins, were it of hemp gallows-ropes: that function was yours, and from immemorial time has been; yours, and as yet no other's. These poor shirt-spinners have forgotten much, which by the virtual unwritten law of their position they should have remembered: but by any written recognised law of their position, what have they forgotten? They were set to make shirts. The Community with all its voices commanded them, saying, 'Make shirts' – and there the shirts are! Too many shirts? Well, that is a novelty, in this intemperate Earth, with its nine-hundred millions of bare backs! But the Community commanded you, saying, 'See that the shirts are well apportioned, that our Human Laws be emblem of God's Laws' – and where is the apportionment? Two million shirtless or ill-shirted workers sit enchanted in Workhouse Bastilles, five million more (according to some) in Ugolino Hunger-cellars; and for remedy, you say, what say you? – 'Raise our rents! I have not in my time heard any stranger speech, not even on the Shores of the Dead Sea'.

CONCLUSION

The Luddites were not, as the popular use of the term suggests, indiscriminate opponents of new machinery. The Luddite movement was a reaction to the continued use of wide frames and 'colts' in a deep recession, to produce shoddy goods which would undermine the market for superior work produced on traditional frames by skilled workers. Their concerns were justified – as the subsequent decline of the Nottingham industry shows.

This case illustrates that it was not the use of new technology on its own that was damaging. It was the confluence of several factors: the macroeconomic conditions, especially in the Napoleonic Wars; the use of wide frames for a purpose other than that for which they were originally designed; the attempts by the owners to maintain their revenues by quality reduction; and the ownership of the machinery by capital (rather than by a co-operative).

Nonetheless, it emphasises that new technology does have the power to cause widespread destruction of the interests of those who it displaces. And as Lord Byron said – see the longer quotation above – was it really wrong of anyone to imagine that, 'the maintenance and well doing of the industrious poor, were objects of greater consequence than the enrichment of a few individuals by any improvement in the implements of trade which threw the workmen out of employment'? At the very least it is a lesson that when creative destruction causes so much destruction many will question whether the creation is really worth having – until we can evolve commensurate innovations in the socio-economic environment which insure the displaced against their losses.

NOTES

1   Several excellent studies have discussed the historical role of business innovation in wealth creation – notably, Rosenberg et al. (1992), Baumol (2002), and Landes (2003).

2   Many of the most important historical episodes took place in Nottinghamshire, only a few miles from where I live, but the movement was also active outside Nottinghamshire – see Thomis (1970) for an overview.

3   'In this town, about twenty years ago certain people invented an instrument for weaving, with which a single person could weave more cloth, and more easily, than many others in the same length of time. As a result there arose disturbances and complaints from the weavers, until the Town Council finally prohibited the use of this instrument.' – translation from http://www. marxists.org/archive/marx/works/1867-c1/ch15.htm#S5

8. The Division of Labour

Adam Smith did not discuss the idea of creative destruction as such. That did not come until the work of Sombart and Schumpeter. Nonetheless, Smith's *Wealth of Nations* does indeed contain a discussion of what we could now describe as the creative destruction caused by the division of labour. Book I contains his well known discussion of the creative side of the division of labour, while Book V contains the less well known discussion of the destructive side. Smith discusses this contrast with such care that it is worthy of a short chapter here.

PRODUCTIVE POWER

Adam Smith put the division of labour at the heart of his theory of wealth creation. In Book I of the *Wealth of Nations*, he analyses in detail how the division of labour can lead to massively increased productivity. I quote him at length because he explains all this with such clarity (Smith, 1776/1904a, pp. 5–6):

> The greatest improvement in the productive powers of labour, and the greater part of the skill, dexterity, and judgment with which it is anywhere directed, or applied, seem to have been the effects of the division of labour ...
> To take an example, therefore, from a very trifling manufacture; but one in which the division of labour has been very often taken notice of, the trade of the pin-maker; a workman not educated to this business (which the division of labour has rendered a distinct trade), nor acquainted with the use of the machinery employed in it (to the invention of which the same division of labour has probably given occasion), could scarce, perhaps, with his utmost industry, make one pin in a day, and certainly could not make twenty. But in the way in which this business is now carried on, not only the whole work is a peculiar trade, but it is divided into a number of branches, of which the greater part are likewise peculiar trades. One man draws out the wire, another straights it, a third cuts it, a fourth points it, a fifth grinds it at the top for receiving, the head; to make the head requires two or three distinct operations; to put it on is a peculiar business, to whiten the pins is another; it is even a trade by itself to put them into the paper; and the important business of making a pin is, in this manner, divided into about eighteen distinct operations, which, in some manufactories, are all performed by distinct hands, though in others the same man will sometimes perform two or three of them. I have seen a small manufactory of this kind where ten men only were employed, and where

some of them consequently performed two or three distinct operations. But though they were very poor, and therefore but indifferently accommodated with the necessary machinery, they could, when they exerted themselves, make among them about twelve pounds of pins in a day. There are in a pound upwards of four thousand pins of a middling size. Those ten persons, therefore, could make among them upwards of forty-eight thousand pins in a day. Each person, therefore, making a tenth part of forty-eight thousand pins, might be considered as making four thousand eight hundred pins in a day. But if they had all wrought separately and independently, and without any of them having been educated to this peculiar business, they certainly could not each of them have made twenty, perhaps not one pin in a day; that is, certainly, not the two hundred and fortieth, perhaps not the four thousand eight hundredth part of what they are at present capable of performing, in consequence of a proper division and combination of their different operations.

In every other art and manufacture, the effects of the division of labour are similar to what they are in this very trifling one; though, in many of them, the labour can neither be so much subdivided, nor reduced to so great a simplicity of operation. The division of labour, however, so far as it can be introduced, occasions, in every art, a proportionable increase of the productive powers of labour. The separation of different trades and employments from one another seems to have taken place in consequence of this advantage.

... the improvement of the dexterity of the workman necessarily increases the quantity of the work he can perform; and the division of labour, by reducing every man's business to some one simple operation, and by making this operation the sole employment of his life, necessarily increased very much dexterity of the workman. A common smith, who, though accustomed to handle the hammer, has never been used to make nails, if upon some particular occasion he is obliged to attempt it, will scarce, I am assured, be able to make above two or three hundred nails in a day, and those too very bad ones. A smith who has been accustomed to make nails, but whose sole or principal business has not been that of a nailer, can seldom with his utmost diligence make more than eight hundred or a thousand nails in a day. I have seen several boys under twenty years of age who had never exercised any other trade but that of making nails, and who, when they exerted themselves, could make, each of them, upwards of two thousand three hundred nails in a day. The making of a nail, however, is by no means one of the simplest operations. The same person blows the bellows, stirs or mends the fire as there is occasion, heats the iron, and forges every part of the nail: in forging the head too he is obliged to change his tools. The different operations into which the making of a pin, or of a metal button, is subdivided, are all of them much more simple, and the dexterity of the person, of whose life it has been the sole business to perform them, is usually much greater. The rapidity with which some of the operations of those manufacturers are performed, exceeds what the human hand could, by those who had never seen them, be supposed capable of acquiring.

The idea was further developed by several other economists, most notably by Charles Babbage. In his book, *On the Economy of Machinery and Manufactures*, he articulated what is now known as the 'Babbage Principle' (1835, pp. 175–6):

the master manufacturer, by dividing the work to be executed into different processes, each requiring different degrees of skill or of force, can purchase exactly that precise quantity of both which is necessary for each process; whereas, if the whole work were executed by one workman, that person must possess sufficient skill to perform the most difficult, and sufficient strength to execute the most laborious, of the operations into which the art is divided.

We can appreciate the importance of the Babbage effect as follows. In Smith's analysis, the division of labour increases productivity through 'learning by doing'. The Babbage effect divides labour into two components: for example, those requiring skill, and those requiring strength. If the division of labour were not a practicality, workers would need to have skill *and* strength. But when the division of labour is possible, we can allocate different tasks to different workers according to their endowments of skill and strength. As Swann (2009a, p. 178) argues, it would be hard to assemble a truly world class cricket team without the Babbage effect.[1]

DESTRUCTIVE POWER

But while Smith extolled the creative power of the division of labour in Book 1 of the *Wealth of Nations*, he did not flinch from describing its *destructive* power in Book V (Smith, 1776/1904b, p. 267):[2]

In the progress of the division of labour, the employment of the far greater part of those who live by labour, that is, of the great body of the people, comes to be confined to a few very simple operations, frequently to one or two. But the understandings of the greater part of men are necessarily formed by their ordinary employments. The man whose whole life is spent in performing a few simple operations, of which the effects are perhaps always the same, or very nearly the same, has no occasion to exert his understanding or to exercise his invention in finding out expedients for removing difficulties which never occur. He naturally loses, therefore, the habit of such exertion, and generally becomes as stupid and ignorant as it is possible for a human creature to become. The torpor of his mind renders him not only incapable of relishing or bearing a part in any rational conversation, but of conceiving any generous, noble, or tender sentiment, and consequently of forming any just judgement concerning many even of the ordinary duties of private life. Of the great and extensive interests of his country he is altogether incapable of judging, and unless very particular pains have been taken to render him otherwise, he is equally incapable of defending his country in war. The uniformity of his stationary life naturally corrupts the courage of his mind, and makes him regard with abhorrence the irregular, uncertain, and adventurous life of a soldier. It corrupts even the activity of his body, and renders him incapable of exerting his strength with vigour and perseverance in any other employment than that to which he has been bred. His dexterity at his own particular trade seems, in this manner, to be acquired at the expense of his intellectual, social, and martial virtues. But in every improved and civilised society this is the state into which the labouring poor, that is, the great body of the people, must necessarily fall, unless government takes some pains to prevent it.

Smith argued that the situation was different in simple societies that had not developed such a division of labour (Smith, 1776/1904b, p. 268):

> In such societies the varied occupations of every man oblige every man to exert his capacity and to invent expedients for removing difficulties which are continually occurring. Invention is kept alive, and the mind is not suffered to fall into that drowsy stupidity which, in a civilized society, seems to benumb the understanding of almost all the inferior ranks of people.

Later writers have developed this theme with great passion. One of the most emotional critics was John Ruskin:[3]

> We have much studied and much perfected, of late, the great civilized invention of the division of labour; only we give it a false name. It is not, truly speaking, the labour that is divided; but the men:—Divided into mere segments of men—broken into small fragments and crumbs of life; so that all the little piece of intelligence that is left in a man is not enough to make a pin, or a nail, but exhausts itself in making the point of a pin or the head of a nail. Now it is a good and desirable thing, truly, to make many pins in a day; but if we could only see with what crystal sand their points were polished,—sand of human soul, much to be magnified before it can be discerned for what it is—we should think there might be some loss in it also. And the great cry that rises from all our manufacturing cities, louder than their furnace blast, is all in very deed for this,—that we manufacture everything there except men; we blanch cotton, and strengthen steel, and refine sugar, and shape pottery; but to brighten, to strengthen, to refine, or to form a single living spirit, never enters into our estimate of advantages.

Marx (1844) developed this further:

> With this division of labour on the one hand and the accumulation of capital on the other, the worker becomes ever more exclusively dependent on labour, and on a particular, very one-sided, machine-like labour at that. Just as he is thus depressed spiritually and physically to the condition of a machine and from being a man becomes an abstract activity and a belly, so he also becomes ever more dependent on every fluctuation in market price, on the application of capital, and on the whim of the rich.

And Durkheim (1893/1984, p. 307) emphasised that it is not just repetitive manual labour that can be damaging:

> If we have often rightly deplored on the material plane the fact of the worker exclusively occupied throughout his life in making knife handles or pinheads, a healthy philosophy must not, all in all, cause us to regret any the less on the intellectual plane the exclusive and continual use of the brain to resolve a few equations or classify a few insects: the moral effect, in both cases, is unfortunately

very similar.

All of this provides the foundation for William Morris's memorable and scathing attack on the division of labour (1879/1966, p. 82):

> the division of labour, once the servant, and now the master of competitive commerce, itself once the servant, and now the master of civilization.

In contrast, Ludwig von Mises (1951) argued that these negative effects are exaggerated, because even if labour is monotonous, the citizen can recreate himself with a judicious use of leisure time. Indeed, many working people today exercise their common innovation in the time they have for recreation. However, there is one very widespread negative effect of the division of labour that is rarely repaired in this way. We can call it the *limited vision* of specialised labour: the inability of one type of specialised labour to understand the perspectives and concerns of other types of specialised labour.[4]

PUBLIC POLICY TOWARDS BASIC EDUCATION

Having identified these problems, Smith proposes a solution: public funding of basic education (Smith, 1776/1904b, p. 269):

> The education of the common people requires, perhaps, in a civilized and commercial society the attention of the public more than that of people of some rank and fortune.

He argued that the children of people of 'rank and fortune' would not work until perhaps 18 or 19 years old, and their parents or guardians would generally spend enough to ensure that they were well educated before starting their work. Moreover, he argued (Smith, 1776/1904b, p. 269):

> The employments, too, in which people of some rank or fortune spend the greater part of their lives are not, like those of the common people, simple and uniform. They are almost all of them extremely complicated, and such as exercise the head more than the hands. The understandings of those who are engaged in such employments can seldom grow torpid for want of exercise. The employments of people of some rank and fortune, besides, are seldom such as harass them from morning to night. They generally have a good deal of leisure, during which they may perfect themselves in every branch either of useful or ornamental knowledge of which they may have laid the foundation, or for which they may have acquired some taste in the earlier part of life.

How different it is for ordinary people (Smith, 1776/1904b, p. 269):

It is otherwise with the common people. They have little time to spare for education. Their parents can scarce afford to maintain them even in infancy. As soon as they are able to work they must apply to some trade by which they can earn their subsistence. That trade, too, is generally so simple and uniform as to give little exercise to the understanding, while, at the same time, their labour is both so constant and so severe, that it leaves them little leisure and less inclination to apply to, or even to think of, anything else.

But Smith argues that for a small expense, the public can ensure that the whole population acquire a basic education (Smith, 1776/1904b, p. 270):

> The public can facilitate this acquisition by establishing in every parish or district a little school, where children may be taught for a reward so moderate that even a common labourer may afford it; the master being partly, but not wholly, paid by the public, because, if he was wholly, or even principally, paid by it, he would soon learn to neglect his business. In Scotland the establishment of such parish schools has taught almost the whole common people to read, and a very great proportion of them to write and account. In England the establishment of charity schools has had an effect of the same kind, though not so universally, because the establishment is not so universal.

Smith argues that instruction in Latin would be better replaced by instruction in elementary geometry and mechanics, because (Smith, 1776/1904b, p. 270):

> There is scarce a common trade which does not afford some opportunities of applying to it the principles of geometry and mechanics, and which would not therefore gradually exercise and improve the common people in those principles, the necessary introduction to the most sublime as well as to the most useful sciences.

Smith develops quite detailed proposals along these lines, and notes that this was the approach used in ancient Greece and Rome to maintain the spirit of their citizens. And he discusses the value of this to society (Smith, 1776/1904b, p. 272):

> Even though the martial spirit of the people were of no use towards the defence of the society, yet to prevent that sort of mental mutilation, deformity, and wretchedness, which cowardice necessarily involves in it, from spreading themselves through the great body of the people, would still deserve the most serious attention of government, in the same manner as it would deserve its most serious attention to prevent a leprosy or any other loathsome and offensive disease, though neither mortal nor dangerous, from spreading itself among them, though perhaps no other public good might result from such attention besides the prevention of so great a public evil.

And Smith proposes a similar rationale for the basic education of those who have been broken by the division of labour (Smith, 1776/1904b, pp. 272–3):

> The same thing may be said of the gross ignorance and stupidity which, in a civilized society, seem so frequently to benumb the understandings of all the inferior ranks of people. A man without the proper use of the intellectual faculties of a man, is, if possible, more contemptible than even a coward, and seems to be mutilated and deformed in a still more essential part of the character of human nature. Though the state was to derive no advantage from the instruction of the inferior ranks of people, it would still deserve its attention that they should not be altogether uninstructed. The state, however, derives no inconsiderable advantage from their instruction. The more they are instructed the less liable they are to the delusions of enthusiasm and superstition, which, among ignorant nations, frequently occasion the most dreadful disorders. An instructed and intelligent people, besides, are always more decent and orderly than an ignorant and stupid one. They feel themselves, each individually, more respectable and more likely to obtain the respect of their lawful superiors, and they are therefore more disposed to respect those superiors. They are more disposed to examine, and more capable of seeing through, the interested complaints of faction and sedition, and they are, upon that account, less apt to be misled into any wanton or unnecessary opposition to the measures of government. In free countries, where the safety of government depends very much upon the favourable judgment which the people may form of its conduct, it must surely be of the highest importance that they should not be disposed to judge rashly or capriciously concerning it.

CONCLUSION

As we said at the start of this chapter, Adam Smith did not use the concept of creative destruction but, as we have seen, Smith's *Wealth of Nations* contains a discussion of what we could now describe as the creative destruction caused by the division of labour. He started by describing the huge contribution of that organisational innovation to productivity, and then examined the dysfunctional effects of the division of labour. He considered that the latter effects were serious enough to call for a publicly-funded policy intervention in basic education.

Some business-people have been quick to criticise the educational system, claiming that it is letting down ordinary people, and that it is letting down business. However, some of these same business people conveniently forget that their predecessors' strategy, the division of labour, played a large part in creating the deeply ingrained education problem. If Adam Smith is correct, then there is little wonder that the educational system faces quite a challenge to put this right!

Some will argue, in a similar way to von Mises, that the problems of division of labour could be overcome by mind-broadening education. Yes, that could be – *if* that education does broaden the mind. And that will only happen if students from one tradition are taught to respect work from another tradition. Without that, education will only reinforce the dysfunctional side of the division of labour.[5]

NOTES

[1]   The point can be readily understood if we consider that very few cricketers have ever achieved world class stature as *all of the following at the same time*: batsman, spin-bowler, fast-bowler, fielder, and captain.

[2]   The arguments of this section are further developed in Swann (2012).

[3]   Ruskin (1904/1996, vol. 10, p. 196)

[4]   There are countless examples of this limited vision of specialised labour in the academic world: the economist who cannot understand the many aspects of wealth that cannot be measured; the engineer who cannot fully understand the economic and social effects of their engines; the scientist who has no sense of the humanities; and those in the arts and humanities who have little or no understanding of science. This is the problem of *Two Cultures* – as described by C.P. Snow (1959).

[5]   Early in my career it was my privilege to teach (or try to teach) economics to scientists and engineers. I recall one of the engineering students telling me that his tutors thought economics was not a serious subject, and had told him he shouldn't take it seriously! And, indeed, he didn't – nor did many of his class-mates! But, much as these students found it very irksome to study economics, we also found them very hard work to teach, partly because they did not make much effort, and partly because most of them were really rather *bad* at economics. While they were undoubtedly very talented at mathematics, they found it hard to spell out a sensible economic argument. I have sometimes reflected on which background (outside economics) is ideal for the study of economics. As an MBA teacher, I taught economics to students from all sorts of backgrounds: maths, science, engineering, humanities, arts, performing arts, music, divinity, classics, and others. The best students usually had an arts or classics background. Indeed, the most naturally talented economist I ever met had a background in classical Greek and ancient history.

9. Online and Local Booksellers

Now we turn to some contemporary examples of creative destruction. The first is one that would, surely, have been of great interest to Joseph Schumpeter. It is the competition between online booksellers, notably Amazon, and traditional bricks and mortar bookstores.

THE INTERNET AND PERFECT COMPETITION

In 2000, the Economist newspaper published a survey of Internet economics, with the bold conclusion (*Economist*, 2000):

> the Internet cuts costs, increases competition and improves the functioning of the price mechanism. It thus moves the economy closer to the textbook model of perfect competition.

While all the assertions in the first sentence are correct, the conclusion in the second sentence has been shown to be quite wrong in some industries. It is true that online retailing may appear to level the playing field, and remove one of the main disadvantages facing small and remote businesses. But when the selling operation enjoys very substantial economies of scale and scope, the outcome is likely to be more concentration, and not perfect competition.

One of the most powerful counterexamples to the idea that the Internet will lead to perfect competition has been in bookselling. Online bookselling has enabled a smaller number of large players (notably Amazon) to exploit economies of scale and has driven many smaller bookshops out of the market. And this is, perhaps, just one example of a more general phenomenon with online retailing.

In his discussion of creative destruction, Joseph Schumpeter (1942, p. 84) was especially interested in:

> competition from the new commodity, the new technology, the new source of supply, the new type of organization (the largest-scale unit of control for instance) —competition which commands a decisive cost or quality advantage and which strikes not at the margins of the profits and the outputs of the existing firms but at their foundations and their very lives.

The online retailing of books is a clear example of that. The business model of Amazon is an object lesson in the use of computer technologies to achieve rapid order processing, speed of delivery and massive economies of scale. Many local 'bricks and mortar' bookstores have found that Amazon has indeed struck, 'at their foundations and their very lives'.

How much difference has it made? An article in the *Daily Telegraph* (2011b) gave the following summary:

> Heavy discounting by supermarkets, the rise of Internet retailers and the growing popularity of e-readers such as the Kindle have forced nearly 2,000 bookshops to close since 2005. There were 2,178 high street bookshops left in Britain in July, according to research carried out by Experian, the data company, compared with 4,000 in 2005. A total of 580 towns do not have a single bookshop.

And it is not just small bookstores that find themselves unable to compete. In June 2012, it was announced that the World's biggest bookstore (in Toronto) would close (Quill and Quire, 2012). In the UK, even the large chains have had to shut some of their branches. Moreover, a submission from the Booksellers Association to the Office of Fair Trading in 2011 estimated that Internet-only booksellers in UK account for 31 percent of book sales by value, and that Amazon accounts for 70 percent of book sales on the Internet (Booksellers Association, 2011).

DOES IT MATTER?

Suppose, for a moment, that everybody has the same tastes, that everybody is active online, and that everybody chooses to buy books online rather than from their local bookstore. In that case, it could be that the demise of the local bookstore doesn't matter much to this homogeneous group of consumers. It does of course matter to the proprietors of local bookstores, and as such it is, definitely, creative destruction. But this supposedly homogeneous group of consumers don't seem too concerned about this element of destruction.

However, a cursory look at the newspapers makes it clear that feelings about the demise of the local bookstore run very high indeed. It matters a great deal to many people. For one thing, the assumptions in the last paragraph do not apply. People do not all have the same tastes, not everyone is active on line, nor do they wish to be, and plenty of people do not want to buy books online. They buy from local bookstores because these stores are more than just a source of books; they play an important and thoroughly benign part in the local community. A headline in the *Daily Telegraph* (2011a) put it very well: 'every bookshop closure creates a hole in our communities'. The Booksellers Association (n.d.) identifies several benign effects of local bookstores:

- Bookshops are havens for everyone, building community character and contributing to the distinct flavour of a neighbourhood.
- Bookshops are literary and cultural hubs, bringing members of the community together to discuss books, exchange ideas and meet authors.
- Bookshops support local and national causes and events, including reading groups, schools, libraries, arts organisations, festivals and charities.

Some value other features of the service offered at 'bricks and mortar' bookshops, in particular the availability of knowledgeable staff, and the opportunity to browse before purchase.[1]

But, despite their loyal followers, the profitability of local bookstores is generally fairly precarious. Suppose that 30 percent of customers switch to buying online. That loss of 30 percent of sales is enough to break the local store. In effect, the survival of the local bookstore requires that a large majority (perhaps 80 percent plus) of local book-buyers vote – as it were – in favour of the local store. A simple majority of book-buyers is not enough; it must be a large majority. And after the local store has gone out of business, it is the 70 percent who did not want to buy online who lose out, while the 30 percent who switched do not lose much.

Moreover, it is likely that the losers feel their losses particularly acutely. They are the ones who appreciate the benign properties of the bookstore in the local community, and who feel (understandably) that big bookstores and, especially, online booksellers simply don't offer those other benign characteristics. By contrast, those who switch to online buying are probably the ones that care much less about these benign properties, and to them, the demise of the local bookstore is much less important.

It is a well recognised principle in marketing that the extent to which someone complains or expresses dissatisfaction is inversely related to his/her elasticity of demand. Those with a high elasticity of demand simply switch to another source, but those who do not have another comparable source are the ones who will complain. Those with a low elasticity of demand for buying from 'bricks and mortar' stores do, presumably, attach some considerable value to that service. This observation might, in principle, be exploited by local bookstores as a route to survival. They may be able to 'tap' the loyal followers' inelasticity of demand, and charge for some of the other services they provide, thus making up some of the shortfall in revenue. We consider in the next section whether that strategy is likely to work.

REVIVAL OF THE LOCAL?

At this point I shall appear to change the subject completely! But in fact there is a close connection between this apparent detour, and the future of independent booksellers.

As we shall see in Chapter 11, between 1900 and 1975, the number of breweries in England declined from about 1319 to 139. But then, thanks to the efforts of CAMRA (The Campaign for Real Ale), that trend was reversed, and by 2004, there were 480 breweries (Swann, 2010), and by 2010, a total of 767 (BBC, 2010). This represents a marked, and very exciting, 'revival of the local'. The long process of industrial and geographical concentration of breweries was followed by a process of horizontal product innovation and geographical dispersion. Admittedly, many of the new breweries are small businesses, with only a small volume of production, and the industry is still dominated by the big brewers. Nonetheless, the significant thing is that the small brewers can still survive.

Could independent booksellers enjoy a similar, 'revival of the local'? Some optimists believe so. One article in *The Bookseller* (2009) ran with a very optimistic title: 'Indies predict golden age for bookselling' (The term 'Indies' is a abbreviation of 'Independents'.)

As we saw above, the net figures are gloomy, with a continuing downward trend in the number of independent booksellers. But Booksellers Association statistics showed that although 83 independent stores closed in 2008, 66 new ones opened (*Bookseller*, 2009). Some of the entrants are managed by exceptionally experienced staff who know the business very well. These managers emphasise the importance of employing well-read staff who know their stock very well. Some were planning to combine sales of new books with sales of high quality second-hand books. One of these managers was quoted saying (*Bookseller*, 2009):

> The indie bookseller is set for a return for several reasons: people value a knowledgeable bookseller, they like an individual shop which does not look the same as every other, and they are tired of the hard sell.

But the downward trend has continued. In 2006, there were 1483 independent bookstores affiliated to the Booksellers Association; by 2011, that number had fallen to 1099 (BBC, 2011a).

There are of course some important differences between the economics of the micro-brewery and the economics of book-selling. Three in particular stand out.

Economies of Scale and Scope

Amazon is successful because it has been successful in exploiting economics of scale and scope. They stock everything while the local bookstore cannot hope to stock everything. In that sense, the local bookstore simply cannot cover the whole range in the way that online bookstores can do.

By contrast, while large brewers may enjoy the advantage of economies of scale, they do not appear to enjoy economies of scope. This is partly because the large brewer produces the final product in very large batches, and it is not economic to produce a wide variety of beers in small quantities. But even more important that that, big brewers rely on branding to sell their beers, and because of the large economies of scale in branding, they do not want a large number of beers in their portfolio.

Difference in Consumer Behaviour

Some readers may approach the bookstore with no clear idea of what it is they wish to buy, apart perhaps from the generality that they want some good fiction to read on holiday. Such readers will surely be guided by knowledgeable staff and will emerge with a satisfactory purchase. But many readers have a very specific title in mind from the start – or a very small number of specific titles – and unless the bookstore has this specific book, they will emerge empty-handed. Before online booksellers, we would ask the bookstore to order the book, but now, if the book has to be ordered specially, then it is quicker and cheaper to do it online.

Those who appreciate real ale, however, have a rather different approach. First and foremost, very few people emerge from a pub without having had a drink! Even the most demanding beer drinker will usually find something acceptable, even if the pub keeps at most a small array of beers. And many will take some pleasure in trying a real ale with which they are unfamiliar.

Transporting the Product

Online booksellers can provide an efficient book supply service from a small number of warehouses. For example, Amazon has (in 2013) seven 'fulfilment centres' for Great Britain: Brogborough, Peterborough, Doncaster and Hemel Hempstead (England), Gourock and Dunfermline (Scotland), and Swansea (Wales).[2] Because the product is easily transported, Amazon can easily supply the whole of the Great Britain market from these seven warehouses. The online buyer will probably not know, and will almost certainly not care, which of these centres supplies his order – unless something goes wrong. And the online buyer in Nottingham, say, would not be at all impressed if the online bookstore said, 'we cannot supply your order, as it is only stocked in our Swansea warehouse'.

The story is different with brewing. The national brands produced by the big brewers are treated in the brewery so that they can be transported around the whole country. By contrast, real ale does not travel very well, and is usually only found in the region where it is brewed. The discerning real ale drinker will certainly want to know where the beer is brewed, and would fully understand and approve if the publican in Nottingham were to say, 'I cannot offer that beer because it is brewed too far away – in Cornwall'.

These three factors mean that small brewers can still survive in a market dominated by big brewers, because so few of those who prefer real ale will desert it in favour of one of the big brewers' national brands. By contrast, many book buyers will not find what they want in the local bookstore, and will chose to buy online instead.

SECOND-HAND BOOKSELLERS

The story so far concerns the sale of *new* books. Interestingly enough, however, in the market for second hand and antiquarian books, the effect of the Internet has been somewhat different. Use of the Internet has enabled small, specialist booksellers to improve their performance by exploiting the much larger marketplace accessible online. Several sites offer an easy way to search the stock of thousands of second-hand booksellers, including: Abebooks, Alibris and Biblio. And the communities served by these sites are large. For example, Abebooks has (in 2012) a community of 2053 booksellers in the UK and 7058 in the USA.[3] Many of these booksellers are very small organisations, and yet they survive.

Of course, the economics of second-hand and antiquarian bookselling is rather different from the economics of new bookselling. First of all, the large discounts that online sellers can negotiate from publishers are not relevant in the case of second-hand books. Second, the supply of second-hand books is rather unpredictable, and it would be hard for an online seller to commit to keeping a stock of all old titles. And third, it would be hard to see how a 'sale or return' deal could operate with second-hand books.

In the light of that, small second-hand bookstores are unlikely to be undermined by the online bookselling giants. However, it is highly likely that the online giants may seek to capture some of the profit in second-hand book sales by acquiring the second-hand book sites listed above and increasing their charges to booksellers. Indeed, Amazon already acquired Abebooks in 2008 (Abe Books, 2012).

CONCLUSION

Although some optimists still think that independent 'bricks and mortar' bookstores will survive, it seems that online bookselling is steadily driving more and more independents out of business.

This is a powerful example of creative destruction. The creative side is a powerful business model that can supply even the most obscure books at low cost and great speed. But there is a highly destructive side too. There is the loss of business and livelihood for independent booksellers. But there is also the loss to book buyers who would greatly prefer to browse and buy their books at the local bookstore, but can no longer do so.

And there are, potentially, some further destructive effects which may not be felt until some time later. For example, some predict that the death of the local bookstore will lead to a decline in literacy, and certainly that would impact on an individual's M-wealth *and* R-wealth. And some have gone as far as to suggest that the decline of bookshops and libraries will lead to an increase in anti-social behaviour (*Daily Telegraph*, 2011b).

NOTES

[1]   Some small independent bookstores complain that customers browse in their stores, but then buy the book online. It is obviously hard to say how common this is.

[2]   Information from Wikipedia (2013a). The Dunfermline centre replaced the centre in Glenrothes at the end of 2011.

[3]   These figures were obtained by searching Abe Books (2012) for sellers in the UK and USA, respectively.

10. Software Innovation and e-Waste

In this chapter, we look at an unexpected example of the destructive side of innovation. We shall see that software innovation has been an important contributor to personal computer e-waste – that is, the disposal of personal computers that are still in perfect working order, but are unable to run the most recent software.

When I first taught a class on this to our MBA students, a few years ago, they were astonished that there should be any connection between software innovation, which they saw as a very 'clean' activity, and e-waste, which is clearly a very 'toxic' problem. And indeed, the issue of personal computer e-waste did not really surface as a problem until 2002, and the connection to software innovation was only recognised from about 2005. Be that as it may, Greenpeace now recognises e-waste as one of the fastest growing types of hazardous waste.

In this chapter we shall start with a short summary of the creative side of software innovation. Then we show, by means of a very simple model, why there is a connection between the rate of software innovation and the growth of e-waste. Next, we discuss why the problem is exacerbated by a tendency towards 'software bloat' and by some of the marketing strategies adopted by software companies. Finally, we assess the size of the e-waste problem and the damage it does.[1]

THE CREATIVE SIDE OF SOFTWARE INNOVATION

Software innovation for personal computers is one of the most creative and powerful innovations of our age. I have written about this at length in Swann (2009c). But, in line with my argument above that the creative side of creative destruction is well understood while the destructive side is not, I shall only give a brief summary here.

Firstly, what did these innovations do for the innovators? There is no doubt that they have delivered massive competitive advantage to the innovators. For example, innovations in operating systems helped to secure Microsoft's position as supplier of industry standard operating systems software. But innovations in Windows were, in fact, even more significant than that, because they also enhanced Microsoft's competitive position in applications software. In particular, because their Windows operating system was the industry standard, Microsoft were also able to achieve integration between 'office' packages (e.g. word processor, spreadsheet, database and presentation software) in a way that other companies could not. In the MSDOS era, before Windows, Microsoft were market leaders in operating systems but not in word processors, spreadsheets, databases or presentation software. By the Windows era, however, Microsoft were market leaders in all these segments.

Secondly, were these innovations of equal value to the user? Or did they just lead to Microsoft winning market share from other software rivals? In my view, these innovations in operating systems and applications software contributed value to the user in three specific ways. First, the operating system standards and the stream of innovations within the standards have encouraged a proliferation of software. This includes more choice of software within each category of application but also new types of applications software. Second, the integration between packages and 'look and feel' standardisation of the Windows era has probably enhanced the productivity and versatility of software users. And third, the enhanced features of successive software versions are of value to some users, at least. However, many consider it is probable that diminishing returns have now set in, and relatively few users will benefit from further innovations of these sorts.

In view of these positive contributions, some suggest that I am being pedantic (and even Luddite) to fuss about environmental side-effects. I don't agree with that assessment. But more important, I think their objection misses the point. The level of software innovation achieved ten years ago (2002) gave most PC users all the functionality they could possibly need. By that time, e-waste was emerging as an issue, but was nothing like the problem it has now become. It is software innovations since then that have made a far larger contribution to e-waste – and arguably these innovations, and the consequent waste, were not necessary for most users.

FROM SOFTWARE INNOVATION TO E-WASTE

A very simple model can illustrate why there is a link from software innovation to e-waste. It is based on three principles.

The first is Moore's Law (Intel, n.d.), illustrated in Figure 10.1 which states that the capacity of a new computer doubles every two years. In 1965, Gordon Moore – one of the founders of Intel Corporation – observed that during the first five years of integrated circuit history, the number of active components per chip had doubled every year and that it was reasonable to expect this to continue.[2] Later, Moore said that this very steep exponential rate of growth could not continue, but that a doubling in components per chip every two years was still quite feasible. And indeed, if we look at the numbers of components on each of the new generations of Intel microprocessor introduced over the period 1971–2010, these fit Moore's Law very accurately indeed.

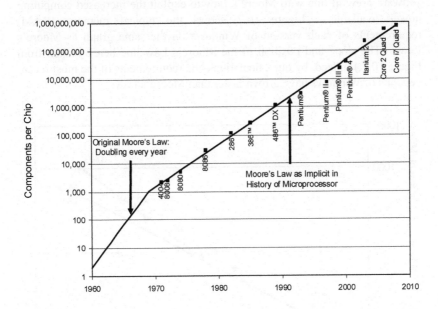

Figure 10.1 Moore's Law

Source: Author's graph based on data from www.Intel.com.

Moreover, Moore's Law is not just an accurate forecast, but has been used as a technology vision in the electronics and computer industries around which all players coordinate their technology strategies.

The second principle is that the resource demands of new software increase at the same rate as Moore's Law. In parallel with Moore's Law, there have been remarkable developments in PC software. The very first PCs all had their own individual interpreters or monitors in ROM, and there was no disk operating system as such. The first operating system to get anywhere near the status of a standard was CP/M, produced by Digital Research. The introduction of the IBM PC in December 1981 would change all that. IBM turned to Microsoft to supply their MS-DOS operating system for use on the IBM PC. It did not take long for MS-DOS to replace CP/M as the most common standard operating system. But from 1990 onwards, Windows Version 3.0, and especially Version 3.1 quite quickly replaced MS-DOS as the standard operating system. As with MS-DOS, Windows went through several successive versions from the first popular version (3.0) in 1990, up to Vista (in 2007), Windows 7 (in 2009) and Windows 8 (in 2012).

The functionality and hardware requirements of this operating system software grew in line with Moore's Law to exploit the increased computing power available. Figure 10.2 shows the typical memory (RAM) requirements of each version of Windows on the same graph as Moore's Law. (The slope and position of the Moore's Law line here is taken from Figure 10.1.) Indeed, by our calculations, the requirements of the most recent versions of Windows have grown faster than Moore's Law.

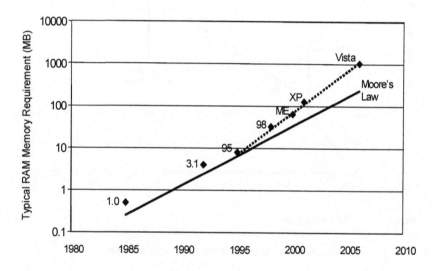

Figure 10.2   Memory Requirements of Software

Source: Author's graph (Swann 2009c, 2009d), based on data from www.microsoft.com and other trade sources.

For the purposes of our simple model, however, we shall assume that the resource demands of new software increase at the same rate as Moore's Law. And, for simplicity, we assume that the resource demands of new software are equal to one eighth (12.5 percent) of the capacity of a new computer.

Third, the time taken for a computer to run software is inversely proportional to unused resources. The mathematics of computer system measurement offers a simple principle describing the time it takes for a computer to perform a particular task. This is the throughput-delay curve. It shows that delay increases as the total demand on the computer system increase.

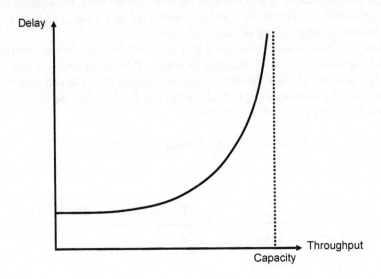

Figure 10.3   Throughput-Delay Curve

There is one special case of particular interest, which we shall use here: the delay (or time taken) for a computer to run software is inversely proportional to unused resources. So for example, if the resource capacity of the computer is C and it runs one piece of software which demands computing resources of S, then the delay is given by:

$$D = \frac{k}{(C-S)} \qquad (10.1)$$

Where k is a constant – and for simplicity, we assume below that k=1. Note what this means: as the resources demanded by the software (S) approach the computer's capacity (C), delay becomes indefinitely large. I suspect that many readers have experienced very long delays when their old computer starts up and wondered what was happening. This is what was happening!

Using these principles, we can complete Table 10.1. It describes, in outline, six years in the life of a personal computer, from its introduction in year T. Row (a) follows Moore's Law in describing the capacity of a new computer in years T, T+2, T+4 and T+6. In line with Moore's Law, capacity doubles every two years. Row (b) describes the resource demands of new software introduced in these years. Again, as assumed above (principle 2), these demands increase at the same rate as Moore's Law. The choice of units for the computer capacity and software demands are arbitrary, but selected so that the usable lifetime of the computer works out at 6 years, which is the approximate average across all classes of users.

Row (c) simply divides row (b) by row (a), while row (d) divides row (b) by the capacity of a year T computer (8 units). Row (e) is simply 1 minus row (d), and row (f) uses the special case in equation (10.1) to compute the delay. (It is assumed that k=1). And finally, row (g) describes the economic status of a year T computer at each date.

Table 10.1   The Link from Software Innovation to e-Waste

		Year		
	T	T+2	T+4	T+6
(a) Capacity of new computer	8	16	32	64
(b) Demands of new software	1	2	4	8
(c) Demands of new software / Capacity of new computer	12.5%	12.5%	12.5%	12.5%
(d) Demands of new software / Capacity of year T computer	12.5%	25%	50%	100%
(e) Unused resources on a year T computer running new software	87.5%	75%	50%	0%
(f) Time taken for year T computer to run new software	1.14	1.33	2.00	∞
(g) Viability of year T computer	As new	Very good	Slowing down	e-Waste!

As we follow the history from left to right, we observe three things:

- The increase in the demands of new software as a proportion of the total computing capacity in a year T computer;
- The corresponding decline in unused resource as a year T computer runs new software; and
- An increase in the time it takes for a year T computer to run new software.

By year T+6, the year T computer has reached saturation. It takes all of the resources of the computer to run the most recent software (row d). There are no spare resource left (row e), and that means it takes the computer an indefinitely long time to run new software (row f). At year T+6, in effect, the year T computer has become e-waste. It still works well as a piece of hardware, but it cannot run the most recent software.

SOFTWARE 'BLOAT' AND MARKETING STRATEGIES

So much for this very simple model; but the reader may well be wondering whether things need to be like this. Why must the resource demands of new software increase at the same rate as Moore's Law? Why is necessary for the user to run new software on the old computer? Why doesn't the user just continue to run old software on the old computer? We shall try to answer these questions in this section.

Why must the resource demands of new software increase at the same rate as Moore's Law? 'Software bloat' is a term used to describe the tendency for new versions of software to use greater quantities of system resources (processing power and memory) than necessary in order to deliver the same functionality as earlier versions of the software. Some have suggested that the problem of software bloat is so bad that most users experience little net benefit from Moore's Law. One observation of this sort is often called *Wirth's Law*. It states that as hardware gets faster, software gets slower, so that the net effect is no change. Some would say that this view is too pessimistic and that even if software bloat is a reality, there are some net gains from Moore's Law.

Perhaps the underlying cause of software bloat is Moore's Law itself. In the early days of the PC, the 1970s, software developers faced very severe constraints on available memory, storage space and processor speed. Accordingly, these software developers had to design their programmes very carefully if they were to get them to work on the primitive PCs of that time. But as Moore's Law brought down the price of memory, the constraints on software developers were relaxed. Indeed, Cusumano and Selby (1996, pp. 5–6) show how Microsoft's early recognition of the strategic implications of 'free hardware' played an important role in that company's software success.

Today, Moore's Law has made computer memory so cheap that software developers rarely face any binding hardware constraints. As a result, these software developers see no economic need to optimise software designs so as to minimise hardware use.

Instead, the marketing imperatives of rich software features and rapid speed to market are dominant. Software developers have to design under pressure because the 'standards race' character of competition between rival software programmes tend to put a premium on being early to market (Grindley, 1995; Church and Gandal, 1992; Langlois, 1992; Rohlfs, 2001). In such races, the ability to build up a network of users at an early stage is often more important than quality per se. This means that software vendors often choose to make 'beta' versions of software available to selected users at an early stage in order to build up a user base as fast as possible. Sometimes marketers wish to do this before designers are happy with the product – a common source of tension.

Swann (2009d) gives a detailed account of some of the sources of software bloat, including 'lazy' design, bundling of pre-installed software, 'featuritis' and security upgrades.

Why is necessary for the user to run new software on the old computer? Why doesn't the user just continue to run old software on the old computer? Consider a user who has no wish to upgrade existing software as (s)he is quite content with the functionality offered by their original software. Would (s)he be able to run the same PC indefinitely without unmanageable demands on the hardware resources of their PCs? The answer to that is, generally, 'no'. Common marketing strategies adopted by many software vendors may push these PC users to upgrade to new versions of software even if they have no particular wish to upgrade.

Three strategies in particular deserve attention here. First, a fairly standard strategy on the part of software vendors is to keep a relatively short life cycle for each version of their software. This is so common in so many industries that it may seem unexceptional, but limited life cycles in this context imply more than in other contexts. Limited life cycles mean not only that a particular version of software is only marketed for a limited period, but also that the software vendor will only provide support for that software for a limited period. After that period, the vendor no longer supports that version of the software. Microsoft's lifecycle policy towards product support is described in Microsoft (n.d.)

This is especially relevant for items such as operating systems software where it is generally recognised that out of date software can be a security risk. If the vendor no longer supports the operating system, that means that the user can no longer download those security patches and updates required to ensure the security of the operating system. In view of that, a PC that uses a 'legacy' version of the operating system cannot be guaranteed to be secure for connection to the Internet and therefore becomes unusable for that purpose. Even if the old operating system is quite adequate for the user's needs, (s)he is obliged to update to the new version of the operating system, or if that will not run on the limited resources of an existing PC, then the user is obliged to upgrade his/her hardware as well. This strategy is therefore one of the factors that contributes to premature obsolescence of otherwise perfectly operable PCs.

Secondly, almost all software is licensed rather than sold. When we install a piece of software on a computer, we enter into a licence agreement. This gives us rather different rights than we would have if we owned the software outright. There are several implications of this. In the present context, it is relevant because it severely constrains the second hand market for 'refurbished' PCs.

If one user is obliged to upgrade his PC because the software (s)he needs to run makes excessive demands on the resources of his/her existing PC, then it would be reassuring to think that this otherwise viable second hand PC could find a market amongst users with less demanding requirements. However, even if a hardware refurbisher could make this second hand PC perfectly viable, it will only be marketable if the refurbisher can reinstall older versions of operating systems and other software which are compatible with the resources of this machine. But if the software proprietor no longer licenses the refurbisher to use legacy software, then that option is not viable. Indeed, there will be a risk that when the currently licensed version of the software is installed, the PC will be no more viable for a new user than it was for the original user.

A third strategy can be especially damaging in terms of causing premature obsolescence. This could be called the strategy of asymmetric compatibility between different versions of (say) a word processing package. This means, in brief, that documents produced on Version N+1 of the software cannot be read by users of Version N, even though documents produced on Version N can readily be accessed by users of the new version N+1.

The reason why this contributes to premature obsolescence is clear enough. If I am a team-worker and collaborate with a series of colleagues in editing text files, then it is essential that we can all work in the same standard. This is the simple story of standards and network effects which has been well analysed by innovation economists. If I have Version N of the software while the others have Version N+1, then sooner or later I will find the situation unworkable. For there will be files generated by the others which I cannot read. For that reason, if for no other, I will eventually feel obliged to update my software to version N+1. And if that upgrade puts excessive demand on the resources of my PC, then a software incompatibility triggers not just a software upgrade but also a hardware upgrade. Once again, this leads to premature obsolescence of otherwise perfectly viable hardware.

One other strategy has also contributed to premature hardware obsolescence, though this strategy is not the exclusive preserve of software vendors, but is adopted by many users of the WWW. This is the increasingly extravagant use of graphics on websites. The ability to view websites with a lot of graphics may not directly put undue pressure on an old PC, but such websites may only be visible using the latest versions of Internet browsers[3] and graphics software, and these in turn can only be run on computers with considerable hardware resources. So once again, we find the same type of phenomenon. To keep up, PC users need to be able to use the sorts of software developed for state of the art PCs. But this software cannot run properly on older PCs. So once again we find a further pressure for premature obsolescence.

Why are these strategies adopted? I don't suggest that companies adopt these strategies out of disrespect for environmental concerns per se. Rather, the rationale for these strategies lies in competitive strategy:

• the desire to encourage upgrading to generate repeat sales
• the desire to keep control of the source of economic rents
• the desire to achieve competitive distinction and attract attention

Nonetheless, these strategies all play a part (albeit unintended) in generating premature obsolescence and, probably, e-waste.

THE SIZE OF THE E-WASTE PROBLEM

If a user decides to upgrade his/her PC because it is no longer of running the software (s)he wishes (or is obliged) to use, then it is not automatic that the old PC will become waste. Sometimes, such PCs are passed from the more demanding to the less demanding users in an organisation or family. Sometimes, old PCs are refurbished and sold in the second hand market. And a growing number of charities aim to recycle old PCs to deserving causes in the least developed countries.

However, the optimists who think that all old computers – unless they develop an electronic fault – can and will find a useful home as will be disappointed. A simple way to show this is to compare the cumulative global shipments of PCs (i.e. all PCs shipped since the first PCs in 1975) and the world-wide installed base of PCs (i.e. all PCs still in use), it is immediately apparent that the former is larger than the latter, and there is a rapidly growing gap between the two. By definition, the cumulative number of unused PCs is equal to the cumulative shipments of PCs less the installed base of PCs.

Figure 10.4 gives an indication of how the e-waste problem has grown. Note that in 2008, the cumulative number of unused PCs exceeds the installed base of PCs in use. That means that of all the PCs sold up to the end of 2008, only a half were still in use at the end of 2008.

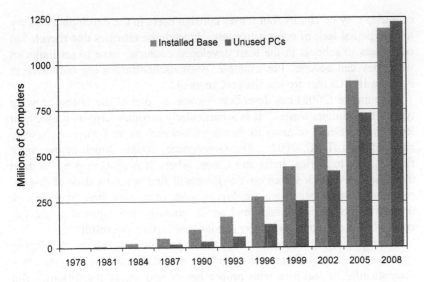

Figure 10.4   Installed PC Base and Unused PCs

Source: Swann (2009d).

Some commentators interpret this cumulative number of unused PCs as an estimate of cumulative e-waste. But use of the term 'e-waste' is not standardised. Some use a broad definition of e-waste which, in the PC context, covers all old computers that are stored rather than used, because they can no longer be used for their original purpose. This is indeed what Figure 10.4 shows.

Others prefer a much narrower definition of 'e-waste' which, in the PC context, covers only those computers or computer parts that are discarded into landfill. This is much harder to measure accurately, because it leaves no paper-trail. Indeed, Greenpeace (2008) fear that much e-waste is deliberately hidden, as developed countries seek to reduce the costs of recycling legislation by shipping old computers to less developed countries, supposedly for re-use, but where they end up in landfill.

Why is it not possible to find a use for all old computers (so long as they work)? The simple answer is that there is only limited scope to find less demanding users who can make productive use of these old machines where the users of developed countries could not. This is partly a result of the design and marketing strategies described above. And even where legacy software (with modest hardware requirements) is still available, it is doubtful whether users of the old PCs and legacy software can achieve international competitiveness when using such tools. Passing off old tools to developing countries may be charity, but it may consign users in the developing country to a perpetual lack of competitiveness. Indeed, the charities that recycle old computers to schools in the least developed countries have to set limits on what they can accept. For example, www.itschoolsafrica.org only accepts Pentium III PCs that are less than six years old.

Greenpeace (2008) has described e-waste as 'one of the fastest growing types of hazardous waste'. It is a particularly noxious form of waste, as it leads to the release of many toxic ingredients such as lead, mercury, arsenic and cadmium (BBC, 2002, 2006; Greenpeace, 2008). Much of the waste finds it way to Africa, India and China, where it is processed by 'cottage industries'. A quick search on YouTube will find several videos of this PC recycling businesses, where employees work over open fires, without any protective clothing or masks, and are in consequence exposed to the full cocktail of toxic fumes and suffer serious health risks as a result.

In principle, legislation restricts the export of old PCs to developing countries for recycling, and requires manufacturers to recycle PCs domestically, in facilities with proper health and safety regulations. But there seem to be many loopholes allowing manufacturers to get around these restrictions. It has been estimated that as much as 80 percent of America's electronic waste is shipped out of the country (BBC, 2002). In part, this is because the sheer volume of e-waste did, for some time, put an unmanageable strain on an already stretched e-waste recycling industry: 'E-waste is already beyond the capacity of recycling, which is why an illegal trade in e-waste has developed … Hardware changes because of Vista will compound the problem' (Young, 2007).[4]

However, there have also been some important advances in the ethical recycling of e-waste. A striking example is the initiative by Network to Supplies (n.d.), who aim for 99 percent recycling of computer equipment.

CONCLUSION

The influential Stern Review on The Economics of Climate Change (Stern, 2006) said that innovation would have an essential role to play in achieving sustainability: 'Innovation driven by strong policy will ultimately reduce the carbon intensity of our economies.'

In this chapter, by contrast, we have seen an example of where innovation can be the very force that leads an industry onto an unsustainable path. Some readers may think the case study described here is a 'one-off' and that examples of innovations that threaten sustainability are rare. On the contrary, my view is that such examples are remarkably common, but that we have only recently started to understand how much innovation is in tension with sustainability.

Quite a bit of work has been done on possible solutions to the e-waste issue. We can distinguish two basic approaches: (a) trying to slow down the rate at which e-waste is created; (b) improving the e-waste recycling process. As this work lies outside the main scope of this book, I refer the interested reader to Swann (2009d).

NOTES

[1] Most of this is discussed in two unpublished papers of mine, Swann (2009c, 2009d).

[2] Moore (1965).

[3] Another, recently introduced measure that also forces users to upgrade their Internet browser is in effect a 'tax' on users of old browsers. An Australian online retailer was the first to introduce such a 'tax'. Customers using Internet Explorer 7 have to pay extra for online purchases. The company chose to do this because of the amount of time they were wasting to make pages designed for current software look right when viewed with old software. See BBC (2012b) for further details.

[4] Some believe the use of Linux could help, because the typical hardware 'refresh period' for Linux is twice as long as for Microsoft Windows (Onktush, 2007; Office of Government Commerce, 2004). This would double the lifetime of a computer and halve the rate of waste.

11. Parkinson's Law of Traffic

This chapter concerns *Parkinson's Law of Traffic* – a striking example of the dysfunctional and destructive side-effects of a particular business and government innovation.

When I was young, car journeys took a long time and I was not a very patient passenger! Then one year, my father said that the journey would now be quicker because of the new 'motorway'. That sounded pretty good news to me! Before long, however, we learnt that motorways were not always the super-efficient highways that we hoped they would be. While they were relatively empty in the early years, the level of traffic soon increased, so that at peak times, and in the holiday season, they could be seriously congested. Moreover, it only took one accident to create a massive tail-back of many, many miles.

Some people suggested that new motorways create new traffic. Indeed, it was suggested that the famous Parkinson's Law ('work expands to fill the time available for its completion') has a corollary. *Parkinson's Law of Traffic* states that 'traffic expands to fill the available road-capacity'. This suggestion was met with much amusement in some quarters. The 'official line' remained that roads do not create traffic: the growth of traffic was simply evidence of just how much latent demand there was for long-distance road travel. But, on the contrary, *Parkinson's Law of Traffic* makes perfectly good economic sense, as we shall see in this chapter.

NEW ROADS AND NEW TRADE

At the simplest level, new roads reduce the costs of trading over distance. Consider the case of two nearby small towns, A and B, and their various businesses. Many of the businesses in A and B are similar, and it is unlikely that the inhabitant of A would bother to trade with a grocer in B when there is an equivalent grocer in A. But some of the businesses in A may be unique to A, and some of those in B may be unique to B. (For example, A may have a high quality furniture maker specialising in chairs, while B has a renowned second-hand bookshop specialising in books on political economy.) The Venn diagram in Figure 11.1 illustrates this.[1]

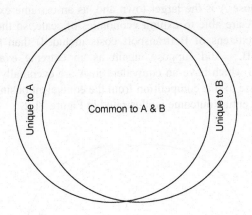

Figure 11.1   Businesses in Towns A and B before Competition

The businesses in A and B are represented by the left hand and right hand circles respectively. The intersection of these sets is large, and represents the businesses that are common to both towns. The crescent-shaped segments to the left and the right represent the businesses unique to A and B respectively.

When travel between the two times is slow and expensive, inhabitants of one town may do little or no trade with the unique businesses in the other. But when there is a new road between the two towns, making travel much quicker and cheaper, the inhabitant of one may wish to trade with the unique businesses in the other. I leave it open as to how that trade takes place. In some cases, the inhabitant of one town will travel to the other town to visit the unique businesses. In other cases, the unique businesses will arrange to deliver their goods to customers in the other town. But either way, there will be an increase in traffic.

However, these 'unique' segments in Figure 11.1 are only a relatively small percentage of the total, so this simple framework would suggest that there will only be a small volume of traffic in each direction to take advantage of the stores unique to A and B.

NEW ROADS AND CONCENTRATION

A much more significant effect of transport infrastructure on traffic takes place if the existence of the roads start to influence market structure and hence, the geographical distribution of activity.

The most obvious case of this is when these businesses enjoy economies of scale. Suppose A is the larger town and, as an extreme example, all the businesses in A are able to exploit economies of scale, so they can offer a better deal to citizens of B (transport costs included) than the equivalent businesses in B.   And suppose, again as an extreme example, all the businesses in B which have an equivalent in A are eventually driven out of business, because of this competition from the equivalent businesses in A.   In that case, the eventual outcome is illustrated in Figure 11.2.

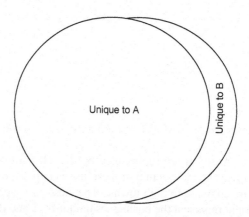

Figure 11.2   Town A Dominates after Road Building

While this is an extreme and, mercifully, unrealistic example, it serves as a useful benchmark.   In this case, a huge volume of goods will be transported from businesses in A to customers in B, and that will lead to a substantial increase in traffic.

A less extreme, and more realistic variation on this theme is shown in Figure 11.3.   In this case, many, but not all of the businesses in A are able to exploit economies of scale, so they can offer a better deal to citizens of B than the equivalent businesses in B.   And, in consequence, many but not all the businesses in B which have an equivalent in A are eventually driven out of business, because of this competition from the equivalent businesses in A.

The Venn diagram of Figure 11.3 then is divided into three parts: the businesses unique to A (after any equivalents in B are driven out of business), the businesses that are found in A and B, and the businesses that are unique to B.   In this case, the amount of traffic generated is not so great as in Figure 11.2, but it is substantially much larger than in Figure 11.1, because customers in B depend on businesses in A for a large share of their purchases.

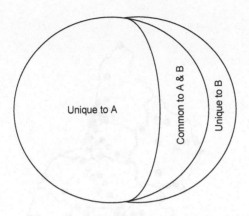

Figure 11.3   Town A Dominates but Some Companies in B Survive

So far, we have considered a rather extreme case, where businesses in the larger town A may drive their equivalents in B out of business, but the reverse does not happen.[2] That is, we observe industrial concentration (fewer businesses) *and* geographical concentration (most are located in A). An obvious variation on Figures 11.2 and 11.3, therefore, is where the introduction of a new road between A and B leads to a decline in the number of businesses in A as well as B. This is the case of industrial concentration *without* geographical concentration.

AN EXAMPLE OF BREWERIES

A striking example of the way in which declining transport costs have lead to industrial concentration and geographical concentration is found the English brewing industry during the first 75 years of the twentieth century. Consider Figures 11.4 and 11.5 on the next pages.

   In Figures 11.4 and 11.5, there are four different marks which describe the density in each 'location' (of 1 square km). A small circle indicates 1 brewery per location; a medium circle indicates 2–4 breweries per location; a medium square indicates 5–8 breweries per location; and a large square indicates 9 or more breweries per location.

Figure 11.4 Geographical Dispersion of Breweries in England, 1900

Source: Author's graph using data from Brewery History Society (2005).

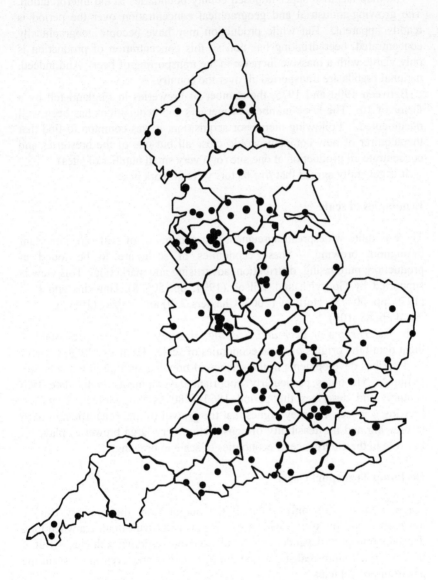

Figure 11.5   Geographical Dispersion of Breweries in England, 1975

Source: Author's graph using data from Brewery History Society (2005).

The map has also super-imposed county boundaries to aid interpretation. The growing industrial and geographical concentration over the period is readily apparent. But while production may have become geographically concentrated, beer drinking has not, so this concentration of production is only viable with a massive increase in the transporting of beer. And indeed, national brands are transported all over the country.

Between 1900 and 1975, the number of breweries in England fell by a factor of 10. The large numbers of mergers and acquisitions has been well documented.[3] Following merger or acquisition, it was common to find that the acquirer or new company would close all but one of the breweries and concentrate all production at one site (or a very small number of sites).

It is generally agreed that *five* factors were at work here.

Economies of scale

There is quite widespread agreement that economies of scale are important throughout brewing. These economies of scale are to be found in production, purchasing, distribution, advertising and marketing. This view is supported by Gourvish and Wilson (1994, pp. 505–8), Hawkins and Pass (1979, pp. 60–78), Hornsey (2003, Chapters 7, 9) and Vaizey (1960, pp. 83–7 and pp. 88–100). [4]

In his, *History of Beer and Brewing*, Hornsey (2003) has described in great detail the origins of these economies of scale. Hornsey (2003, Chapter 7) describes developments in the science of brewing starting in the late 17th Century. He notes particularly important developments in the late 19th century, and describes the period 1860–1880 as the 'Golden Years' of brewing science. Hornsey argues that the growth of this scientific approach to brewing and the feasibility of constructing very large breweries played a key role in the emergence of economies of scale in brewing.

Declining Transport Costs

Large breweries are only viable if the output from the brewery can be transported cheaply over a wide area. That was difficult in an era when long distance transport depended on canals and horse-drawn vehicles. But it became much more realistic in the era of railways and even more so in the age of motor vehicles.

Vaizey (1960, Chapter 7) notes that the cost of transporting raw materials to a brewery are not very significant. The really important source of transport costs is the retail delivery of beer. Gourvish and Wilson (1994, pp. 149–51) describe how the growth of the railways played a huge role in developing Burton-on-Trent as one of the main centres of the brewing industry in England: 'Perhaps no other town and industry in Victorian Britain demonstrated better the benefit of the railways' (Gourvish and Wilson, 1994, p. 151).

Hornsey notes that before 1900, brewery amalgamations mainly involved small local firms within a few miles of each other and it was rare for any local monopolies to emerge. Thereafter, much more ambitious mergers took place: 'with improved transport connections, such moves were now quite feasible' (Hornsey, 2003, p. 592). Hornsey (2003, pp. 549–56) also notes that up to 1939, brewers used a mix of road, rail and horse-draw carriages to transport their beers. After the end of petrol rationing in the 1950s, this situation changed rapidly and road transport soon dominated all aspects of retail delivery.

Greater Transportability of Beers

Even with economies of scale and declining transport costs, large breweries are only viable if the beer will travel well. It is fair to say that for a long time, traditional beers did not travel very well. The advent of brewery-conditioned beers from the 1930s onwards made such transportation much more realistic.

Brewery-conditioning was a 20th Century innovation. Scientific developments in filtration, carbonisation, refrigeration and pasteurisation had revolutionised bottled beer manufacture (Hornsey, 2003, p. 595). The beer was biologically 'dead', which means that it was chemically stable. This means that it could be stored for much longer periods and that it would travel much better than 'live' beers. These developments were then applied to production of 'keg' beer – biologically 'dead' beer in steel barrels. The first experiments were by Watneys in the 1930s but the main impetus towards 'keg' beers started in 1946 (Hornsey, 2003, pp. 670 ff).

Consumer Tastes

Merger activity in the brewing industry and the consequent growth in industrial and geographical concentration lead to a steady decline in the number of brands (Hall, 1979). While not everyone was happy with that trend,[5] many consumers *were* content with a limited range of national brands. Following customer reaction to mediocre and unpredictable beers in the 1940s (Hawkins and Pass, 1979, p. 54), consumer demand for quality and reliability was stronger than the demand for variety *per se*.[6] Using the classification of consumer types described in Swann (2009a, Chapter 15) it is arguable that many beer drinkers during this period behaved like 'Galbraith' consumers – that is, consumers whose tastes and buying behaviour are receptive to advertising and marketing efforts by the large brewers, and who are attracted to the 'big name' national brands.   And this consumer characteristic in turn reinforces the process of concentration: regional brewers could not compete in supplying 'keg' bitters and lagers because they could not afford the huge advertising campaigns required to create 'big name' national brands.

'History Matters'

We noted above that reaction to mediocre draft beer during and after World War 2 had helped to build the momentum behind national 'keg' brands. Far from real ale at its best, as we see it today, these mediocre beers were cloudy, full of sediment and unpleasant to drink. One historical 'accident' is said to have played an important role in helping to promote 'brewery conditioned' beer. Hornsey (2003, p. 671) describes how the brewer J.W. Green (later Flower's Breweries) of Luton, Bedfordshire, started experimenting with 'keg' beer when locally stationed US airmen were very disenchanted with drinking murky draft beer. This 'keg' (later known as Flower's 'keg') soon gained a widespread following, and by around 1960, two 'big name' national brands of 'keg' (Double Diamond and Watneys Red Barrel) had become 'vogue drinks' (Hornsey, 2003, p. 672).

Implications

The result of these five factors was a steady growth of industrial and geographical concentration. Does this matter? Well, it certainly mattered to the founders of CAMRA (the Campaign for Real Ale) who fought a bold and successful action to re-educate drinkers of the pleasures of real ale and the desirability of having a wide choice of locally-brewed beers. Thanks to their efforts, the number of breweries in England has risen from 139, in 1975, to 767, in 2010 – a five-fold increase. We mentioned this briefly in Chapter 9.[7]

TRAFFIC AND THE ENVIRONMENT

Does it matter if new roads (or new transport infrastructure more generally) create a substantial increase in traffic? It hardly needs to be said that heavy traffic imposes a substantial environmental cost on our towns and the countryside in the form of noise, pollution, danger, health hazards,[8] and so on.

This is a difficult issue, but some would argue that so long as the price of additional transport (fuel prices, vehicle taxes, road tariffs, congestion charging, and so on) fully covers the social and environmental costs of additional transport, then an increase in traffic is justified. So long as the price is set equal to the environmental cost, then the benefits of further transport offset the costs.

However, the problem, in a nutshell, is that many think that the price of transport is substantially less than its full environmental cost, but at the same time, industries that depend on transport for their business (e.g. the haulage industry) say they cannot remain competitive if the price of transport is raised any further. As a result, it seems inevitable that traffic will grow faster that is justified by a comparison of costs and benefits.

Moreover, the cost of growing traffic is not only reflected in the natural environment. It also impacts on the socio-economic environment. A common outcome of the rapid growth of transport is that economic activity becomes very unevenly distributed across the country – and the world, indeed. I think it is fair to generalise that most people in Great Britain would agree that too high a proportion of economic activity and economic growth is concentrated in London and the South East, and too little in the North of England, in Wales and in much of Scotland. And at a global level, few surely could dispute that the uneven distribution of economic activity between the developed and developing world is grossly inequitable.

Here, indeed, it could be said that politicians have sold citizens a false hope. New roads from the core of a nation's economy to the peripheral regions are supposed to level the playing-field in favour of the peripheral regions. And that can sometimes be the outcome. But, as we saw in this chapter, when economies of scale are important, the outcome can be to further concentrate activity in the core and further disadvantage the periphery.

CONCLUSION

In this chapter, I have tried to explain why *Parkinson's Law of Traffic* is not just an amusing irony, but is sound economic theory. We have discussed it in the context of road and other forms of transport, where the outcome is that increased transport capacity leads to more traffic coupled with an increase in industrial and, often, geographical concentration. This is the destructive side of innovations in transport networks.

Moreover, this principle doesn't only apply to physical transport networks. It can also apply to broadband networks. Indeed, there is probably also a Parkinson's Law of Broadband, which asserts that the amount of broadband traffic expands to fill the available bandwidth. Why should this be? In part it arises because, in the world of online business, competitive pressure means we may need ever more spectacular websites to attract attention. These website innovations are ever more memory intensive, meaning a substantial increase in the amount of traffic. If all web users have equal access to high-speed bandwidth and the latest design tools, then perhaps there is no harm in this. But if, as is much more plausible, different web users have very different endowments in terms of bandwidth and tools, then this trend can create an uneven playing field. In practice, it means that regions with lower bandwidth are economically marginalised.

NOTES

[1]   The crude model here draws on Krugman's sophisticated analysis of geography and trade – see Krugman (1980, 1991, 1992).

[2]   Although it sometimes feels that all business in England is congregating in London and the South East, and driving many companies in the North out of business, things are not quite as dire as that – or not yet, anyway.

[3]   See Gourvish and Wilson (1994), Hall (1979), Hawkins and Pass (1979), Hornsey (2003), Mark (1985) and Millns (1998).

[4]   But not all share this view. By contrast, Protz (1978) argues that the much-vaunted economies of scale never arose and cites the higher prices charged for national beer brands than for local brands. A middle view would be that these economies of scale do indeed exist, but did not result in lower prices for consumers – partly because of the market power of the big six brewers and some x-inefficiency in those companies.

[5]   Indeed, CAMRA was founded by drinkers who were far from happy at this trend, and CAMRA played a substantial role in the partial reversal of that trend from 1975 onwards. This is all discussed in more detail in Swann (2010).

[6]   Advertisements for Ind Coope's beer *Long Life*, which was very popular in the 1960s, stressed that, 'it never varies!'

[7]   See Swann (2010) for a detailed account of the fall and rise of the local brew.

[8]   For example, a recent American study has suggested that autism may be linked to traffic pollution. It found that children exposed to high levels of pollution were three times more likely to suffer from autism than children who grew up with cleaner air (BBC, 2012e).

12. Innovation and Consumerism

Some politicians think it quite inappropriate that Church men and women – even the most senior Churchman in Britain – should 'interfere' in politics and the economy. I have never understood this point of view. After all, few politicians are shy to give their opinion on anything and everything – including many things that they are quite evidently unqualified to speak about.

Rowan Williams, Archbishop of Canterbury from 2003–2012, is not the first Archbishop or Bishop of modern times to speak out against what he considers to be a fundamental error in our political economy.[1] Moreover, as I have argued above, the relevant concept of wealth for our purposes is not M-wealth but R-wealth ('no wealth but life'). Who could be better qualified to talk about the relationship between innovation and life?

By chance, my work on this chapter coincided with the publication of Dr Williams' book, *Faith in the Public Square* (2012), once described as his 'valedictory work as Archbishop' (*Guardian*, 2012b). In this he sets out some very deep concerns about our current political economy, and these seem to me so important that I decided they must be addressed here. In the context of this book, this chapter describes the potentially destructive effects of innovation on the consumer as a person – as a human being.

'FAITH IN THE PUBLIC SQUARE'

Dr Williams' book, *Faith in the Public Square* is not a work of theology. It is a book about the role of religion in public life. Indeed it is a wide-ranging critique of our modern political economy. Here I shall focus on one part of it: his critique of consumerism.

Williams has written critically of consumerism on many earlier occasions. In his book, *Lost Icons*, he made this memorable observation on marketing and the child as consumer (Williams, 2000, pp. 22–3):[2]

> The perception of the child as consumer is clearly more dominant than it was a few decades ago. The child is the (usually vicarious) purchaser of any number of graded and variegated packages – that is, of goods designed to stimulate further consumer desires. A relatively innocuous example is the familiar 'tie-in', the

association of comics, sweets, toys and so on, with a major new film or television serial; the Disney empire has developed this to an unprecedented pitch of professionalism. Rather less innocuous (more obsessive, more expensive) is the computer game designed to lead on to ever more challenging and sophisticated levels. Anything but innocuous is the conscription of children into the fetishistic hysteria of style wars: it is still mercifully rare to murder for a pair of trainers, or to commit suicide because of an inability to keep up with peer group fashion; but what can we say about a marketing culture that so openly feeds and colludes with obsession? What picture of the acting or choosing self is being promoted?

Williams questions our obsession with materialism and the worship of consumer goods. He is critical of many of the assumptions that, as he sees it, are now built into life in the 21st century. In particular, he questions the idea that economic growth is by definition a good thing (Williams, 2009):

> Practically speaking, at the individual and the national level, we have to question what we mean by growth. The ability to produce more and more consumer goods (not to mention financial products) is in itself an entirely mechanical measure of wealth. It sets up a vicious cycle in which it is necessary all the time to create new demand for goods and thus new demands on a limited material environment for energy sources and raw materials. By the hectic inflation of demand it creates personal anxiety and rivalry. By systematically depleting the resources of the planet, it systematically destroys the basis for long-term wellbeing. In a nutshell, it is investing in the wrong things.

He says that it is the church's role to ask such questions, and argues that religion, 'is committed to serious public debate about common good' (Williams, 2012, p. 96). There is certainly a pressing need for serious debate about the assumed need for growth, because many ordinary people do not understand why it is necessary.

AN ECONOMIST'S VIEW: PART 1

There are two main lessons from the last section. The first lesson is that the value of economic growth is in doubt. Although this means a slight detour from the main plan of the book, the question, 'do we need growth?' is so important that I shall take a little space here to discuss it.

Do we need growth, and why? The short answer to this is that it depends what we mean by 'we'? If 'we' are all the citizens in an economy, Williams is probably right that a substantial proportion do not need growth. Yes, those in poverty and those in poor countries badly need growth in their incomes and M-wealth. But some (perhaps *many*) individuals in developed countries do not need any more growth. They have enough M-wealth as it is, and rather than accumulating more M-wealth, they would be better advised to learn how to turn their M-wealth into R-wealth.

But if 'we' means the current market economy as a 'machine', then the answer is that it needs growth even if the citizens of the economy do not. Why is that? The short answer is that the current market economy, as a machine, needs growth (even if the citizens don't) because in the absence of growth the economy starts to behave in a dysfunctional way. There are several aspects to this dysfunctional behaviour.

First, when there are innovations that enhance labour productivity but there is no growth in the economy, then there will be growing unemployment. This will not be a case of an equal reduction in hours all round (which might actually be welcome) but will be very unevenly spread. Second, without growth, the economy is liable to suffer from serious debt problems. This is what we have seen in the fallout from the credit crunch of 2007 onwards. Third, when the functioning of a modern economy depends on businesses borrowing loans from banks and repaying with interest, then there must be growth in the borrowers' businesses or otherwise the borrowers will not be able to repay their loans.

All in all, without growth, there will be increasing and uneven unemployment, the distribution of M-wealth will become more uneven, and the role of the government will expand. But because government revenues from tax do not grow, there will not be the resources to pay for the expanded role of government.

Many of our economic institutions are designed on the assumption of continuing growth. For example: pension funds depend on a buoyant stock market which in turn depends on growth. Joint stock companies are based on it. Capitalism itself is dependent on growth: capital is invested for a return, and without growth there can be no return. And so on.

In short, our economy as a machine is entirely dependent on growth. But, to quote the celebrated remark attributed to Kenneth Boulding, 'anyone who believes exponential growth can go on forever in a finite world is either a madman or an economist'. Given that continuing growth is not sustainable, the dependence of the economy on continuing growth is definitely not a desirable state of affairs. But – as we saw so clearly in the recent recession – neither is it very satisfactory to live in an economy of the present 'design' when there is no growth. I cannot begin to resolve these issues in the present text, and for that reason, this section is very short.[3]

AN ECONOMIST'S VIEW: PART 2

We can sum up the second lesson from the previous section as follows: innovation can damage the consumer as a person. To economists brought up in a mainstream or neoclassical tradition, that is a strange conclusion. Here I shall explain why it may seem strange, but why it is indeed *right*. In what follows, I shall refer to several different theories of the consumer – drawing heavily on Swann (2009a, Chapter 15).

Neoclassical economics typically assumes a particular type of consumer, who we may call the *economic* consumer. This consumer has some rather special characteristics. In particular, (s)he:

- has fixed and pre-determined tastes
- is not influenced by others
- has no need to experiment
- knows what (s)he wants
- cannot be persuaded that (s)he needs anything else
- is resistant to persuasive advertising
- cannot be manipulated

How does the economic consumer react to innovation? (S)he will welcome cost-reducing process innovations that offer desired goods and services at lower cost. And (s)he will welcome product innovations that offer more of the product characteristics that (s)he values. But (s)he will not be interested in product innovations that add new characteristics which (s)he does not need.

In short, this sort of consumer is not fazed by innovation or marketing strategies. Moreover, it is pretty clear that the consumers described by Williams are not *economic* consumers. So what type(s) of consumers can be manipulated into consumerism? I shall list here four types.

Galbraith Consumer

In his celebrated book, *The Affluent Society*, Galbraith (1958) described a very different type of consumer. This is one that:

- does not have fixed and pre-determined tastes
- is certainly influenced by others
- is open to persuasive advertising
- can be manipulated

Indeed, he defined this consumer thus (Galbraith, 1958, pp. 152–3):

> As a society becomes increasingly affluent, wants are increasingly created by the process by which they are satisfied. This may operate passively. Increases in consumption, the counterpart of increases in production, act by suggestion or emulation to create wants. Or producers may proceed actively to create wants

through advertising and salesmanship. Wants thus come to depend on output.

Many people would be reluctant to accept that they could be so open to persuasion and manipulation as this. But the very fact that the advertising industry has grown to its present size suggests that they cannot all be right. Indeed, we could say that one of Bertrand Russell's 'irregular verbs' operates here: I am immune to advertising, you are not beyond persuasion, he is easily manipulated. And, of special relevance in the present context, many young consumers are obviously impressionable, and persuasive advertising is very effective at exploiting that.[4]

Douglas Consumer

This consumer is named after the economic anthropologist, Mary Douglas. She was interested in the social character of much consumption, which is not found in the behaviour of the stereotypical economic consumer. Douglas argued that, 'the real moment of choosing is ... choice of comrades and their way of life'.[5] And once the individual has made that choice, subsequent decisions often follow some sort of group norm, and purchase decisions offer a way to bond with your peer group.

Like the Galbraith consumer, the Douglas consumer is influenced by others, and is open to persuasion, but the forces that influence him/her are different. Often, consumption decisions will follow those made by influential members of the group. Selling to a Douglas consumer poses a different and perhaps more subtle challenge to the marketer, but marketers have not been slow to rise to this challenge.

Veblen Consumer

This consumer, named after Veblen's (1899) theory of conspicuous consumption, is driven by a desire to be distinctive. The Veblen consumer wants to display his/her distinction, and does this with a conspicuous display of consumption.[6] Some product innovations offer a welcome opportunity to demonstrate distinction, so long as they are not consumed widely. The demand for distinction is subtle, because it is a signal of being different from those who consume other products and this means demand is contingent on the whole array of consumption behaviour. In earlier work (Swann, 2001a), I identified two particular types of Veblen consumer in the market for prestige cars. One seeks distinction in the aristocracy of recent innovations – for example, the Ferrari 458 Italia. The other seeks distinction in the rare classic car – such as the Ferrari 250 GTO, of which only 39 were produced from 1962 to 1964.[7]

Like the Galbraith consumer and the Douglas consumer, this Veblen consumer is open to persuasion, but the forces that influence him/her are different again.   And moreover, selling to the Veblen consumer poses perhaps the most subtle of challenges of all. Having said that, Enzo Ferrari, founder of the Ferrari company, said that he only had one marketing policy, which was to produce exactly one car less than the market demands. It is rather like the children's game, 'musical chairs': when the music stops, we can be sure that there will be a frenzied rush as the N children try to occupy the N-1 available chairs.

Dutiful Consumer

This final consumer can be called a dutiful consumer. This term has come to mean two rather different things. In this context, we mean consumers who buy as if they are acting from a sense of duty. It is almost as if 'Uncle Sam' is pointing at them saying, 'your economy needs you to consume' – and so they do.[8] Economists used to thinking about the economic consumer tend to think such consumption behaviour is very strange. Who in their right mind would consume out of a sense of duty? But in fact, such behaviour is more common that we may realise.

There are simple examples, where we consume out a sense of loyalty to a friend or relative, or to our local community.   We dutifully consume the rather inedible scones cooked by an elderly neighbour, and we dutifully sit through a three-hour concert at a child's school. And we dutifully buy some cakes at the local church fete, or support a new bookshop – in the hope that somehow, it will survive the competitive pressures described in Chapter 9.

But the dutiful consumer does not just stop there. The first-time parent may buy all kinds of baby 'stuff' out of a well-intentioned desire to do all he or she can to give the child a good start in life, and this will include many items that are later found to be completely unnecessary. The same parent may later buy an excess of Christmas or birthday presents for their children, just to be sure that there are no broken hearts on the day. And indeed, there a quite a few occasions on which the dutiful consumer must not forget to consume dutifully.[9]

But, the critic may be thinking, there it must stop. Surely we do not consume out of a sense of duty to keep companies in business? Well, I think that some of us do. For example, I remember being reproached by an elderly relative when I told her I was a vegetarian. She did not approve at all! For what would happen, she asked, to all the livestock farmers, fishermen, butchers and fishmongers if everyone were vegetarian? I forbore to say that vegetarians are good news for dairy farmers, arable farmers and market gardeners.

Another example is the attempt to appeal to 'patriotic duty'. I still have a badge I bought in the 1960s as a teenager, which reads 'I'm Backing Britain'. The initiative of that name was originally a grass-roots attempt to boost the flagging competitiveness of British business, and was not very successful. But it led into a somewhat more successful campaign to persuade British consumers to buy British products (BBC, 2011b). In particular, quite a few people believed it was deeply unpatriotic to buy a non-British car. And this is by no means unique to the UK.

Indeed, it is not clear where the duties of the most dutiful consumer will end. I have encountered consumers who express a duty to support their football team by buying an expensive replica shirt every year, a duty to support their national economy regardless of price, a duty to support the innovations of their national scientists by buying the latest electronic gadget, and so on. And, in a way, this dutiful consumer is the Galbraith Consumer, Douglas Consumer and Veblen consumer rolled into one.

CONSUMERISM AND CREATIVE DESTRUCTION

While the economic consumer cannot be manipulated in the way described above, it should be clear from the last section that marketers have many routes to manipulating the Galbraith, the Douglas, the Veblen and the Dutiful consumer. In this section, we explain why innovation, accompanied to this manipulation, can do so much damage.

Marketers look at innovation in a slightly different way from economists. Economists stress the objective characteristics of the product, and why these might persuade consumers to choose this product rather than another. Marketers pay less attention to these considerations, and more to the 'position' of the product in the mind of the prospective buyer. In their famous book, Ries and Trout (2001), put it very succinctly:

> Positioning is not what you do to a product. Positioning is what you do to the mind of the prospect. That is, you position the product in the mind of the prospect.

To those unused to the language of marketing, the use of the word 'prospect' is a bit disturbing. But setting this concern aside, what can we say about the way marketers manipulate the Galbraith, Douglas, Veblen and Dutiful consumers? How does the manipulation that accompanies innovation damage the consumer?

At the very least, it leads to a waste of money on something that is neither wanted nor needed, disappointment at this waste of money, and feelings of being cheated. But it can be much worse than that. Such manipulation can turn the consumer into a *pathological* consumer. This may sound a bit too melodramatic, but unfortunately it is not. There is little doubt that continued manipulation of these consumers by advertising and marketing can cause mental illness.

Indeed, the term, pathological consumption is used to describe the dysfunctional behaviour of individuals for whom over-consumption has become a norm and a response to social pressures and expectations. Pathological consumption is an addiction and should not be regarded lightly: it is a serious health problem.

Now, although marketers can certainly manipulate Douglas and Veblen consumers to buy things they wouldn't otherwise buy, these consumers are not the creation of marketers. Douglas and Veblen consumers would exist even if there were no advertising and no marketing strategies. But Galbraith consumers are indeed the creation of advertising and marketing. In the absence of that, the Galbraith consumer would not exist. And as for Dutiful consumers, some of them would exist in the absence of advertising and marketing, but some would not.

CONCLUSION

While using *Google Scholar* to explore some of the psychological and medical literature on pathological consumption, I came across a book (apparently dated 2010) by J.M.W. Kitchen, entitled, *Consumption: Its Nature, Causes, Prevention and Cure*. For a few seconds, I was shocked: has all consumption become so pathological that it needs *prevention and cure*? But then it dawned on me: this is a medical book about pulmonary tuberculosis – known in the nineteenth century as *consumption*. Kitchen's path-breaking book was originally published in 1885, and re-published by print-on-demand in 2010.

However, this accidental association begs a very important and interesting question. If capitalism requires continuing growth of production, and that requires continuing growth of consumption, will there come a time when the majority of consumption is indeed pathological? Will there come a time when consumption (in the sense understood by economists) is such a problem that it does indeed require a book to explain its, *Nature, Causes, Prevention and Cure*?

Such a suggestion may seem puerile and silly! I only wish it were! For it can, without doubt, be argued that pathological consumers play an essential role in servicing the needs of the economic machine. If these pathological consumers don't exist, then the economic machine will have to invent them.

Veblen turned the old proverb, 'necessity is the mother of invention' on its head, and concluded: 'invention is the mother of necessity'.[10] The producer producing new products needs to ensure that there is a demand for those new products, and if there is not, he needs to create such a demand. Innovation may have been the servant of the consumer, but is now becoming the master. Or, indeed, have we already reached the point where innovation is already the master?

In, *To Have or To Be?*, Erich Fromm (1976/1997, p. 143) argues that *homo sapiens* has been turned into *homo consumens* by a capitalist society that demands continuing growth of production and therefore continuing growth of consumption:

> If human beings are ever to become free and cease feeding industry by pathological consumption, a radical change in the economic system is necessary: we must put an end to the present situation where a healthy economy is possible only at the price of unhealthy people.

Many economists will think this is too melodramatic. I sincerely hope they are right, but I fear they are wrong.

NOTES

[1] I am very pleased that Pope Francis has done the same, with very great effect. And David Jenkins, sometime Bishop of Durham, launched a sustained attack on economic theory, and those economists who treat their theory as a branch of theology (Jenkins, 2000).

[2] On occasions, Williams was even blunter. For example: 'Every transaction in the developed economies of the west can be interpreted as an act of aggression against the economic losers in the worldwide game' (quoted in Hare, 2011).

[3] Essential reading for the interested scholar will include work by Douthwaite (1999a), Hirsch (1977), Schumacher (1974), Victor (2008).

[4] Advertisers are always interested in television audiences dominated by younger viewers. They are usually less interested in audience dominated by older people.

[5] Douglas (1983, p. 45), here quoted from Becker (1996, p. 13).

[6] Several writers before Veblen also talked about the demand for distinction, notably Adam Smith and Nassau Senior – see Swann (2009a, Chapter 15).

[7] The idea of distinction as a driving force in consumption has been thoroughly developed in the modern sociological analysis of consumption by Bourdieu (1984). As Bourdieu shows, distinctive consumption does not necessarily have to be very expensive consumption, but just has to be distinctively different. We can identify a *Bourdieu consumer*, who is interested in distinctive consumption, but does not have the means to achieve this by *expensive* consumption. The Bourdieu consumer is often, indeed, the intellectual counterpart to the Veblen consumer. So the Bourdieu consumer usually chooses to signal distinction by high-brow consumption – listening to sophisticated (and sometimes obscure) music and reading sophisticated (and sometimes obscure) books.

[8] Some use the term, dutiful consumer, to mean a responsible consumer who is not profligate, who does not waste, and who buys products that are environmentally friendly. To avoid confusion, I prefer to call these *ethical consumers* or *green consumers*.

[9] In the UK, this list could include Christmas, Easter, birthdays, anniversaries, Mother's day, Father's day and Valentine's day.

[10] Veblen (1914).

13. High Frequency Trading

Originally, I resolved not to include any material on financial innovation in this book. Why? Although I can claim some expertise in industrial innovation, I do not have equivalent expertise in financial innovation. However, I later decided that there simply must be a chapter on the destructive side of financial innovation, for one reason, if no other. It appears that financial innovation is one of the more destructive innovations, in terms of its effects on the real economy.[1]

In Greek mythology, Pandora had a beautiful box, which she had been told not to open under any circumstances. But curiosity got the better of her, and she opened the box, allowing all the contents to escape and do untold harm. Only hope remained inside the box.[2] It is tempting to use the tale of Pandora's box as a metaphor for what happened in Britain after 'Big Bang' – the dramatic deregulation of financial markets in October 1986, endorsed by Prime Minister Margaret Thatcher and managed by Chancellor Nigel Lawson. True, the opening of Pandora's box at the time of deregulation did not bring immediate crisis, but many believe that deregulation was ultimately responsible for many of the most dysfunctional activities of the City of London in recent years.[3]

This chapter concerns the destructive effects of high frequency trading. This is but one example of the increasingly dysfunctional innovations emanating from the financial sector. But it is one of the easiest cases in which to perceive the destructive side of innovation.

A ROSE-TINTED VIEW OF SHAREHOLDERS

In the days when companies were small and were owned by their managers, the interests of the owners and managers were in effect the same. Therefore, what we now call the principal-agent problem did not arise. But as companies grew into large corporations, and when the owners (or shareholders) were distinct from managers, the principal-agent problem emerged as a real concern for many companies. Managers had a great deal of scope to run the corporation in their own interests and not in the interests of the owners. And only the most vigilant Board of Directors, under constant scrutiny by supposedly vigilant shareholder-owners, could expect to notice this sort of opportunistic behaviour and to take steps to curtail it.

A particular concern was that the time horizon of managers was typically a good deal shorter than the time horizon of the owners. This would be true when managers are hired and fired fairly regularly, or appointed only on relatively short-term contracts, while the shareholders were there for the long term. In that case, the principal-agent problem would turn into a problem of short-termism. Managers would run the company for relatively short-term benefits (because that is what their remuneration depends on) while the owners would like to give much more attention to the long term value of the company.

These differing objectives would not always be in conflict. But they would not be consistent over issues like R&D and radical innovation, and over long-term brand value. Managers may be cautious about risky long term investments in R&D and radical innovation, and may be prepared to compromise on quality and 'milk' the brand in the short term, even though that is not in the long term interests of the brand. Owners who are in there for the long term would be concerned about what their managers are doing.

Nonetheless, a rose-tinted view suggests that active shareholders can help to limit the principal-agent problem. This view would be correct if both of the following criteria are true:

a) The shareholders are investing for the long term, and therefore care about the long term value of the company.
b) The shareholders vigilantly scrutinise corporate governance, and bring pressure on the Board of Directors at every opportunity. They make full use of their voting opportunities at the AGM to block any proposals that may damage their interests.

But are all shareholders really like this? Unfortunately, not. At best, a relatively small fraction and, certainly, a declining fraction of shareholders meet these three criteria.

REAL SHAREHOLDERS AND TRADERS

So, if the rose-tinted view is wrong, what are real shareholders like? It is quite common to distinguish four categories of investors:

- Dedicated shareholders
- 'Quasi-indexers'
- Transient shareholders

• High-frequency traders

The first category, 'dedicated' shareholders, are those described in the previous section: they meet both the criteria (a and b) listed above.

The second category, 'quasi-indexers', simply want an investment that approximately follows the index. They are not interested in getting involved in corporate governance. So, while they meet criterion (a), they don't meet criterion (b).

The third category, 'transient' shareholders, are the mirror image of 'quasi-Indexers': they don't satisfy the first criterion (a), but do satisfy criterion (b). They are not long-term investors, but invest for short- to medium-term gain. However, they can be active in corporate governance – sometimes in a good way (e.g. stamping on corrupt practices) but sometimes in a dysfunctional way (pressurising for short-term objectives to be prioritised, at the expense of long-term growth).

The fourth type, high-frequency traders, are the complete opposite to 'dedicated' shareholders. They are not interested in the long term success of the company, because they only own the shares for minutes, seconds or even milliseconds. Indeed, they are barely 'shareholders' at all. And because of that, they have no interest in corporate governance.

We can also compare the different ways in which these different investors seek to make money from shares. Consider the movement of a share price over time, and suppose that the movement can be broken down into three components as follows:

$$Price = Trend + Wave + Noise \qquad (13.1)$$

Dedicated shareholders seek to gain from the long-term trend. They simply sit out the noise and the waves around that trend. They are the most valuable shareholders to the company, because: (a) they are prepared to stay long-term and are not deterred by short-to medium-term fluctuations in the share price; and (b) their vigilance helps to ensure proper corporate governance.

Quasi-Indexers also seek to gain from the long-term trend, though because their portfolio is diversified, they face a lower proportionate noise and lower proportionate waves around that trend. They are also quite valuable shareholders to the company, because they are prepared to stay long-term and are not deterred by short-to medium-term fluctuations in the share price. However, they do not make a contribution to corporate governance.

Transient shareholders seek to make money from the upswing of the wave. That is, they seek to buy at or near the trough and sell at or near the crest of the wave. They are not such valuable shareholders to the company, because they will not stay long-term precisely because they deterred by short-to medium-term fluctuations in the share price. They sell to avoid losing on the downward phase of the wave. However, they are 'fair weather friends' to the company. In addition they are active in corporate governance, which can be beneficial to the company. But their activity can be double edged: we said above that they may pressurise the company for short-term gains in the share price, at the expense of long-term growth.

High Frequency Traders seek to make money by exploiting the noise – and their superior ability to predict very short-term movements. If they predict a rise in a period, they buy to sell at the end of the period. If they predict a fall, they sell short to buy back at the end of the period. These traders are probably of no value at all to the company issuing shares. Indeed, they are barely even 'shareholders' and they do nothing for corporate governance. Some high frequency traders claim they are valuable because they contribute liquidity to the market, but most others are pretty sceptical about this.

Table 13.1 Comparison of Four Types of Investor

Type of Investor	Long Term Shareholder?	Active in Governance?	Source of Profit	Value to Company Issuing Shares
Dedicated	Yes	Yes	Trend	High
Quasi-Indexer	Yes	No	Trend	Medium
Transient	No	Yes (but biased)	Upswing	Some
High-Frequency	No	No	Noise	None at all

Table 13.1 summarises the four types of investor. In the battle for corporate governance, the outcome will depend on the mix of these.

LESS DEDICATION AND MORE TRANSIENTS

Why has the dedicated shareholder declined as a species to be replaced by transient shareholders and high frequency traders? A quick look at Figure 13.1 gives us a pretty good idea! It shows daily closing prices for the FTSE-100 share price index from 2 April 1984 to 22 August 2012.

Over the period, 2 April 1984 to 31 December 1999, the FTSE-100 index exhibited a fairly steady upward trend. There were some reversals, of course – notably in 1987 and 1998–99. But the patient and dedicated shareholder, prepared to ride out these reversals, saw the index rise from 1,108 to 6,930 over the period: that is a trend rate of growth of 12.3 percent.

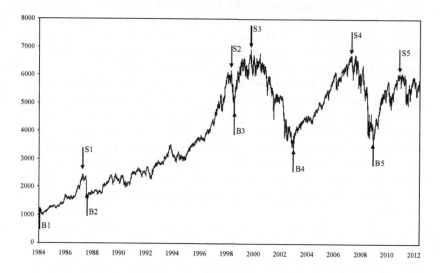

Figure 13.1　FTSE-100 Index: 2 April 1984–22 August 2012

From January 2000 onwards, however, the pattern was completely different. From that date, the dedicated shareholder has been unable to make any gain (on this index) – even over 12 years and more. It is hardly surprising, therefore, that an increasing proportion of investors sought to make money from transient shareholdings.

To see this, consider the following simple example. We shall compare the profits of the dedicated shareholder and a transient shareholder who is lucky enough to buy and sell at the points marked on Figure 13.1. (S)he buys at B1, sells at S1, buys at B2, sells at S2, and so on at B3, S3, B4, S4, B5 and S5.

Table 13.2 compares the profits of these two types of shareholders, firstly from 1984–1999, secondly from 2000–2012, and then over the whole period (1984–2012). The units of measurement are the units of the FTSE-100 index.

In the first period (1984–1999), the dedicated shareholder does well enough (profit of 5,822). The transient shareholder does about 40 percent better (profit of 8,180). But this additional profit must be won at the expense of someone else. And indeed, the losers are those shareholders unlucky enough to buy the shares from our transient shareholder at S1 and S2, and who therefore make losses in the ensuing downswing. The size of their losses (-2,358) is shown in the column headed 'Losses to Other Traders'.

Table 13.2 Profits of Dedicated and Transient Shareholders

From	To	Shareholder Type	(a) Profit	(b) Losses to Other Traders	Sum (a)+(b)
02/04/1984	30/12/1999	Dedicated	5,822	0	5,822
02/04/1984	30/12/1999	Transient	8,180	-2,358	5,822
30/12/1999	22/08/2012	Dedicated	-1,156	0	-1,156
30/12/1999	22/08/2012	Transient	6,005	-7,161	-1,156
02/04/1984	22/08/2012	Dedicated	4,666	0	4,666
02/04/1984	22/08/2012	Transient	14,185	-9,519	4,666

In the second period (2000–2012), however, the difference between the dedicated and transient shareholder is far larger. The dedicated shareholder makes a loss of -1,156 while the transient shareholder makes a profit of 6,005. In this case the loss to the unfortunates who buy the shares at S3, S4 and S5, is -7,161.

The contrast between these two different periods gives us a pretty clear idea of why the dedicated shareholder is a declining species in the second period. It also shows how the good performance of the transient shareholder is only possible because this shareholder avoids some of the losses that the dedicated shareholder has to bear. But these losses can only be avoided if there are other unfortunate investors around to suffer the losses. These unfortunates are sometimes called 'dumb money' – small private investors who 'underperform', or to put it bluntly, are exploited by 'smart' investors.

The last two rows show the combined profits (and losses) over the two periods taken together. Here the transient shareholder makes about three times the profit made by a dedicated shareholder. But as we see in the next section, the high frequency trader can do much better still!

ROBBING PETER TO PAY PAUL?

High Frequency Traders generate their money by exploiting the high-frequency noise in share prices. In practice, these traders may trade hundreds or thousands of times in a day, and hold an investment 'position' for only a very brief period of time (seconds or minutes). However, to get a feel of how profitable it can be, let us consider the case of traders who trade in any share on a daily basis.

Imagine a (hypothetical) trader with perfect powers of forecast, but too small to influence market prices. (S)he trades every day. If (s)he expects a price rise, she buys at the start of the day and sells at the end. If she expects a price fall, she sells short and buys back at the end of the day. In short, this hypothetical trader can make a profit each day equal to the absolute size of the price change on that day.

We shall call this extraordinary trader a '100 percent HF Trader', meaning that they can make 100 percent of the profit to be made from daily trading. Of course, it is surely (we hope!?) inconceivable that any trader can do as well as that. So we shall also consider another high frequency trader who we shall call a '10 percent HF Trader'. This one can make 10 percent of the profit made by the '100 percent HF Trader'. That may not seem nearly so good, but we shall see that it is still pretty good.

Table 13.3 provides the same information as Table 13.2, but now augmented to show the profits made by the 100 percent HF Trader and the 10 percent HF Trader.

Table 13.3　Profits of Shareholders and High Frequency Traders

From	To		(a) Profit	(b) Losses to Other Traders	Sum
02/04/1984	30/12/1999	Dedicated	5,822	0	5,822
02/04/1984	30/12/1999	Transient	8,180	-2,358	5,822
02/04/1984	30/12/1999	100% HF Trader	85,778	-79,956	5,822
02/04/1984	30/12/1999	10% HF Trader	8,578	-2,756	5,822
30/12/1999	22/08/2012	Dedicated	-1,156	0	-1,156
30/12/1999	22/08/2012	Transient	6,005	-7,161	-1,156
30/12/1999	22/08/2012	100% HF Trader	150,675	-151,831	-1,156
30/12/1999	22/08/2012	10% HF Trader	15,068	-16,224	-1,156
02/04/1984	22/08/2012	Dedicated	4,666	0	4,666
02/04/1984	22/08/2012	Transient	14,185	-9,519	4,666
02/04/1984	22/08/2012	100% HF Trader	236,453	-231,787	4,666
02/04/1984	22/08/2012	10% HF Trader	23,645	-18,979	4,666

In the first period (1984–1999) the 100 percent HF trader makes a massive profit of 85,778. Compare this to the profit of the transient shareholder

(8,180) and the profit of the dedicated shareholder (5,822). But this massive profit can only be made at the expense of those unfortunate enough to trade with the 100 percent HF Trader. These unfortunates ('dumb money') make a massive loss of -79,956. And even the 10 percent HF Trader can outperform the transient and dedicated shareholders. This 10 percent HF Trader makes a profit of 8,578 – and once again, some of this is at the expense of 'dumb money'.

The difference is even more marked in the second period (2000–2012). Here the 100 percent HF Trader makes a massive profit of 150,675. Compare this to the profit of the transient shareholder (6,005) and the loss of the dedicated shareholder (-1,156)! All of the 100 percent HF Trader's profit is at the expense of 'dumb money', which takes a huge loss of -151,831. And the 10 percent HF Trader also easily outperforms the transient and dedicated shareholders – again, all of it at the expense of 'dumb money'.

Some economists describe high-frequency trading as 'rent seeking'. This is something of a euphemism and doesn't capture the damage being done here. Apart from any long-term rise in the market, all of the massive profit made by the high frequency trader is made at the expense of others. There is no wealth creation (neither M- nor R-wealth) and no economic benefit from the activity. Few outside the high-frequency trading community believe the argument about enhanced liquidity is anything more than a smoke-screen. Indeed, it is more likely that markets will become less liquid, because few people are willing to play the role of 'dumb money' in this game.

Table 13.4 Further Comparison of Four Types of Investor

	Long Term?	Governance Activity?	Profit Source	Value of Investor?	Negative Effects
Dedicated	Yes	Yes	Trend	High	None
Quasi-Indexer	Yes	No	Trend	Medium	None
Transient	No	Yes (biased?)	Upswing	Some	Some
High-Frequency	No	No	Noise	None at all	Massive

In view of this, it seems essential to revise Table 13.1. I have added a final column describing 'negative effects' – as shown in Table 13.4. This column describes the negative effects (if any) of this investor's activity on others in the market. We saw that some of the transient shareholders profit was made at the expense of other investors. But the real damage here is done by high frequency traders: almost all their profit is made at the expense of other investors, who bear a massive loss as a result.

ULTRA HIGH FREQUENCY TRADING?

We could be forgiven for thinking that high-frequency trading as it stands now is bad enough. But there may be *even worse* to come. To understand why, we need to go back to the pioneering work of Mandelbrot (1967) on the subject of fractals. (This section draws on Swann, 2009b, pp. 72–3).[4]

Mandelbrot started with an apparently simple question: how long is the coastline of Britain? Though the question seems simple, the answer is not simple at all. Why? Because it depends entirely on the length of the rule you use to measure the coast. To see why, it is best to consider a particularly 'jagged' or undulating coastline – such as the far north-west of Scotland.[5]

Imagine that a giant used a giant ruler to measure the coast-line. Then, having done that, he broke the ruler in half, and repeated the exercise with the smaller ruler. Suppose that this process is repeated many times, until the ruler is (say) 100 metres long. How do these different measurements compare? Mandelbrot showed that smaller the ruler, the larger the resulting measurement of length. The reason is that when a large ruler is used, it jumps across bays, estuaries and so on, and thus approximates a complex coast-line by a straight line. But when a smaller ruler is used, it starts to explore these bays and estuaries, and thus makes a more detailed approximation to the coast-line.

Now one might suppose that as the size of the ruler is reduced and further reduced, the computed length of the coastline would eventually converge to a finite number, which could be called the 'true' length of the coastline. But Mandelbrot's argument is because these coastlines have the mathematical properties of a fractal, the measured lengths of the coastline increases *without limit* as the unit of measurement is made smaller. The logical limit of the argument is this. With an arbitrarily small ruler, the length of the coast-line is arbitrarily large.

Building on this analysis of the coastline problem, Mandelbrot (1967, 1982) developed a general theory of fractals. He showed that all kinds of space-filling curves have this fractal property – and one of the cases he considered was the movement of share prices! He demonstrated that the length of a fractal curve could be approximated as follows:

$$L = k\lambda^{(1-D)} \tag{13.2}$$

Using the coastline example, these variables and parameters are interpreted as follows: L is the length of the coastline, λ is the length of the ruler, k is a constant and D is the *fractal dimension* – a measure of the complexity of the coastline.[6] From Equation (13.1), we obtain:

$$\frac{\partial \ln L}{\partial \ln \lambda} = 1 - D \qquad (13.3)$$

If the fractal dimension (D) is 1, then the length of the coastline is constant, regardless of λ. If the fractal dimension is greater than one, on the other hand, the measured length increases as the length of the ruler (λ) is reduced.

We can easily translate equation (13.2) to the context of share prices.[7] In this case: L is the maximum amount of money that could be made by the 100 percent HF trader (as described above), and also the amount lost by 'dumb money'; λ is the interval between trades; and D is the fractal dimension.

How large is D in the context of share prices? One useful source (Valdez-Cepeda and Solano-Herrera, 1999) found the following point estimates of D for different share price indices:

Industrial Dow Jones: D = 1.332
Nikkei Cash: D=1.474
British FTSE-100: D=1.495
Australian Share Price (all ordinaries): D=1.506
German DAX Composite index: D = 1.688

Their estimate of D = 1.495 for the FTSE-100 is almost identical to the estimate I obtained (D = 1.493) for the data in Figure 13.1. Roughly speaking, this value of D means that if we cut the interval between trades from 4 to 1, then we increase the maximum amount that could be made by the 100 percent HF trader (and also the amount lost by 'dumb money'), by a factor of 2. Little wonder then that HF traders wish to become ultra-high frequency traders!

Table 13.5 spells this out in more detail. It extrapolates the maximum profit from high frequency trading (and the maximum losses to unsuccessful traders), assuming, for convenience, a fractal dimension of 1.5.

SOME CONCLUDING OBSERVATIONS

While this example of financial innovation could be called creative destruction, it could just as well be called *destructive creation*. It is hard to think of an example where there is so little social value to an innovation and yet the returns to the innovator are so huge. Indeed, I think there is a good case for claiming that the social value of this innovation is, if anything, negative. In these concluding observations, I shall give some reasons for this point of view.

Table 13.5 The Attractions and Hazards of High Frequency Trading

days	hours	minutes	seconds	milli-seconds	Maximum Profit	Maximum Loss
1024	......	......	......	......	1	−1
256	......	......	......	......	2	−2
64	......	......	......	......	4	−4
16	......	......	......	......	8	−8
4	......	......	......	......	16	−16
1	24	......	......	......	32	−32
	6	......	......	......	64	−64
	1.5	90	......	......	128	−128
		22.5	......	......	256	−256
		5.6	......	......	512	−512
		1.4	84	......	1,024	−1,024
			21.1	......	2,048	−2,048
			5.3	......	4,096	−4,096
			1.3	1318	8,192	−8,192
				330	16,384	−16,384
				82	32,768	−32,768
				21	65,536	−65,536
				5	131,072	−131,072
				1.3	262,144	−262,144

The Kay Review of *UK Equity Markets and Long-Term Decision Making* (2012) described how high frequency trading is part of a broader trend towards trading in shares rather than investing in shares (Kay, 2012, p. 11):

> We focus on the important, though not clear-cut, distinction among asset managers between those who 'invest' on the basis of their understanding of the fundamental value of the company and those who 'trade' based on their expectations of likely short term movements in share price. While some trading is necessary to assist the provision of liquidity to investors, current levels of trading activity exceed those necessary to support the core purposes of equity markets.

And he went on to observe (Kay, 2012, p. 11):

> This conflict between the imperatives of the business model of asset managers,

and the interests of UK business and those who invest in it, is at the heart of our analysis of the problem of short-termism.

But while Kay noted that the growth of high frequency trading concerned many of those he spoke to while writing the report, he argued (Kay, 2012, p. 39):

> We do not, however, believe that the recent growth of high frequency trading is, in itself, a major contributor to short-term behaviour on the part of either savers or companies, although the phenomenon of high frequency trading has emerged as an aspect of a broader trend which favours trading over trust relationships.

On the face of it, this last argument may seem surprising. But, on reflection, I think Kay is right. Short-termism was already a fact of life in a world of transient shareholders. The damage was already done before the emergence of high frequency trading.

What high frequency trading does is further to marginalise the long-term investor on whom corporate governance depends. An ever smaller proportion of those who own shares know or care about the long-term value of the company or will do anything to ensure that the long term value is maintained. I think we could say that this undermining of corporate governance is a definite negative.

Mitchell (2010) has argued that the above is part of a wider and even more damaging phenomenon. This is the replacement of capitalism by what he calls *financialism* (Mitchell, 2010, p.1, his emphasis):

> While capitalism still characterizes a portion of the American economy, it has become subordinated to a new economic order. This economic system is one in which the financial markets exist primarily to serve themselves. In this system, capital is raised for the purpose of creating, selling, and trading securities and derivative securities that do not finance industry but rather trade within markets that exist as an economy unto themselves. At the same time, those markets have profound and adverse effects on the real economy. This new economic system is *Financialism*.

In *financialism*, the financial sector is no longer the servant of the real economy, it does not support the real economy, and sees no obligation to support it. In financialism, financial markets exist to serve the interests of the financial sector – full stop. Mitchell's analysis makes explicit reference to the negative effects of financialism on the real economy.

Paul Volcker has also made some sceptical remarks about the effects of financial innovation on the real economy – most famously arguing that the ATM was the only financial innovation he could think of that has been of social benefit. In an interview with the *Wall Street Journal* (2009), Volker described a presentation he had heard about the 'joys of financial innovation and financial engineering':

> I was listening to this, and I found myself sitting next to one of the inventors of financial engineering. I didn't know him, but I knew who he was and that he had won a Nobel Prize, and I nudged him and asked what all the financial engineering does for the economy and what it does for productivity. Much to my surprise, he leaned over and whispered in my ear that it does nothing—and this was from a leader in the world of financial engineering. I asked him what it did do, and he said that it moves around the rents in the financial system—and besides, it's a lot of intellectual fun.

So there, via Mr Volcker, we hear it from the *horse's mouth*: financial innovation and financial engineering does nothing for the economy or for productivity. On the contrary, it can do much harm.[8]

Despite this zero, or even negative, social value, financial innovation is able to attract a mass of investment. For example, the massive and expensive 7,800km Asia Submarine-cable Express (ASE) – which connects Japan, Malaysia, Singapore and the Philippines – was built with high-frequency trading in mind (BBC, 2012c). It offers a three millisecond speed advantage above any other cable between Singapore and Tokyo, and while that speed gain may sound modest, it could prove critical to financial trades made in this region. How perverse that such the global economy finds it worthwhile to invest in such a complex and expensive engineering feat for the sake of trades of no social value! And this is not an unique example by any means. The UK government has also developed an obsession for an ever-accelerating speed from broadband networks. Former Culture Secretary, Jeremy Hunt, is quoted as saying that, 'we must never fall into the trap of saying any speed is "enough"' (BBC, 2012d).

Plenty of ordinary people see the negative social value of this activity, and support the idea of a 'Tobin tax' – or a tax on financial transactions. This would certainly reign in high-frequency trading. But the consensus amongst city traders is that this would simply shift high-frequency trading abroad, and thus deprive the UK of much needed invisible earnings. If the analysis of this chapter is correct, the invisible earnings cannot compensate for the damage done by this activity, but that point is conveniently forgotten by traders. When I hear such self-serving arguments, I can't help thinking of Samuel Johnson's famous dictum: 'patriotism is the last refuge of a scoundrel'.[9]

NOTES

[1]   Some time after I wrote this chapter, moves were announced in New York to place constraints on high-frequency trading (BBC, 2014b): 'New York's attorney general has

called for curbs on services provided to high-frequency traders. In particular Eric Schneiderman highlighted services that allow traders to get faster access to information. He said traders can make rapid and often risk-free trades before the rest of the market can react'. It seems long overdue that something is done to constrain this most dysfunctional activity.

2   *Oxford Dictionary of Phrase, Saying and Quotation* (1997, p. 353).

3   Some dispute this and claim that the problems stem from excessive regulation. I am not an expert on financial economics, but they 'doth protest too much, methinks'. I have talked to many financial economists in this country and other countries, and the consensus I hear is that financial institutions in the tightly regulated economies were prevented *by regulation* from doing some of the most reckless things that have been done in the City of London. Moreover, if those in the City of London really believe they were under-regulated, then presumably they would welcome additional regulation. But, on the contrary, any attempt to increase regulation of the City is not met with enthusiasm (*Guardian*, 2012c).

4   While the modern pioneer of fractals is Mandelbrot, the idea goes back to earlier work by the mathematician, Lewis Fry Richardson – see Swann (2009b, p. 72).

5   I have not reproduced the map here for reasons of space, but a suitable length of coast-line is that north of the 'Great Glen' – from Fort William to Cape Wrath.

6   The term D is also the *Hausdorff* dimension of the space-filling curve, but in this context, it is more commonly called the *fractal* dimension.

7   Indeed, some of Mandelbrot's earliest studies of fractals relate to stock price movements. Mandelbrot (1997) collects many of his papers on the application of fractals in finance.

8   Warren Buffett has made his concerns about financial innovation very well known (BBC, 2003).

9   Samuel Johnson to James Boswell, April 7, 1775; here quoted from *Oxford Dictionary of Quotations* (1979, p. 276).

14. Summary of Part II

This chapter summarises what we have learned in Part II about the destructive side of business innovation. It is offered as a brief summary for the convenience of those who feel they cannot *see the wood for the trees*. We have studied seven case studies of business innovation and have focussed on the destructive side of these innovations. This focus does not imply that there is no creative side, nor that the destructive side will *generally* dominate the creative side. We simply adopt this focus on the destructive side because, despite our familiarity with Schumpeter's concept of creative destruction, the destructive side is most often ignored in the study of innovation.

Figure 14.1 summarises what we have found. For each case, it indicates where the negative or destructive effects are to be found.

The most obvious destructive effect is the way that innovation by one company can undermine the sales, the market share or the profitability of other businesses. Put like that, it is perhaps seen as one of the least dysfunctional side-effects – and indeed, some would say it is no more dysfunctional than the evolutionary principle of 'survival of the fittest'. However, in some cases, that may mask the true hardship implied by this aspect of creative destruction. In some cases, the destructive effects were substantial. Small-scale weavers suffered severely from the advent of the wide frame. Many local booksellers were driven out of business by online book-selling. The concentration of beer production drove many small brewers out of business. And we argued that high frequency trading is little more than 'robbing Peter to pay Paul'. Moreover, high frequency traders do nothing for corporate governance, and the survival of good corporate governance depends on the dedicated long-term shareholder – a dying breed.

Another category refers to the destructive effects on consumption. For example, wide frames may have produced far cheaper products, but the quality was inferior and consumers lost out as a result. The decline of local bookstores was an undesirable side effect of the growth of online book-selling and some consumers bitterly regret the death of the local store. Real-ale enthusiasts felt the same about the growing concentration of production in brewing. Software innovation led to unwanted pressure on many computers users to upgrade their hardware. And consumerism has, at the very least, disoriented the consumer – see below.

Chapter:		Education	Science	Art	Business	Marketplace	Socio-Econ. Environment	Natural Environment	Consumption	Health
7	Wide Frames			−	−	−	−		−	
8	Division of Labour	−		−			−			−
9	Bookstores				−	−	−		−	
10	Software & e-Waste						−	−	−	−
11	Traffic				−	−	−	−	−	−
12	Consumerism	−							−	−
13	High Freq. Trading				−	−	−			

Figure 14.1 Destructive Effects of Business Innovation

Some have destructive effects on health. The division of labour has had dysfunctional effects on the worker as a human being. The processing of e-waste is a hazardous business, but carried out in many countries as a cottage industry without proper concern for health and safety. The continuing growth of traffic has several adverse effects on health. And consumerism, in truth, does more than disorient the consumer (as per the last paragraph): consumerism can create pathological consumption, which is an illness.

Most of these innovations also had some destructive effects on the socio-economic environment. Wide frames created poverty and the workhouse. Ruskin suggested that it was the workers who broken into pieces – not just the work. The loss of local bookstores and local brews undermined the local environment. And high frequency trading replaced trust relationships with trading activity. Some of these innovations also had destructive effects on the natural environment. Software innovation led to hardware waste. The centralisation of brewing placed more reliance on long-distance transport. And, finally, there were also some smaller effects on education and arts. In short, there are plenty of negatives here.

PART III

The Benign Breeze of C-Innovation

The Rough Breeze of C-Innovation

15. Introduction to Part III

Part III of the book is concerned with common innovation (or C-innovation). It can be seen as a discussion of some of the large amounts of creativity that are not used in business, but in other areas of human activity to increase R-wealth and wellbeing. Each chapter in Part III examines common innovation in one of the categories identified in Part I (Chapter 6). Each chapter starts either with a sketch of a few examples of common innovation in that context, or with a single longer case study.

The reader should bear in mind the following points while reading these chapters. In each chapter, we can in principle divide the innovative activity into three components. If the chapter refers to common innovation in Y, where Y is one of the categories identified in Chapter 6 (consumption, natural environment, etc.), then the three components are:

- common innovation that adds directly to Y
- common innovation that exploits other categories (e.g. X) to enhance Y
- common innovation that exploits activities in Y to enhance other categories (e.g. Z)

So for example, Chapter 17 on common innovation in the natural environment, has three sections:

- common innovation that adds directly to the natural environment
- common innovation that exploits other categories (e.g. science) to enhance the natural environment
- common innovation that exploits the natural environment to enhance other categories (e.g. education)

The reader will see that this can lead to some duplication. For example, exploitation of the natural environment to enhance education could arise in two chapters: the chapter on the natural environment and the chapter on education. We have decided to leave this duplication, where it occurs, because it is essential that each chapter gives a full picture of common innovation in and around a given category.

In principle, there may well be examples of common innovation that link every pair of categories. If we were to draw a matrix (like Figure 6.3) representing the flows from one category to another, we could, in principle, find an example to fill every cell in that matrix. Indeed, when I started to write this book, I considered whether I could produce an exhaustive set of examples to fill every cell. However, it became clear that the end result would be unreadable in this traditional book format. And moreover, my objective here is to use a general framework to illustrate how common innovation works, rather than get bogged down in the details of particular examples.

Instead, I provide some examples for a subset of these cells, as an illustration. This does not mean that the other cells are empty. And moreover, even if there are no links *today* from one category to another, this does not mean that there will be no link *in future*. For an essential characteristic of common innovation is that it builds linkages between categories where none exist. And, in doing so, common innovation contributes to R-wealth creation.

After reading these chapters in Part III, the reader may be tempted to say that these examples of common innovation are both obvious and trivial! As to the first point, my response is, good! There is so much 'evidence' in economics (notably econometric evidence) that is not in the least bit obvious, so it is nice to have something obvious for a change! As to the second point, yes, many examples of common innovation do seem pretty modest. For as I argued in Chapter 3, if business innovation is a 'perennial gale', common innovation is a 'gentle and benign breeze', and many common innovations would have a low score on the 'Beaufort Scale'. But when we add them all together, and when the linkages in the framework on Chapter 6 are well developed, we find that common innovation can have a notable impact on R-wealth.

At this stage, we are a long way away from attempting to quantify the elements of this matrix. But if this could be done, even roughly, the matrix offers a simple and convenient way to quantify the overall effects of common innovation on R-wealth creation – and how that compares with the effects of business innovation on M-wealth creation. This would be done by a straightforward application of Leontief's Input-Output analysis. We shall return to this in Part IV (Chapter 25), and some further details are provided in the Appendix.

16. Consumption and the Home

In this chapter, we simply survey some of the forms of common innovation that are found in the home. This is not an exhaustive list, and does not need to be, for I am sure that the reader can fill in the gaps for him/herself.

COMMON INNOVATION IN THE KITCHEN

A good place to start a discussion of common innovation is in the domestic kitchen. One of the simplest and most common forms of common innovation is found there. The subtitle of Valerio's (1988) cook-book captures this perfectly: *I piatti ricchi della cucina povera.*[1] The creative but impecunious cook turns ordinary and inexpensive ingredients into a delicious and nutritious meal. Note that it is the common innovation of the cook in the domestic kitchen that adds this value – not the investments of agribusiness, nor the innovations of the food industry, nor the innovation of the supermarkets.

This does not in the least deny the importance of high quality raw materials. Nor does it deny that there are innovations in the food supply chain. Nor does it deny that 'rich dishes' can also be created by professional cooks in restaurants. And nor does it deny that the domestic cook may be guided by recipes from cook-books, television programmes, and so on.

While this example is good place to start, some may think this is utterly trivial.[2] Certainly, if we compare the innovative effort expended in a single domestic kitchen with the innovative effort involved in creating a new generation of personal computer or a new generation of airliner, then the former does seem very modest indeed. But that is not the appropriate calculation: it ranks innovations in terms of their technological complexity and cost, rather than their contribution to R-wealth creation.

A more sensible calculation would be to compare the R-wealth created by common innovation in all domestic kitchens across world, with the R-wealth and M-wealth created by a new generation of personal computer across the world. This is by no means an easy calculation, and I cannot provide an answer here. But I am absolutely confident to say that the contribution of common innovation in all domestic kitchens across the world is certainly not trivial. I would not be at all surprised, indeed, if it exceeded the R-wealth created by the new generation of personal computer or the new generation of airliner.

In short, common innovation in the domestic kitchen is not in the least bit trivial because, even if it seems very modest from a technological point of view, it is very common, which makes it economically important. And this is just the first of many important examples of common innovation by the consumer in his/her own home.

COMMON INNOVATION IN THE HOME

It is helpful to divide the various types of common innovation in the home into two broad categories.

(a) The first could be described as the domestic equivalent of product innovation. It is where final consumers use their own creativity to make new objects to place or use in the home. This could be, for example, a new work of art or a new piece of furniture.

(b) The second could be described as the domestic equivalent of Henderson and Clark's (1990) concept of 'architectural' innovation. In its original context, 'architectural innovation' means reconfiguring components to make a new end result, while the components themselves are unchanged. In this context, it means that final consumer uses their own creativity to use and rearrange existing objects (or professional innovations) within the home to good effect.

The use of (a) alone is quite rare. The closest example of this I can think of is the home of two of our neighbours. This couple are both artists, and many or most of the decorations and objects in their home are of their own making. In its purest form, however, the use of (a) only would imply that the design of the objects comes first and the layout of the home is subordinate to the objects themselves. That is rather rare.

The use of (b) alone is much more common. The final consumer uses existing objects and professional innovations, so there is little or no 'common innovation' in the objects themselves. But the final consumer uses a lot of creativity in arranging and configuring these objects. This 'interior design' is common innovation when the final consumers work out the designs for themselves, but is a professional innovation when they employ professional interior designers.[3]

The use of (a) and (b) together is much more common than (a) alone.

Even when final consumers create a lot of their own designs and objects, they give careful consideration of how their own designs are to fit into the home. This sort of common innovation relates to a wide variety of household effects: furniture, fabrics, paintings and wall-hangings, decoration, fireplaces, lighting, electrical appliances, and so on.

COMMON INNOVATION IN THE GARDEN

Another obvious example is common innovation in the garden. Here the greater part of common innovation is probably the domestic equivalent of 'architectural' innovation – rather than product innovation.

Why is that? I make that assertion because very few domestic gardeners do their own plant breeding! Most buy, or are given, seeds and cuttings that will grow into plants that are recognised species or hybrids. Very few produce their own hybrids.[4] The innovation is not in the plants themselves, but in the way they are arranged, configured and cared for. As with interior design, it is common innovation when the final consumers produce their own garden designs, but not if they hire a professional garden designer.

Again, this may seem obvious and therefore trivial. But even if it is obvious, it is not trivial. Time use studies find that gardening is a popular hobby in itself and that time spent in the garden enjoys great amenity – even if we don't know what proportion of this time could be described as common innovation. The garden is an important source of R-wealth.

Moreover, common innovation in one garden does not just create R-wealth for the owner of that garden. There can be pleasant positive externalities for passers-by. I have in mind the beautiful garden of a very modest bungalow near where I live. While the house is very modest, and we would normally pass it without taking notice, the garden is a source of delight to those who pass on foot, on the bus or in a car.

COMMON INNOVATION IN HOBBIES

Moving on from the 'real estate' of the home, we can now turn to another category of common innovation that takes place in the home. This happens when final consumers uses their creativity to support and develop their hobbies. We can divide the consumer's use of their own creativity here into three categories.

Product Innovation

The first is, once again, the domestic equivalent of product innovation. The final consumers use their own ideas to create something new and of value. So, for example, I might paint a new painting, write a new poem, or write new music for a song. Obvious examples are to be found in the following as hobbies: arts and crafts, music and composition, making clothes, writing, family history research, and so on.

Architectural Innovation

The second is something similar to 'architectural' innovation.   More specifically, we could call it 'common innovation by collecting'. We can perhaps identify two categories of collecting. The first is where the items are of value in themselves: works of art, valuable books, studio pottery, jewellery, and so on. But even so, the intelligent collector can use common innovation to ensure that the value of the collection is more than the sum of its parts. We shall describe how in a moment, The second is where the items on their own are of little or no value: matchboxes, beer-mats, postcards, and so on. Most of these 'collectibles' are modest commercial items, though some collect objects found in the wild – such as leaves from trees and seashells.[5] They only gain any significant value when placed in a collection. And here the intelligent use of common innovation by the collector is essential to turn these ordinary objects into an interesting collection.

How does the intelligent collector use common innovation to enhance the interest and value of the collection?   In addition to the basic steps of collection (finding and acquiring) the intelligent collector can add value by researching, organising, cataloguing and maintaining these items. It is in these last activities that common innovation is to be found.

We could also say that family history research (which I would include in category a) involves some collecting. Details about one ancestor become more interesting when they are combined with details about many other ancestors.

Active Consumption[6]

The third is more subtle, and at first sight it might look as if there is no common innovation here. This is the use of the consumer's creativity in the active consumption of professional innovations.

For example, there are perhaps two ways I could listen to a professional recording of some keyboard pieces by J.S. Bach. One is to listen to it in a casual way, enjoying it at a 'superficial' level, but without delving deep into the structure and interpretation of the music. In this case, there is no common innovation. All the innovation was that by J.S. Bach himself, or by the pianist/harpsichordist, or perhaps by the sound recorder and production team. The other is to listen with great care – perhaps over and over again – taking repeated notes, so as to develop a much deeper understanding of the music. In this case, the creativity involved in active consumption adds something to the R-wealth gained from listening. Indeed, in this latter case there is common innovation, and it can be quite important.

We find many other such examples of common innovation amongst active consumers, when they are using creativity and intelligence while viewing works of art and architecture, or when they are using creativity and intelligence while reading works of literature.

And, if we extend the definition of hobbies to include those involving a lot of activity outside the home, then obvious examples include tourism, exploring, and research on local history. Although these activities may also depend on business innovation (package tours, transport, and so on) there are many opportunities for common innovation when active consumers using creativity and intelligence to make more out of their tourism, exploring and research.

OVERVIEW OF COMMON INNOVATION

In this section, we move on from the motivating examples listed above to discuss the three generic aspects of common innovation in this context.

Common Innovation that Adds Directly to Consumption

Many of the examples of common innovation described above fit into this category. This means that new ideas are used to enhance what is obtained from consumption, but the ideas do not stem directly from any of the other categories in our analytical framework. In addition, the effects of these common innovations are found within the consumption category and do not directly influence other categories – apart from health and R-wealth.

Indeed, there is a good reason for this. In English, we sometimes use the word 'recreation' to describe the desired effect of some consumption activities and hobbies. If we use the literal meaning of the word, and interpret it in the context of our analytical framework, we can think of these activities as repairing the damage done to our R-wealth by some other aspects of our life (work, commuting, etc). This repair may be best achieved if the final consumer keeps well clear of these negative influences on R-wealth.

Common Innovation that Exploits other Categories to Enhance Consumption

However, some consumers do make use of ideas stemming from other categories to enhance consumption. Some intelligent consumers are informed by science. An obvious example of this is where the wise consumer is guided by scientific knowledge to consume in a way that is good for their health. This is obviously relevant in the context of diet, but applies more broadly to a variety of consumption activities and hobbies. A simple example would be a preference for active consumption (country walks) over passive consumption (watching lots of television). A more complex example would be planning consumption activity to counter depression or other mental health problems.

In a similar way, intelligent consumers are guided by their education. It is not hard to think of consumption activities where the educated consumer can achieve more R-wealth than the uneducated consumer. One example is common innovation by collecting – as described above. The educated collector can derive much from an otherwise unexceptional item, which would not attract or rouse the interest of an uneducated collector. Another example is the active consumption of works of art. While the uneducated consumer can certainly appreciate these at a certain level, the educated consumer can often achieve an even greater level of appreciation.

Some consumers are skilful at exploiting the natural environment to enhance their consumption. An obvious example is the picnic: a meal of ordinary items can be turned into a memorable experience if the meal is eaten at the top of a hill with a fine view, or by the seaside. And those who design golf courses understand this principle very well. The attraction of a golf course to many players is not just the design of the course itself, but also the surrounding environment. Other consumers know that the socio-economic environment can enhance their consumption. People will pay large sums for tickets to rock concerts because, 'being there' is such an important part of the experience. The same applied to the FA Cup Final: for a clear view of the match, it may be easier to watch on the television, but once again, 'being there' is so important.

And, although I said above that recreation may work best if it removes the consumer from everyday sources of stress, it is nonetheless true that we can use knowledge and skills we learn in our business and in the marketplace to enhance consumption. So, for example, many academics develop some portable skills that can enhance a variety of consumption activities. One is the ability to write reasonable prose at speed and without undue pain. A second is the ability to 'skim read': that is, to read through a large document at speed to see if it is of relevance and to find the sections of interest. A third is the ability to speak to a large group of people without undue anxiety. And many of us learn financial lessons in working life that make us better at managing the financial side of our consumption activities.

Common Innovation that Exploits Consumption to Enhance other Categories

I suspect that for most consumers, consumption is primarily an activity directed at enhancing health and R-wealth. For most consumers, the issue of what lessons might be taken from consumption activity to enhance other categories would probably be a secondary matter. However, there are examples of innovation that exploit consumption to enhance other categories.

The obvious place to start here is the research of von Hippel (1988, 2005), though much of this relates to business innovation rather than common innovation. In his early work, von Hippel (1988) argued that information or feedback from the consumer was an important input to the business innovation process. In his later work, von Hippel (2005) wrote of *democratic* innovation, where the consumer was not just a source of information or feedback, but could be said to play a role in driving the direction of innovation. In the same way, the consumer's experience in consumption is an important input to focus groups and market research.

This may be a part of business innovation, but it is also an input to common innovation in academic research and policy-making. However, it is not only business that learns from the consumer. The consumer can provide important information to science and education – most obviously as a 'research object', but sometimes as a 'research observatory', and occasionally as an amateur (or 'citizen') researcher (see Chapters 19 and 21). In a similar way, lessons learnt from the consumer can make an important contribution to common innovation in the socio-economic environment (see Chapter 18).

CONCLUSION

When compared to Part II of the book, it appears that these examples of common innovation are mostly creative and that the destructive element here is limited.

So, for example, common innovation in the kitchen makes a better meal from given ingredients. Common innovation in the living room creates a better space in which to live. Common innovation in the garden creates a better space in which to relax. Common innovation in collecting creates a more interesting and valuable collection. And common innovation in tourism creates a more memorable holiday. The destructive element of these examples of common innovation is limited, because my 'quiet' use of common innovation in my own home creates R-wealth for me and my family, but does not obviously reduce the R-wealth of my neighbours.

There is one potentially destructive side to common innovation, of course. This would be found if the common innovation of the final consumer replaces the professional innovation of the trader. An example of this could be where the final consumer, as DIY ('do it yourself') painter and decorator, damages the livelihood of the professional painter and decorator. Another would be when the common innovation of the final consumer in the kitchen undermines the livelihood of a local restaurant. But this must be a very limited effect. I cannot ever remember meeting professional decorators or professional plumbers who complain that they have no work because of DIY!

The reason why this DIY has such a limited destructive effect is that it operates in a different segment of the market to the high quality professional. The DIY approach to innovation is either much cheaper or it allows the final consumer to obtain a much closer fit to what is wanted at a manageable price. DIY therefore appeals to two groups:

- those who have a low opportunity cost to their time – and can therefore afford the time for DIY;
- those who attach a very high value to getting the design exactly right – and who would therefore find it expensive to use the services of a high quality professional.

By contrast, the high quality professional is more expensive, and especially so if the customer wants a 'bespoke' design. The professional service therefore appeals to two groups:

- those who have a high opportunity cost to their time – and cannot therefore afford the time for DIY;
- those who do not have strong views on getting the design exactly right – and who would therefore find it quite acceptable to use a standard service (rather than a bespoke service).

In short, the extent to which these common innovations undermine professional innovation is usually limited.

All these examples of common innovation seem obvious and, as a result, the reader may be tempted to assume they are therefore trivial. But even if obvious, they are definitely not trivial. We know from time use surveys that a lot of time is spent in the home, garden and in leisure, even if we don't know how much of that time is spent in common innovation. It is reasonable to estimate that common innovation by the consumer at home can have a substantial effect on creation of R-wealth.

In conclusion there is one other important lesson here. The R-wealth generated at home depends not only on professional innovators and what they do to the products and services we buy. It also depends, in large degree, on the extent to which final consumers use common innovation in the home. The essential point is that we are talking here of active, rather than passive consumers. While passive consumers simply benefit from professional innovations, and have none of their own, active consumers use common innovation to create more R-wealth from given M-wealth. A hundred years ago, Wesley Mitchell (1912) wrote:

> Important as the art of spending is, we have developed less skill in its practice than in the practice of making money. Common sense forbids our wasting dollars earned by irksome efforts; and yet we are notoriously extravagant. Ignorance of qualities, uncertainty of taste, lack of accounting, carelessness about prices – faults which would ruin a merchant – prevail in our housekeeping. Many of us scarcely know what becomes of our money; though well-schooled citizens of a Money Economy ought to plan for their outgoes no less carefully than for their incomes.

More generally, consumption was then, and still is, an underdeveloped art – especially when compared to production. But the theme of this chapter is that we can get better at it, and common innovation will help us to do so.

NOTES

1   'Rich dishes from the poor kitchen'.
2   The reader's perception of the importance of common innovation in the domestic kitchen will also depend on location and economic circumstances. Take a highly paid worker in the City of London, for example, who may rarely eat at home: *common innovation* in that domestic kitchen is a rarity. Then take a retired person living in a quiet suburb of a less wealthy city, or in the countryside: eating out is an uncommon treat, and *common innovation* in the domestic kitchen is of the greatest importance. And then take an unemployed person in a poor country …
3   The Chinese art of Feng Shui seeks to orientate of buildings and their contents in an auspicious manner so as to enhance the wellbeing and quality of life of those who live and work in these buildings.
4   A few amateurs do, however, do try to cultivate their own hybrids or do other research on their plants. This could be described as a form of common innovation in science – a topic we shall discuss in Chapter 21.
5   Large private collections of natural objects could also be classified as common innovation in natural science – see Chapter 21.
6   This term is due to Bianchi (1998). Swann (1999) also discusses the role of a particular type of active consumer, the *Marshall consumer* (named after Alfred Marshall), who is, in effect, an innovator.

17. Natural Environment

Chapter 16 was concerned with common innovation by an individual or a small group of individuals: the final consumer(s) in the home. This chapter is mainly concerned with common innovation by larger organisations – often public sector or third sector. There is an element in common but a difference in scale. Final consumers use common innovation to make a pleasant environment in their gardens, while the organisations of this chapter use common innovation to make a pleasant environment from much larger areas of land.

While the examples of common innovation listed in the Chapter 16 needed little explanation because they are all so well known, we do need a more detailed explanation in this chapter. For that reason, I have chosen to examine a single case study of common innovation which I know very well.

A CASE STUDY

This case study describes how an old industrial site has been transformed into a nature reserve. It is true that nature, working without human intervention, would have made much of the transformation by itself. But the transformation has been directed and accelerated by human intervention.

Attenborough Nature Reserve lies about seven kilometres south west of Nottingham. It occupies a long strip of land between the village of Attenborough and the River Trent – one of the three largest rivers in England. Originally, this land was wet meadow land by the River Trent. From early photographs, it appears that this landscape was very similar to the present landscape along other nearby stretches of the river.

When the Trent flooded, this land was prone to flooding, and that happened in most years. This history of flooding meant that the grassland was rich in mineral deposits. And underneath the soil, there were large deposits of sand and gravel from the ice age. In 1929, excavation work started in the area to create Attenborough Quarry. After the topsoil was removed, the quarry was worked to collect gravel and sand for industrial and building use. When each particular part of the site was exhausted, the topsoil thus removed was then deposited in a series of mounds, and the exhausted site made a very ugly landscape. Excavation would then move on to a fresh part of the site. Indeed, excavation still continues today some distance upstream from the main reserve.

The initial effect of this industrial development, therefore, was to turn pleasant meadow land into a barren wasteland. However, as these gravel pits were repeatedly flooded by the River Trent, the landscape was naturally transformed into a series of lagoons in amongst the original grassland and scrub, and a patchwork of tiny islands (the mounds of topsoil) in the lagoons. Over a few years, a wide variety of plants started to re-colonise the area. The lagoons provided an ideal habitat for a wide variety of water birds, and the patchwork of tiny islands provided food, shelter and safe nesting sites for the birds. Over time, and as the site has matured, a wider variety of habitats naturally emerged, and this in turn attracted a wider variety of wildlife.

As a nature reserve, Attenborough is best known for its birdlife. It is an important site for winter wildfowl, and important breeding ground in the summer. It also attracts many birds of passage in the spring and autumn. But other wildlife are also to be found, including: wildflowers, wild shrubs and trees, butterflies, dragonflies, foxes, voles, shrews, otters and bats.

However, just as the industrial landscape of Attenborough was partly man-made, so also the new landscape of Attenborough was partly man-made. The process of re-colonisation was in part a natural process, but this natural process was shaped and accelerated by human intervention. The area became a nature reserve in 1966, and was designated a Site of Special Scientific Interest (SSSI) in 1982. Staff and volunteers working for with Nottinghamshire Wildlife Trust have been active in developing and maintaining the different habitats in the reserve.[1]

If we compare the landscape of today[2] with the original landscape, we see that a splendid nature reserve has replaced a pleasant but unexceptional rural landscape. For most people, the value of the landscape has been enhanced. But, the important lesson here is that this value was not achieved *despite* the earlier period of industrial use. On the contrary, the present landscape is the direct result of many years of sand and gravel extraction, followed by a period of natural and man-made re-colonisation. Indeed, the period of industrial use contributed, in the longer term, to enhance the natural value of the site. It is a wonderful, if (at first) unexpected, legacy from an industrial site. It also serves as a interesting counterpoint to Ruskin's memorable and apocalyptic vision about industrial desecration of natural landscape:[3]

> Last week, I drove from Rochdale to Bolton Abbey ... Naturally, the valley has been one of the most beautiful in the Lancashire hills ... (but) at this time there are not ... more than a thousand yards of road to be traversed anywhere, without passing a furnace or mill.
> Now, is that the kind of thing you want to come to everywhere? Because, if it

be, and you tell me so distinctly, I think I can make several suggestions to-night, and could make more if you give me time, which would materially advance your object. The extent of our operations at present is more or less limited by the extent of coal and iron-stone, but we have not yet learned to make proper use of our clay. Over the greater part of England, south of the manufacturing districts, there are magnificent beds of various kinds of useful clay; and I believe that it would not be difficult to point out modes of employing it which might enable us to turn nearly the whole of the south of England into a brick-field, as we have already turned nearly the whole of the north into a coal-pit. I say 'nearly' the whole, because, as you are doubtless aware, there are considerable districts in the south composed of chalk, renowned up to the present time for their downs and mutton. But, I think, by examining carefully into the conceivable uses of chalk, we might discover a quite feasible probability of turning all the chalk districts into a limekiln, as we turn the clay districts into a brick-field. There would then remain nothing but the mountain districts to be dealt with; but, as we have not yet ascertained all the uses of clay and chalk, still less have we ascertained those of stone; and I think, by draining the useless inlets of the Cumberland, Welsh, and Scotch lakes, and turning them, with their rivers, into navigable reservoirs and canals, there would be no difficulty in working the whole of our mountain districts as a gigantic quarry of slate and granite, from which all the rest of the world might be supplied with roofing and building stone.

Is this, then, what you want? You are going straight at it at present ...

Ruskin's concern was understandable.   And for the short term, the excavations at Attenborough had a destructive effect. But in the long term, the outcome is probably better than the starting point.

Common Innovation?

Some readers may think this is an interesting story, perhaps, but they doubt whether it is really common innovation. To answer this, we need to break the question into two subsidiary questions.

First, suppose the transformation of this unused industrial landscape into a nature reserve had been an entirely natural process, with no human intervention – beyond a policy of non-intervention. In that case, is there any common innovation in this case study? Second, if we focus purely on what human intervention has added – over and above the transformation that nature would have accomplished on its own – what common innovation has occurred?

Taking the first question, we might say that this case is purely an illustration of natural innovation. Now, thankfully, natural innovation is often very benign, and is also very common. But the definition of 'common innovation' used in this book refers to human activity alone, and so does not include purely natural innovation. However, the innovation at work here is not just the natural transformation of a wasteland. Any active decision to allow that natural transformation to continue, and to prevent the wasteland being turned into an even worse type of wasteland, would fall into my definition of 'common innovation'. After all, many derelict industrial sites are used for the disposal of waste of one sort or another.

The early phase of natural transformation was probably a case of benign neglect by the then owner of the site – and not an active decision to allow a natural reserve to emerge. But as McDaid (2005) recalls, an active decision had to be made in the 1960s:

> When proposals to fill many of the lagoons with fuel ash from a nearby power station were put forward in the 1960s local people decided to stand up to protect the site and its wildlife. As a result, a vigorous campaign to safeguard the site was established with the support of naturalists from other parts of the county.

At the very least, there was common innovation by all those local people and naturalists who made these interventions in the 1960s. Their vision, tenacity and determination changed the trajectory from 'industrial wasteland' to 'nature reserve'. Figure 17.1 provides a simple illustration.

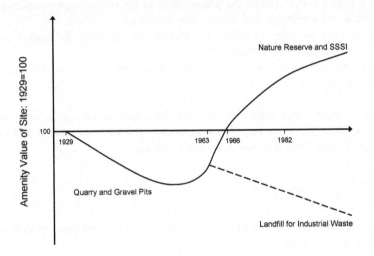

Figure 17.1   Amenity Value of Attenborough Site

Now let us turn to the second question. What has common innovation added to the transformation over and above what might have happened naturally? There are two main aspects to this. First, the Wildlife Trust has sought to develop a greater diversity in the habitats at Attenborough. This has involved:

- creation of many new reed beds, and the extension and maintenance of existing reed beds;
- maintenance of a diverse flora and fauna consistent with the diversity of habitats;
- landscaping some areas of the nature reserve to attract more wildlife.

Second, the Trust has worked to maintain the footpaths and public areas of the reserve, but also to limit access to certain areas where 'shy' birds are being encouraged to settle. The Trust has also worked improve access for those with limited mobility on the main routes through the reserve. In addition, one of the most important developments in recent years has been the building of an eco-friendly Nature Centre, which attracts many visitors in its own right, with its conference rooms, education facilities and interactive displays.

Taking these two questions together, we can say that the three main episodes of common innovation have involved:

- taking action to ensure the preservation of the site as a nature reserve, and to avoid it being turned into another industrial wasteland;
- working to 'improve upon' the natural condition of the reserve and to accelerate its transformation;
- improving access, or in a few cases, controlling access to sheltered parts of the site.

All of these come within the meaning of common innovation used in this book, and all of them have been important. But do some have a destructive side to them? We shall return to this a little later.

AN OVERVIEW

Let us now consider the three generic types of common innovation that can arise in this context.

Common Innovation that Adds Directly to the Natural Environment

Some of the examples of common innovation in our case study fit into this category. This means that new ideas are used to enhance the natural environment in itself, but the ideas do not stem directly from any of the other categories in our analytical framework. In addition, the effects of these common innovations are effects on the natural environment itself and do not directly influence other categories – apart from health and R-wealth.

The biggest piece of common innovation in our case study fits here: the decision by the local community to fight to keep the derelict industrial site as a nature reserve and to prevent it from further desecration. Some of the other, more modest pieces of common innovation also fit here: the development of new reed beds and new habitats to attract a wider variety of wildlife.

Moving on from our case study, similar forms of common innovation can be found when local authorities or charities use creative energies to enhance a public space. This could include enhancements to a public park, a public square or high street, or any public place. A charming example of this which is found in many towns and cities is where school children decorate a large wall with a 'mural' describing life in the local community. I have seen many such examples where a bleak and featureless piece of masonry is turned into a much gentler piece of art.

This remains common innovation so long as the objective is simply to enhance the space. But there can be an obvious overlap with innovation to enhance a marketplace with the explicit objective to increase retail sales or profitability. This would qualify as business innovation if funded by business, or business-supporting innovation policy if funded by local or national government.

Common Innovation that Exploits other Categories to Enhance the Natural Environment

The most obvious classification of this case study is one where people exploited and old industrial site to enhance the natural environment. But the case study also illustrates how the intelligent enhancement of a nature reserve depends on wise use of science – especially, biological sciences and ecology.

Looking beyond our case study, some of the common innovation to enhance a natural environment is based on other knowledge – archaeology, history, social sciences and so on, and not science in a narrow sense. Organisations such as the National Trust and English Heritage need to draw on a variety of knowledge to preserve their monuments and surroundings. Some of this knowledge may be scientific, but much will be archaeological and historical.

Common Innovation that Exploits the Natural Environment to Enhance other Categories

In this case, a large group of common innovations exploit the benign characteristics of the natural environment to enhance other categories. Indeed, a report by the New Economics Foundation (2012) has explored this phenomenon in some depth, and concludes:[4]

> the natural environment contributes to improving mental and physical health, children's development and education, community cohesion and well-being in general.

In the context of our case study, it seems likely that the efforts to enhance accessibility at the nature reserve have lead to directly beneficial effects on the health and R-wealth of those newcomers who are attracted by this enhanced accessibility. I am taking it to be fairly self-evident that more physical exercise in a pleasant natural environment is good both for health and general wellbeing and quality of life – and, hence, R-wealth.

Some of the common innovations impact on other categories. The nature reserve is a popular site for parties of school-children. There is general agreement that children find such visits both enjoyable and educational. Indeed, Nottinghamshire Wildlife Trust have an explicit policy for the use of the reserve for education. This also spills over into an impact on the socio-economic environment: a nature reserve is a particularly inclusive form of public space. It is a particular pleasure for the visitor to see parties of disabled children and youths, and their evident delight, as they find their way around the reserve.

Turning from our specific case study, there are many other examples of this sort. Common innovations that improve the natural environment of a public space can enhance health, R-wealth, consumption activities, education, the socio-economic environment (for example, by increased inclusivity) – and also have beneficial effects on business and the market place.

Moreover, common innovation in the natural environment can be a stimulus for art. Some of the most creative minds of all have found the walk in pleasant parks or countryside to be an excellent 'occasion' for creativity. One of the most celebrated examples is Ludwig van Beethoven. In some of his letters, he described how some of his best musical ideas came to him when he was walking in the countryside:[5]

> You will ask me where I get my ideas. That I cannot tell you with certainty; they come unsummoned, directly, indirectly, – I could seize them with my hands, – out in the open air; in the woods; while walking; in the silence of the nights; early in the morning; incited by moods, which are translated by the poet into words, by me into tones that sound, and roar and storm about me until I have set them down in notes.

And this pastime is also an important occasion for more modest forms of creativity.

CONCLUSION

Is all of this common innovation creative? Or is some of it destructive as well? Let us revisit the three aspects of common innovation in our case study.

a) taking action to ensure the preservation of the site as a nature reserve, and to avoid it being turned into another industrial wasteland;
b) working to 'improve upon' the natural condition of the reserve and to accelerate its transformation;
c) improving access, or in a few cases, controlling access to sheltered parts of the site.

Innovation (a) is almost entirely creative. The reserve has proven a very popular amenity. Every year, more than half a million people visit the reserve and Nature Centre, and hundreds of school and educational visits take place (Broxtowe, 2012). Following the opening of the Nature Centre, the reserve was voted number nine in a 2006 list of popular worldwide 'eco places'.[6] And in 2012, it was ranked as the second most popular nature reserve in a survey by Countryfile (2012).

In principle, innovation (b) might be more controversial amongst conservative naturalists who are sceptical about the idea of 'improving upon' nature. But even critics accept that for the most part, these improvements have been sensitively and appropriately done.

Innovation (c) is the controversial one, however. Increasing access is an admirable goal, but increasing visitor numbers can impinge on some existing users. Some local fishermen and serious birdwatchers complain that they could better enjoy the reserve in the early days when it was not full of people. Others have complained of the attendant problems that come with increasing visitor numbers: problems of car-parking, overdevelopment and overcrowding.

There is nothing exceptional about this. It is an issue for any natural amenity. There is to some extent a trade-off between quality of amenity and the quantity of people enjoying the amenity. As it stands, the reserve has a number of different users: birdwatchers, fishermen, ordinary walkers, dog walkers, cyclists and others. Their objectives and wishes are somewhat different, and sometimes in tension.

In this chapter, I have concentrated on the example of common innovation and the natural environment which I know best. I am sure that most readers will know of many comparable examples. Some of these lie along the boundary of common innovation and business innovation because they are in part commercial operations, charging visitors for access. Examples include:

- The Eden Project, a magnificent 'living theatre' of plants built at a disused china clay pit near St Austell, Cornwall.[7]
- 'Eureka', the National Children's Museum, located on the site of a derelict railway yard in Halifax, West Yorkshire.[8]

Others rank as common innovation because they are funded by charities, local authorities and other public sector sources, and do not charge for access. Examples would include:

- Tissington Trail and High Peak Trail in the Derbyshire Peak District (Derbyshire, n.d.) These trails are old railway lines that have been converted for cycling, horse-riding and walking.

NOTES

[1] The site is owned by CEMEX UK who still extract upstream of the main reserve, and use the waterways for the transport of sand and gravel. The nature reserve is managed by Nottinghamshire Wildlife Trust in partnership with the owners and with support from Broxtowe Borough Council. See Attenborough Nature Centre (2012a) and Cemex (2012).

[2] See Attenborough Nature Centre (2012b).

[3] Ruskin (1904/1996, vol. 16, pp. 336–7).

[4] New Economics Foundation (2012).

[5] Letter to Louis Schlosser, c.1822. Beethoven (2009, para. 54).

[6] *BBC Wildlife Magazine* (2006).

[7] Eden Project (2013) and Smit (2002).

[8] The decision to locate Eureka at this site was the recommendation of HRH Prince Charles. He believed it would help urban regeneration and provide an important learning experience for children and families (Eureka, 2013).

18. Socio-Economic Environment

Following the framework used in Part I (Chapter 6), this chapter concerns common innovation and the socio-economic environment. *Some* of the ideas to be discussed here are better known as *social innovation*,[1] and this will be familiar ground to many readers. But the scope of this chapter is wider than the conventional interpretation of social innovation.

Social innovation is by no means a new idea. We can find important social innovations and innovators from the dawn of the industrial revolution (Mulgan, 2007). One of the earliest and most important innovators was Robert Owen, the enlightened owner of textile mills in New Lanark, Scotland. Owen acquired these mills at the end of the 18th Century, and transformed them from a very harsh working environment into a model community, with facilities, medical care and comprehensive education. His example inspired many other social innovators.

Mulgan (2007, p. 8) offers this definition of social innovation: 'innovative activities and services that are motivated by the goal of meeting a social need and that are predominantly developed and diffused through organisations whose primary purposes are social.' This puts the emphasis on innovations with a social purpose. In this chapter, I shall cast the net even wider – in line with the format of all the chapters in Part III. We shall consider all three of the following:

- innovation that directly enhances the socio-economic environment
- innovation that exploits other categories (e.g. science) to enhance the socio-economic environment
- innovation that exploits the socio-economic environment to enhance other categories (e.g. consumption in the home)

Some may consider that this is too broad for the usual definition of social innovation, and they may well be right. But that does not concern me because, as I said at the start, the scope of this chapter is arguably wider than social innovation alone. I shall consider all three of these in this chapter, because *all three* play a role in the creation of R-wealth.

EXAMPLES

Microcredit

One of the most widely-discussed examples of a social innovation that aims to address pressing social needs is the system of microcredit devised by Grameen Bank (Yunnus, 1998). The principle of microcredit is to make very small loans to borrowers who are rejected by traditional lenders. These borrowers are typically very poor, may lack a proper credit history, may not have steady employment and may be illiterate. For any or all of these reasons they would not be an attractive prospect to traditional lenders. As such, microcredit aims to plug a very large gap in the market.

Many of the borrowers are women, who are sometimes marginalised by the traditional banking system in developing countries. Indeed, Grameen Bank decided to focus its lending on women, partly because giving credit to women produced more rapid effects, and partly because women's repayment rates were higher. While traditional banks were initially sceptical about the principles of microcredit, they also gradually introduced microcredit schemes.

The avowed aims of microcredit are to reduce poverty, support communities and to encourage small-scale entrepreneurship. How successful has it been? Opinion is still divided. Supporters argue that microcredit has led to the growth of new businesses, has helped to reduce poverty, has improved nutrition and education and, in some cases, has empowered women. Critics are more sceptical, doubting whether microcredit has really reduced poverty, empowered women, or improved education and health, and arguing that microcredit has led families into further debt because of the high rates of interest payable on microcredit loans.

For my immediate purpose, however, the very existence of microcredit is important, even if opinion is divided over its efficacy. It is suggestive of how social innovation works, or tries to work, by addressing an urgent social problem. And the scholar of innovation, more familiar with business innovation, should find it interesting to contrast the *modus operandi* of social and business innovation. Moreover, even if microcredit is an imperfect social innovation so far, its creation is surely a step in the right direction.[2]

Finally, the reader may also be wondering: is this really an example of common innovation? It is perhaps a borderline case. I would say that microcredit was an example of common innovation at the start but has now made the transition into a business. It was an innovation that did not seem attractive as a traditional business innovation, and so was started as a social innovation from the 'common' (non-business) domain. But when business saw that it could work, it was also adopted as a business innovation.[3] This is not unusual. The boundary between common innovation and business innovation is by no means an impermeable barrier – and we shall discuss this further in Chapter 23.

Local or Community Currencies[4,5]

Another of the most widely-discussed examples of a social innovation that aims to address social needs is the idea of a local or community currency. Remembering the old proverb that necessity is the mother of invention, it is notable that two of the most-discussed social innovations are attempts to compensate for the shortcomings of the financial services sector.

A local (or community) currency is a currency that can only be used in a limited area. It is not backed by government, and is not usually legal tender (in the conventional sense). It is rarely intended to replace a national currency, but is intended to be complementary. Some more recent variants on this theme provide currencies that can be shared in virtual communities that are not geographically localised.

One of the main reasons for introducing such local currencies is to limit some of the dysfunctional effects noted in Chapter 11 above. When transportable goods and services are subject to economies of scale in production, there is a tendency for production to be firmly concentrated in a few centres, and transported around the country. This means the decline of local production, and localised underemployment. The aim of the local currency is to increase local purchasing power and boost economic activity within the local area. If the local area has underemployment and spare capacity, then the traditional monetarist objection need not apply, and the local currency need not be inflationary. In short, the local currency tries to act as a counter-balance to the centralising tendencies of big business.[6] In my view this is a thoroughly justified objective and I am unmoved by the arguments from some economists that this is economically inefficient as it subverts the power of scale economies.

Once again, the idea of local currencies is not new. Indeed, the pioneering social innovator, Robert Owen (see page 153), had used something similar in the nineteenth century.[7] Moreover, the use of trade tokens by companies, associations or individuals has a much longer history.

Is this *common innovation*? Yes, in general it is. It is a social innovation by citizens of a local area designed to revive the local economy. The objective is to promote the broad social good and not the narrower interests of those issuing the currency.

And how successful are these local currencies? Again the picture is a bit mixed – so far, at least. Some schemes have had considerable success over some years, but have then fallen into decline. For example, the pioneering

Ithaca Hours scheme, founded in 1991, fell into decline by 2011.[8] The *Berkshares* scheme started with a big 'splash' in 2006, and within 9 months there were 1 million shares in circulation. In due course the figure rose to 2.7 million, but then the currency declined, and by 2012, there were only 140,000 shares in circulation.[9]

Nonetheless, there have been some important innovations in the design of local or community currencies in recent years, and the transnational *Community Currencies in Action* project shows particular promise.[10] I shall follow its progress with great interest. But I think we have to keep one essential fact in mind. Like it or not, the local currency has to compete against the convenience and market power of the national currency, and this means competing against one of the most powerful monopolies (or regulated oligopolies) in the country.[11] Currencies can be seen as a 'network technology', where the value of a particular system to each user increases as the size of the network increases (Metcalfe's Law). This gives the national currency a massive advantage, and any local currency needs skilful co-ordination if this disadvantage in terms of network size is not to overwhelm.[12] We saw in Chapter 9 how hard it is for local bookstores to compete against big online booksellers like Amazon. The challenge for local currency is of a similar magnitude – or perhaps even greater.

The Online Help Forum: 1

A Google search for online help forum finds a large number of sites offering support on the repair of cars, computers and household goods, as well as sites offering support on health problems, financial matters and many other topics. In this chapter I shall look at those sites concerning cars, household goods and computers, and in Chapter 22, I shall look at sites concerned with health.

Some of these sites cover a wide variety of products (e.g. ifixit.com), while others are specific to a particular product or technology, and even particular brands. I have made quite a lot of use of those sites offering advice on how to repair cars and computers. These are sometimes managed by the producers of particular products (particular car makers, Microsoft, Linux and so on) but are more often independent of any producer. These sites depend on contributions from a large community of users as well as input from professionals. The users receive no financial reward for their input, but gain a reputational reward when their advice is highly rated or they attain the status of a wise member of the Forum.

Obviously the Internet is an ideal technological platform for this. While the community of car drivers and computer users is not geographically dispersed, the community of users who do their own repairs is indeed quite dispersed. And as most users must make repairs in real time, access to a large, active and experienced network is essential.

Without this source of advice, it is debateable whether the amateur could do such repairs. Some old cars (notably the Land Rovers from the 1950s, 1960s and 1970s) were built to be maintained by the user, and indeed Land Rover produced excellent and detailed user repair manuals. These are universally agreed to be better manuals than any produced by third party manual writers. But many new cars are not built with DIY in mind. On the contrary, they are either designed for professional repair or for a shorter life-cycle.[13] Modern car manufacturers do not write manuals like the old Land Rover manuals, and even though some quite good third party manuals can be found, they do not always answer the really tricky questions. That calls for advice from the online forum.

The position with personal computers is a little different. Software and hardware producers prepare quite detailed manuals. But the range of things that can go wrong is so large that no manual can anticipate everything. Some producers offer their own active forum which posts information from professionals and users. But such information is usually limited to current generations of hardware and software. As discussed in Chapter 10, continuous software innovation means that some PC hardware has a life cycle of 6 years or so, at most, after which it cannot run the latest software. The hardware may still be viable to run old software, but if old software and old hardware is not supported on these producer forums, then the user of a legacy system is again dependent on the community of users.

In my experience, the typical online PC support forum is good enough to help the reasonably computer-literate user to repair some common problems. And indeed, the intelligent user can use these to minimise the rate of e-waste – in particular, the wastage of old hardware that still works, but cannot run new software. This is done by taking an old computer, perhaps scrapping the old and obsolete motherboard, but retaining all the old peripherals. There is still some waste, but far less than the disposal of an entire computer.[14]

This is a clear case of a *common social innovation*. It is a *common* innovation, because it does not aim to operate as a viable business. And it is a *social* innovation as it connects people with specialist questions to people with specialist answers.

This may seem a pretty modest innovation, but viewed as a whole, the online forum concept is surely a success story. I estimate that the online forum user who does some DIY car and computer repairs can expect to save hundreds of pounds (£ Sterling) per annum.[15] Why is this a clear success? Part of the answer is that the online help forum does not usually compete against a great national monopoly. Indeed, some producers are pretty reluctant to give any advice on how to fix their products. After all, they either want to sell new products or charge to repair them. They do not want to tell consumers how to avoid these costs.

Pro Bono[16]

The Latin phrase, *pro bono publico*, often shortened to *pro bono*, refers to work done by professionals at no cost, for the public good. *Pro bono* work is voluntary, but it is different from some forms of 'volunteering', in which people work in fields where they are not expert.[17] By contrast, *pro bono* work is done by experts to their usual professional standards, but without a fee (or for a much reduced fee).

Perhaps the best known example is in the legal profession, where professionals are encouraged to do a small (but significant) amount of *pro bono* work. In the UK, LawWorks is a registered charity offering pro bono services, supported by The Law Society. LawWorks describes its mission as follows:[18]

> LawWorks brokers free legal help for individuals and community groups who cannot afford to pay and who are unable to access legal aid or other forms of financial assistance. LawWorks works with lawyers who volunteer their legal skills to support individuals and community groups.

Pro bono work is also found in other professions, and the term, *corporate pro bono* is used to describe voluntary work done by employees of larger corporations for non-profit organisations and small business. This can involve work as an employee on loan, providing coaching and mentoring, providing services to non-profit organisations as required, and preparing a deliverable (e.g. a software system) that can be used by all non-profit organisations in a sector.[19]

The Taproot Foundation is a leading provider of such corporate pro bono services. Their website describes their activity as follows:[20]

> Most organizations tackling social problems don't have access to the marketing, design, technology, management or strategic planning resources they need to succeed. Without this talent, few are able to have their intended impact on critical issues like the environment, health and education. Taproot is a non-profit organization that makes business talent available to organizations working to improve society. We engage the nation's millions of business professionals in pro bono services ...

University faculty often get involved in *pro bono* work. Some do teaching on *Extra Mural* courses for the University's Extra Mural department. Some do unpaid consultancy for charities, non-profit organisations and local or national government. The innovation here is the way faculty use this unpaid work to generate research of particular interest.[21]

Interest in *pro bono* legal work in the UK has grown in recent years as the Legal Aid system has been cut back. Legal Aid was one of the benign policy innovations of the Attlee government (1945–1951), which met the cost of legal advice and representation for those unable to afford a lawyer. But as the demand for legal services has risen, and the costs have grown, the present coalition government (2014) decided that this growth in funding was no longer sustainable, and that Legal Aid funding must be cut back.[22] Can *pro bono* work really fill the gap left by Legal Aid cuts? The answer from the legal profession is an pretty unequivocal 'no':[23]

> LawWorks boasts of 36,500 pieces of advice for the clinics it supports, a great achievement, but less than seven percent of the total number of cases the government plans to cut from the legal aid scheme next year ... LAG (Legal Action Group) does not decry the achievements of the pro bono movement, but stresses that it needs to keep a sense of proportion about what it can achieve as any claim that it can plug the gap left by the planned cuts really would be hyperbole.

This statement is unsurprising. As I see it, the government and the legal profession are stuck in a 'chicken game' with respect to Legal Aid cuts and *pro bono* work. In the chicken game, neither player wants to give in to the other, and both will indulge in brinkmanship, but the worst possible case occurs when neither side concedes. And that is the situation we see. The government believes that *pro bono* work could fill the gap left by Legal Aid cuts, and that cost savings are achievable. The legal profession obviously does not want to let the *pro bono* movement oversell itself,[24] as this will allow government to go through with Legal Aid cuts. Sadly, the legal profession and the government are locked in a stand-off, and a low-level equilibrium. It is a shame, indeed, that *pro bono* work is thus constrained at the very time that need is the greatest.

OVERVIEW

As in earlier chapters, we can briefly review how these and other forms of common innovation fit into our three-way classification.

Common Innovation that Adds Directly to the Socio-Economic Environment

The two financial social innovations – microcredit and local currencies – are examples of this. The first aims to fill a gap in the market, and the second aims to counterbalance the concentrating effects of a single currency in the face of strong economies of scale. But social innovations in this category are obviously not limited to financial innovations. They can often be categorised as innovations that create institutions, community resources or networks with potentially benign implications for the socio-economic environment.

Common Innovation that Exploits other Categories to Enhance the Socio-Economic Environment

Our fourth example, *pro bono* work, fits here. It exploits the desire of business and other professions (health, education, science and arts) to achieve recognition for social responsibility, and it means that professional advice and services are made available at zero or modest cost.

Common Innovation that Exploits the Socio-Economic Environment to Enhance other Categories

Our third example, the online help forum, fits into this category. The innovator creates an open forum and then individuals fill it with material. We argued that some of the material posted there can save the consumer and the household significant amounts of money and can help to reduce unnecessary waste.

Open source software, which is also a much-discussed example of social innovation, depends on similar good-will from unpaid writers of software code. The 'open source' principle can help to create better software:[25]

> The basic idea behind open source is very simple: When programmers can read, redistribute, and modify the source code for a piece of software, the software evolves ... We in the open source community have learned that this rapid evolutionary process produces better software than the traditional closed model, in which only a very few programmers can see the source and everybody else must blindly use an opaque block of bits.

Why do software writers contribute to such projects for free? Dalle and David (2007) identified four types of software developers who participate in open source projects:[26]

1) Kudos-seeking programmers who are attracted to work on projects for career reasons.
2) Programmers who seek community recognition and esteem.
3) Novices who seek community interaction for self-improvement.
4) Individualist 'user-innovators' who seek the opportunity to build some particular functional capability that they will find useful.

Food Banks could also fit into this category. These also depend on the generosity of donors, not so much for their unpaid intellectual input, but for their vigilance in ensuring that unwanted food is provided to the food bank rather than going to waste. Finally, the 'Round Table' also belongs here.[27]

CONCLUSION

In this conclusion, I wish to make two brief points, and a third, much longer observation.

First, the reader will have noticed that two (or even three) of our examples in the chapter are somewhat problematic. It is not yet clear if they work as we might hope. Opinion is divided on the efficacy of microcredit. Local currencies show some local successes for a period of years, but may fail thereafter. And the potential of *pro bono* work is being held back by a standoff worthy of serious analysis by game theorists. The lesson here is that social innovation can be difficult to implement. It requires co-ordination. It sometimes involves the social innovation in competition with a powerful monopoly, where it is at a serious competitive disadvantage because of Metcalfe's Law. My choice of examples was essentially random, so these problems are revealing. Maybe the wording of this chapter is non-trivial: we should seek innovations in and around the socio-economic environment, because genuine social innovation, in a narrow sense, is rather difficult.

Second, as in other chapters in Part III, I should say a word about the risk, if there is such a risk, of creative destruction in the context of social innovation. Some economists argue that government-led initiatives designed to compensate for 'market failure' may actually 'crowd out' market-based attempts to fill these gaps. Is that what we observe here? Do these social innovations undermine other initiatives? I think the simple answer is no – or not much. In the case of the Grameen Bank's microcredit system, there was nothing else to 'crowd out'. Yunnus (1998) wrote about the various sources of resistance to his initiative, but it seems fair to say that if these systems were adequate, there would have been no need for microcredit. In terms of the analysis of Chapter 5, microcredit is a 'radical' innovation and the M-wealth creating effects dominate any theft of market share. Local currencies may displace the use of national currency in a limited area, but only to a limited extent. And again, in the cases of the online help forum and *pro bono* work, it is not clear there is anything much else to crowd out.

Third, and finally, I would like to reflect on the various roles of welfare state, government policy and social innovation in this context. This will be quite a long discourse – but I think this is the ideal point in the book for such a reflection.

In Chapter 7, we saw how technological change led to severe poverty amongst hand-loom weavers. Before that time, many governments or local authorities resorted to banning the use of some machines for fear that they could not cope with the damage done to the socio-economic environment (in terms of poverty and unemployment). But the wide loom innovations were introduced in this era of free markets, and any such ban would clearly have been inconsistent with the new orthodoxy. Moreover, business has rarely if ever seen that it has any duty to support those who suffer the destructive side of creative destruction, and certainly did not do so at that time. But equally, there was no alternative government policy, at that time, to soften the blow caused by technological change.

Now, in the era of the comprehensive welfare state, there is a safety-net to protect the worst 'losers' from the worst consequences, or most destructive aspects, of creative destruction through business innovation. Such a welfare 'safety net' is quite costly and calls for direct government provision, financed by taxation. Today, it could not be done any other way.[28] So this is strictly an area for policy innovation by government.

In this chapter, by contrast, we are concerned with common innovation: those things that can be done by local communities to enhance their local socio-economic environment. The inclusion of this chapter does not imply that I believe there is something wrong with the idea of the welfare state. Nor do I believe that the 'safety net' described would be better provided by local community initiatives: I doubt that these could ever be sufficient.

However, even those, like myself, who don't see anything wrong with the principle of a welfare state have to recognise that some members of our present (2014) coalition government are lukewarm. And even those politicians who are supportive, recognise the *realpolitik* that the welfare state will be cut back in a period of austerity. In that setting, it is only realistic to ask what local communities have done and can do to improve the condition of their local socio-economic environment. This is only prudent when (as it currently appears) the state is gradually withdrawing from what we thought was an obligation to provide a safety net against creative destruction.

Interestingly, our present government in the UK has a policy, called the *Big Society*, which is intended to encourage precisely this. We are told that the aim of the policy is to empower local people and communities. This is to be achieved by a change in political climate which redistributes power from politicians to people. In more detail, the following aims were articulated, inter alia:[29]

- Give communities more powers through 'localism'.
- Encourage people to take an active role in their communities as volunteers.
- Transfer power from central to local government.

- Support co-ops, mutuals, charities and social enterprises.

While these goals seem admirable, critics fairly say that the policy is very short on detail. In an often-quoted lecture about the Big Society, the former Archbishop of Canterbury, Dr Rowan Williams spoke of, 'aspirational waffle' (*Observer*, 2012; Williams, 2012). But it is essential to read the (former) Archbishop's comments in full, and not just take that sound-bite out of context (Williams, 2012):

> The theme of the Big Society has found its way into a wide range of contexts in the last year or so. Reactions have been varied; but we should not be distracted from recognising that – whatever the detail of rationale and implementation – it represents an extraordinary opportunity. Introduced during the run-up to the last election as a major political idea for the coming generation, it has suffered from a lack of definition about the means by which ideals can be realised. And this in turn has bred a degree of cynicism, intensified by the attempt to argue for devolved political and social responsibility at exactly the same time as imposing rapid and extensive reductions in public expenditure. The result has been that 'Big Society' rhetoric is all too readily heard by many as aspirational waffle designed to conceal a deeply damaging withdrawal of the state from its responsibilities to the most vulnerable.

I entirely agree with this broader assessment: there is a big opportunity here and, from the perspective of this book, it is definitely worthwhile to consider how local communities can contribute to enhancing their socio-economic environment without dependence on centrally controlled policy innovation. But, despite that, the term 'aspirational waffle' is entirely justified. As G.B. Shaw might have observed, the more politicians talk about their desire to see power taken away from politicians and given to the people, the more in reality they wish to centralise all power under their own control.

The former Archbishop also spoke of 'cynicism'. A major reason for this cynicism has been the apparently very modest levels of resources to be made available to support the policy. While there are, as we shall see, some sorts of common innovation that can alter the socio-economic environment for modest resources, it is hard to sell this as a vision when captains of industry demand ever-greater remuneration and ever-smaller tax bills to provide long-familiar goods and services.

Moreover, there is something fundamentally wrong with the accounting that underpins the *Big Society*. How can people with no resources be expected to outperform the most generously rewarded people in society, especially when the task (improving the socio-economic environment) is even more difficult than that faced by the captains of industry? I have heard no answer to this question.

NOTES

[1] Two recent surveys of social innovation are those by Moulaert et al. (2013), Mulgan (2007).

[2] It would be instructive to compare microcredit and its imperfections with the equivalent (commercial) institutions in the UK. It is notable that the present Archbishop of Canterbury (Most Rev. Justin Welby) was sufficiently concerned about these organisations that he pledged the Church would support Credit Unions so as to drive Wonga out of business (BBC, 2013a).

[3] And arguably, some of the criticism that microcredit has received reflects the fact that when a *common social innovation* is replaced by a *business social innovation*, it can no longer be as benign as the original.

[4] New Economics Foundation (2013).

[5] Wikipedia (2014i), New Economics Foundation (2013), Davies, R. (2013).

[6] In ongoing work, I describe this as Cobbett's principle of the 'Wen and the Vortex', after the work of William Cobbett (1830).

[7] Wikipedia (2014h).

[8] Wikipedia (2014h).

[9] *NewStart* (2012).

[10] New Economics Foundation (2013).

[11] Douthwaite (1999b).

[12] By contrast, microcredit does not compete against a giant monopoly. Indeed, there is often no viable competition at all.

[13] This shift in design practice is unsurprising. When car ownership had only diffused to a small proportion of the population, car producers could look forward to continued growth in sales as ownership diffused to a larger proportion of the population. But today, when diffusion in a country like the UK is very high already, any growth in sales requires drivers to replace their old cars at a faster rate.

[14] Some similar examples are described in BBC (2014a). Two common innovation projects seeking to help end users repair their hardware are IFixit (2014) and Restart Project (2014).

[15] This rough estimate is merely based on the work I have done in the period 2012–2014 on our car and computers owned by members of my family. However, I believe it is typical, for I have no great skills as a mechanic or computer 'techie'.

[16] This case, and some others, is not a 'clean' example of the potential of a common innovation. There are other complicating factors. Regardless of that, I have chosen to include it, because it seems to me that all case studies contain 'complicating factors' and it is the duty of the case study writer to record these.

[17] Wikipedia (2014n).

[18] LawWorks (2014).

[19] Taproot Foundation (2014).

[20] Taproot Foundation (2014).

[21] Some work of this sort would rank amongst the most interesting work on economics that I have done. For completeness, however, I should record that some of my work with government departments and government agencies has been paid.

[22] *Guardian* (2014b).

[23] *Guardian* (2011).

[24] *Guardian* (2011).

[25] Open Source Initiative (2014).

[26] Here, I follow the classification in Swann (2009a, pp. 103–4).

[27] See Round Table (2014).

[28] In earlier times it was the obligation of each Church to care for the poor in its Parish.

[29] Wikipedia (2013b) lists some interesting recent reactions to the *Big Society* policy.

19. Education

In this chapter, I shall start with four examples of common innovation around education. The first refers to an ancient example of common innovation – without doubt the most ancient such example quoted in this book. The last refers to one of the most recent educational tools.

EXAMPLES

Board Games

This sections concerns how activities that we might class as consumption (or leisure) can be educational. In particular we consider how 'board games' can educate the player. The common innovation may be in the game itself, or in the way that the player learns from experience – or both. Although I refer to 'board games', the lessons here are not limited to board games alone: they also apply to computer games and other popular games. But I have used the term 'board games' to make it clear that this section is not about game theory!

I start with a very old game, which is perhaps best known as *Oware*, its name in Ghana. It is an abstract strategy game, reckoned to be the oldest board game that is still widely played, and is one of the 'pit and pebbles', or *Mancala* games,[1] which have been around for seven thousand years. The game is believed to have originated in Africa, and diffused across the world (including the Far East, Middle East, Asia, Africa and the Caribbean).[2]

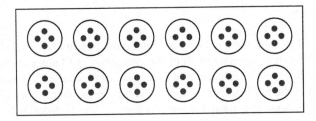

Figure 19.1 Oware Board

On the surface, the game involves two players, but in practice it is never really confined to the two main players, but tends to involve all who watch it, with spectators giving advice and joining in the discussions around the game. And from the start, it has been more than just a game: it is a social institution and an educational tool to teach children skills in calculation, mathematics and strategy.[3] In short, it is a fascinating *common* and *social* innovation.

I suspect that a large number of board games have an important role in educating players about principles of economics. An obvious starting point is the celebrated game, *Monopoly*. This game was marketed in the 1930s by Parker Brothers, and the familiar 4*10 square board was based on Atlantic City, New Jersey. From 1936, the game was licensed for sale outside the USA, and the UK version (with which I am familiar) dates from that time, and is based on London.[4]

The most memorable lesson to be learnt from *Monopoly* is that a monopolist emerges very quickly. While the timescale in which a monopoly emerges is obviously unrealistic, the game of *Monopoly* is a valuable antidote to a neoclassical economics education, in which the student can come to believe that a competitive market (if not exactly a *perfectly competitive* market) can persist indefinitely. The reader can reflect on some of the examples in Part II of this book, in which monopolisation happens remarkably quickly! In particular, those experienced in playing *Monopoly* would have a healthy scepticism for the prediction that the Internet leads to perfect competition! Indeed, we saw in Chapter 9 just how wrong that prediction is in the context of online book-selling!

Board games enthusiasts often prefer some of the more recent games – for example, *Settlers of Catan*. In these games, there is not the same inevitability of a monopolistic outcome, and indeed, at the end of a game, the outcome can still be very finely balanced. I share the idealist's preference for the 'live and let live' attitude of *Settlers of Catan*, and I wish the business world were like this. But the more I look at it, the more I realise that *Monopoly* is, whether we like it or not, close to the mark as a description of business in 'late capitalism'!

School Trips

Enlightened school trips provide an important educational experience by helping children to understand all of our categories in Chapter 6: the natural environment, the socio-economic environment, sciences, health, arts, business and the marketplace. Indeed, I vividly remember school trips from 45–50 years ago, and what I learnt on them. The website School Trips (2014) collects a wide variety of suggested school trips. Many or most of these fit into the categories of Chapter 6. I think that the following lists (derived from that site) are quite instructive, and self-explanatory.

Table 19.1 School Trips

Natural Environment

Environment Centres (see Chapter 17)	Parks and Gardens	Green Awareness
Outdoor Pursuits	Field Studies	Recycling Centres
Farms, Zoos	Boat Trips	Equestrian Activities
Walking Tours	Cycling	

Socio-Economic Environment

Castles	Cathedrals, Abbeys	City Tours
Historic Buildings	Transport Museum	Museum of London
Historical Heritage	English Heritage	

Arts

Arts & Galleries	Cinemas / Film	Crafts
Film Making	Museums	Model Villages
Performing Arts	Storytelling	Theatres

Sciences

Science & Technology	Science Museums	Botanical Gardens
EUREKA – national children's museum	MAGNA – science adventure centre	

Health

Safety Awareness	The Safety Centre	Animal Welfare
Animal and Wildlife Hospital		

Business / Marketplace

Factory Visits	Heritage Railways	Placements
Industrial Museums	Christmas Markets	Cadbury World
Colliery Museums	(Aachen, Lille, Bruges)	(Chocolate Museum)

Source: compiled from entries on the website, School Trips (2014).

The Educated Consumer

In view of what we learnt in Chapter 16 about the power of common innovation in consumption and the home, the link from education to consumption is an important one. There was a famous advertising slogan: 'an educated consumer is our best customer.'[5] While this accurately represent how some companies view the educated consumer, other companies may view educated customers as something of a nuisance: they know too much, they ask difficult questions, and so on. But the educated consumer is an important influence for good, and can have an impact on corporate behaviour and corporate governance.

There are various manifestations of the educated consumer. One type has cultivated 'educated tastes'. This could be a discerning taste for fine wine or real ales, a sophisticated taste for works of art and music, and so on. We saw in Chapter 11 how economies of scale in brewing, brewing innovations to make beer transportable, and the growth of road networks led to massive concentration of brewing in England. The work of CAMRA managed a partial reversal of this trend by creating educated consumers: educated about the brewing process and with an educated taste for real ale.

Another type could be described as the ethical consumer. These consumers want to be informed about the production process that provides the products and services they consume, and about the damage that consumption may do to the environment. Within this broad category, there are several variants.

Some could be described as green consumers. Is the production process clean and sustainable? Those who seek out organic food could be placed in this category. And is consumption sustainable? Or does it entail an unacceptable level of waste? Those who are indignant about the e-waste problem (see Chapter 10) could be placed in this category.

Some ethical consumers are particularly concerned with animal welfare: are the farming methods used humane and free from cruelty? It is striking how, over the last 30–35 years, we have seen in the UK how egg production has switched from the 'battery hen' model, where hens were kept in cages, to the 'free range' model, where hens are allowed access to the open air in daytime. This change is mainly the result of bold and sustained efforts by ethical consumers.

Some are concerned about the treatment of the workforce in the production process. We could call these 'Ruskin Consumers', after Ruskin's famous principle that consumption decisions must take account of the effects of production on the body and mind of the labourer. He argued that we should direct our consumption towards items whose production calls for creativity from the labourer and shun items whose production entails the most destructive aspects of the division of labour.[6]

Another group of educated consumers are skilled at drawing on their education to enhance their consumption activity. In the language of this book, they use their education and knowledge to take better decisions, and to create more R-wealth from a given amount of M-wealth. We saw examples of this in Chapter 16.

And why stop at the concept of an educated consumer? We could broaden this discussion to the idea of an educated *citizen*. We return to that at the end of this chapter.

The Internet and Education

This final example concerns the impact of Internet use on education. The concept of common innovation I have in mind here is the way that the student uses the Internet as a learning tool. Whether the effects of this are benign or otherwise will depend in part on the single-mindedness of the user. The Internet can offer a hugely valuable educational resource to the determined student, and can do much to enhance education. On the other hand, it also offers a high proportion of tempting diversions, which are less constructive to the student's education. The net effect will depend on how determined the student is to use the 'right' things and to shun the temptation to look at low-level entertaining material which does little to educate.

In essence, what the Internet does is increase the variety of ways in which students can access and study resources. Before the Internet, the student was presented with articles and books to read, but there were only some rather limited short-cuts through the material:

- Indexes to a book
- Concordances (e.g. to the Bible)
- Guidance given by a tutor
- Developing skills in 'skim-reading'[7]

With the Internet, search engines and machine readable texts more generally, the student can quickly search a far wider range of sources for relevant material. On the one hand, the enthusiastic student might spend an equal amount of time at his/her studies and exploit this technological advantage to enhance scholarship and learning. On the other hand, the lazy student might exploit this technological advantage to reduce the time-cost of gathering a given sample of relevant material for a particular assignment. The effects of these two responses on education are radically different. Table 21.1 summarises these possibilities.

Clever technologies can be used as labour saving devices to enhance productivity; or they can be used to enhance the education potential of the enthusiastic student. When used in the first way, the effects on education are unhelpful; but when used in the second way, the effects on education are very benign. However the resolution of this is not technologically determined; it depends almost entirely on the student's response – and indeed the way the teacher can shape that response.[8]

Table 19.2 The Internet, the Student and Learning

	Good Student	Lazy Student
Before Internet Era	Reads good number of articles and books in full – enough to pass exams, and good for all-round education.	Reads rather little, and is a marginal pass/fail on many assignments and exams.
Internet Era	Skim-reads many articles and books. Efficient way of completing particular assignments, and good for all-round education.	Skim-reads only the essential articles, so is able to pass assignments and exams, but the overall quality of education declines.

The double-edged character of this tool is hardly a new phenomenon. In my last year at school, we were introduced to an early all-electronic calculator. I recall one of the teachers was less than enthusiastic. He predicted that the availability of calculators would mean that we would forget how to do mental arithmetic and, in due course, we would lose the art of numeracy.

Was he right? Yes and no. Those who have no interest in numbers or mathematics – except those skills they need to manage their finances – find the calculator a convenient labour-saving aid to productivity. And, after years without any practice at 'long division', they have almost certainly forgotten that technique and other techniques of mental arithmetic.

But other students saw a very different side to the effect of the calculator on mathematical ability. In economists' language, the availability of the electronic calculator (especially the scientific calculator) substantially reduced the cost of learning how to apply the more advanced areas of mathematics. As a result, they found it attractive to make greater investments in understanding mathematics.

We could say that the difference here reflects a difference in the elasticity of mathematical ambition with respect to the price of calculation. The master (implicitly) assumed a zero elasticity, and by that assumption, the advent of the electronic calculator would do nothing to stretch our mathematical ambition. By contrast, other students had a more elastic 'ambition curve'.[9]

OVERVIEW

Common Innovation that Adds Directly to Education

Our discussion of how students use the Internet as a learning tool can be seen as this type of common innovation. But there are many other examples.

A well known common innovation which has helped many students over many years is the 'self-help group' or 'self-help tutorial'. This is a group of students who meet together, but without a tutor. A common practice in such groups is a division of labour: each member of the group may read a particular subset of the class reading and then brief his/her class-mates.

Another well-known common innovation is the art of 'skim-reading' – that is, the art of quickly scanning an article or book to see if it contains anything directly relevant to a specific topic. My impression, as a teacher, is that it is very rare to find first-year undergraduates who have this skill. Some final-year undergraduates have developed the skill, but it is more common amongst graduate students and, especially, PhD students. It is not a skill that should be used for all types of reading; for example, we would not encourage a student to skim-read a novel by Jane Austen, or any other great work of literature. But it is a useful skill in many disciplines – certainly in economics.

Another, somewhat more controversial, common innovation is the art of learning by metaphor. Some puritans believe that the use of metaphor is dangerous. They may concede that metaphor should be allowed as an aid to communication, but would argue that the use of metaphor is bad science. But in practice, metaphor is used all the time and in most disciplines. The use of metaphor is a most fundamental problem solving technique. When we face a problem that we do not understand, it can be helpful – at least as a starting point – to liken the problem to something else which we do understand (Ashcraft, 1989, pp. 597–604). Seen in this light, the metaphor is a helpful step on the path to learning – even if it should, in due course, be discarded by the student of more mature understanding.

Common Innovation that Exploits other Categories to Enhance Education

One of the most important learning experiences – certainly in economics, and more widely too – comes when we use examples from the other categories to illustrate a theory. One particular example (concerning the socio-economic environment) springs to mind from my own experience as a teacher.

I was teaching some sessions on consumption behaviour and referred the students to two images on the Internet showing Mrs Thatcher (or Baroness

Thatcher, as she was by then) returning to 10 Downing Street to meet two of her successors as Prime Minister: Gordon Brown and David Cameron. In the first photo, with Brown, she wore bright red. In the second photo, with Cameron, she wore bright blue. Why – I asked our students – should she wear red when visiting Mr Brown but blue when visiting Mr Cameron?

Some suggested that she chose her colours to blend with the political colours of her two hosts: red when visiting a Labour Prime Minister and blue while visiting a Conservative Prime Minister. But, I asked, is it really plausible to expect a 'true blue' Conservative like Mrs Thatcher to wear red to please a Labour Prime Minister? Surely not!

None of them managed to find the true reason. By a curious quirk of misfortune, Mrs Thatcher thought that the colour red suited her best as a woman, but as a Conservative Prime Minister, she did not have many opportunities to wear red. Almost invariably, her personal preference (red) had to be subordinated to her political preference (blue). Clearly, when she visited a Conservative Prime Minister (Cameron) it would have been very strange, and probably disloyal, to wear red. But when visiting a Labour Prime Minister (Brown), she was not obliged to wear her political colour and, for once, she was at liberty to put her personal preferences (red) above her political preferences (blue). In short, when visiting a Conservative prime minister, she was obliged to behave as a 'Douglas Consumer', where consumption decisions are guided by loyalty to the peer group. But when visiting a Labour Prime Minister, she could behave as an 'Economic Consumer', and follow her own personal preferences, without any peer group constraints (Swann, 2009a, p. 192).

Judging from the huge number of essays in the subsequent exam which quoted this example, I could say that if the course achieved nothing else, at least students had learnt how to distinguish different principles of consumption behaviour from simple examples.

Common Innovation that Exploits Education to Enhance other Categories

While discussing the example of the educated consumer, I said that we should really extend the discussion to the educated citizen. The educated citizen should ideally have an understanding of all the categories in our analytical framework: consumption, health, art, science, education itself, the natural environment, the socio-economic environment, business, the marketplace and, indeed, the difference between M-wealth and R-wealth. This knowledge could be a beneficial input to most or all of the other categories in our framework.

Some might dispute this. For example, I have from time to time had discussions with business people about what should be taught on an MBA course. Some of them believe that the MBA should provide students with what they need to 'hit the ground running' in the workplace.

My view is that the MBA simply cannot do that – and should not *try* to do that. No career academic has the deep insights into the details of working practice that the new recruit will learn 'on the job'. As I see it, the MBA course aims to create the sorts of educated citizens that will manage companies well and responsibly. In the same way, the educated citizen will be a valuable recruit to any of the sectors (or categories) in our analytical framework. And the creation of R-wealth requires educated citizens who know about all these categories

CONCLUSION

Most of the discussion so far in Part III suggests that the destructive side of common innovation is not particularly prevalent – certainly not when compared to the creative destruction of business innovation. In the case of the Internet as a learning tool, however, we have seen that it could have a destructive influence – for some students, at least. Arguably it boils down to this. Does the student just want to pass the assignment or pass the exam? Or does the student actually want to learn? If the former, then use of the Internet can be destructive, leading to essays based on sound-bites rather than sustained reasoning, lower standards of understanding, and plagiarism. But if the latter, then I am in no doubt whatever that the creative contribution is substantial. Indeed, the sort of common innovation enabled by the Internet is surely one of the greatest possible contributions to education and learning.

NOTES

[1]   These Mancala games may date as far back as 7000BC (Fagan, 2004, p. 210).
[2]   Oware Society (2014).
[3]   Oware Society (2014).
[4]   A precursor to *Monopoly* was *The Landlord's Game*, created by Elizabeth J. Magie Phillips. The game was designed as an educational tool, to explain the theories of Henry George, and to illustrate the dangers of allowing land ownership to be concentrated in private monopolies (Wikipedia, 2014m).
[5]   Wikipedia (2014s).
[6]   Geddes (1884, p. 37) offers a concise summary of Ruskin's principle.
[7]   Skim-reading is the art of quickly scanning an article or book to see if it contains anything directly relevant to a specific topic.
[8]   *Guardian* (2008b) discusses whether we are losing the art of 'deep reading' in the Internet age. Or do we compensate by developing the art of 'broad reading'?
[9]   Pomerantz (1997) offers a valuable survey of the evidence that calculators can enhance mathematical learning.

20. Arts

At first sight, the relationship between the arts and economics appears to take one of two extreme forms. The first is the common stereotype: that the artist is unworldly, completely absorbed in his/her art, and takes no interest in economic and financial matters. So, for example, Vincent Van Gogh only sold one painting during his lifetime. And, although Mozart had no difficulty in selling his works to many eager patrons, he was constantly in financial difficulties, died in poverty and had a pauper's burial.

At the other extreme, the works of the greatest artists (including Van Gogh, indeed) sell for incomparable prices to the richest collectors, after these great artists have died. And in a similar way, while many musicians struggle to earn a living from their music, a few of the greatest names command exceptional fees for their performances – for example, great classical conductors, pianists, violinists and singers.

In this chapter, however, we are concerned with neither of these extremes. Instead, we shall consider a third, and quite different, type of relationship between the arts and economics. We are interested in the many channels through which innovation around the arts, often common innovation, can contribute to the creation of R-wealth.

I suspect that most of those working in the arts would say that if you want to understand how common innovation adds to the arts and how the arts add to R-wealth creation, you would not ask an economist. I would agree, and I suspect that many other economists would too. But I think it is essential – especially in the context of this book – that economics should develop such an understanding. It is in this spirit that I offer this chapter.

EXAMPLES

Common Innovation and Classical Music

I shall start with an example of common innovation from the area of the arts I know best, classical music: I refer to the use of folk music in classical music. Folk music can reasonably be called a *common innovation*, in contrast to the professional innovation of classical composers.

Folk music is usually defined in a similar way to *folk lore*: 'the traditions, customs and superstitions of the uncultured class' (Scholes, 1970). Classical composers have drawn on themes from folk music for a long time. Scholes (1970) describes how Haydn, Beethoven and Schubert occasionally drew on folk tunes, and how the use of folk music increased in the work of Grieg, Dvorak, Smetana, Albeniz, Granados, De Falla, Stanford, Vaughan Williams, Grainger, Balakirev, Rimsky-Korsakov, Liszt, Bartók and Kodály.[1]

Bartók (1931/1976) gave particular attention to the study of folk music. He distinguished three ways in which folk music (or peasant music, as he called it) can be incorporated into classical music:

> We may, for instance, take over a peasant melody unchanged or only slightly varied, write an accompaniment to it and possibly some opening and concluding phrases. This kind of work would show a certain analogy with Bach's treatment of chorales. ... Another method ... is the following: the composer does not make use of a real peasant melody but invents his own imitation of such melodies. There is no true difference between this method and the one described above. ... There is yet a third way ... Neither peasant melodies nor imitations of peasant melodies can be found in his music, but it is pervaded by the atmosphere of peasant music. In this case we may say, he has completely absorbed the idiom of peasant music which has become his musical mother tongue.

Bartók himself was interested in this 'third way'. In 1905, Bartók and Kodály travelled in the countryside to research and record old folk melodies. It was probably the first substantial piece of research in field musicology. They travelled with a phonograph and waxed cylinders to record the music and performances, and obtained some 16,000 recordings.[2] They made an interesting discovery:[3]

> Magyar folk music had previously been categorised as Gypsy music. The classic example is Franz Liszt's famous Hungarian Rhapsodies for piano, which he based on popular art songs performed by Romani bands of the time. In contrast, Bartók and Kodály discovered that the old Magyar folk melodies were based on pentatonic scales, similar to those in Asian folk traditions, such as those of Central Asia, Anatolia and Siberia.

Bartók's own 'musical mother tongue' derived from what he learnt in his research:[4]

> Bartók was by no means in the general run of 'folklore' composers. It is relatively rare for him to borrow textually from popular folk music, nor does he compose in a 'folk' idiom as did Liszt, the Russians, Grieg and many others. Rather, he was inspired by his fundamental studies of the creative principles of folk art to write profoundly original music.

So, in short, we see how common innovation in folk music does not merely provide some incidental motifs and decoration for classical music, but can provide the foundation for a new 'musical mother tongue'. The reader may respond: 'yes, perhaps, but surely this is still a long way from wealth creation?' No! In the next example, we shall see why this is *not at all far* from the creation of R-wealth.

The V&A Museum in London

If good art is to contribute to the creation of R-Wealth, then it is essential that a wide variety of people and organisations (consumers, educators, business, the marketplace, and others) must learn about good art. The early history of the Victoria and Albert Museum (hereafter V&A) gives the ultimate illustration of how that is to be achieved. Opened in 1857, and originally called the South Kensington Museum (until 1899), it is recognised as a pioneer in the world of museums. According to Conforti (n.d.):[5]

> The first museum to direct its educational objectives toward broad audiences in a systematic and engagingly forceful way was one devoted to the applied arts, the Victoria and Albert Museum.

In contrast, The National Gallery (of London), at that time, was 'a private preserve for picture connoisseurs' and the British Museum had, 'a decidedly academic orientation' (Conforti, n.d.)

In 1835–1836, a Select Committee of the British parliament was asked to report on how to establish better education in the applied arts. They invited the director of the recently opened Berlin Altes Museum, Gustav Waagen, to talk to them. He told them that the best way to rebuild the understanding between workman and artist was:[6]

> ... by giving the people an opportunity of seeing the most beautiful objects of art in the particular branch which they follow; by having collections of the most beautiful models of furniture and of different objects of manufacture ... It is not enough, however, merely to form these collections; there must also be instruction to teach the people on what principles those models have been formed.

None of the museums of that time were suited to this task, and a new institution was required. The government defined the V&A's mission to reform art and design training in Britain, with the objective to improve British goods, making them more competitive in foreign markets. But, over time, the mission became broader than that. The founder, Henry Cole:[7]

> ... expanded the role of the Museum to that of a more public enterprise with a broad educational mandate ... He also spoke of his institution as being directed to workmen of every vocation. Such educational efforts can be considered commercially purposeful — to indoctrinate the present and future consumer while

also training the maker. For a Benthamite idealist like Cole, however, these initiatives also had a more fundamental social benefit. Cole's broadly based public lecture and publication program to 'improve public taste' expanded over time ... (the) commercially driven mission came to be inextricably integrated with contemporary social ideals associated with the belief in a practical, even moral, education for the working classes through their collective experience of art.

From the perspective of this book, this *broader* vision of the V&A's mission can be seen as an attempt to create linkages between the arts and *all* the other categories in our analytical framework – not just business – with the intention of increasing R-wealth (and M-Wealth) for the many.

Cole also adopted a very open admissions policy. The museum was to be open to all classes, and not just an elite, and Cole's objective was to attract large numbers of visitors. The Museum was open free to the public over half the time, and the use of 'student' or 'private' days (when the general public were excluded) was very limited.

After Cole retired in 1873, the Museum's reputation started to decline. Increasingly, the twin requirements of collection and education were in tension with each other. And gradually, the museum was 'recaptured' by an artistic (and social) elite.[8]

Depiction of Industry in Art

An especially important aspect of common innovation in the arts is the depiction of business and industry in art.

From the middle ages, it was quite common for artists to represent the builders, masons, smiths, millers, potters and workers in many other industries. Salzmann's book (1923/1970) on English Industries of the Middle Ages contains many striking mediaeval illustrations of industries and their workers. As Salzmann says, these are interesting from an artistic as well as an industrial standpoint. The illustrations include: masons working on a church, workers prospecting and digging for materials, a mine shaft with miners, furnaces, blacksmiths, iron-mills, women washing ore, men cutting marble with a saw, stonecutters and masons, a potter at his wheel, a brick-maker, a glass-maker and many other subjects.

In a similar way, the famous *Encyclopedie* by Diderot (1751–1772) contained many illustrations of industrial processes at work. One of the best-known of these illustrations represents *epinglier* (the pin-maker), which became famous because of the central position given to pin-making in Smith's *Wealth of Nations*. Indeed, Edwin Cannan, editor of the 1904 edition of *Wealth of Nations*, was in no doubt that Smith's account was based on the this illustration, and the accompanying article in Volume 5 (1755) of the *Encyclopedie* by F. Delaire.[9] These are illustrations of manufacturing before the industrial revolution, and as such, the processes are on a human scale.

Youngner (2006) notes that in the early years of the industrial revolution, many fine artists were reluctant to paint industrial images. Joseph Wright of Derby (1734–1797) was one of the first artists to depict the industrial revolution. His painting of the Ravenhead glass works is an interesting example. Philippe Jacques de Loutherbourg's famous painting of Coalbrookedale by Night (1801) is a striking early example of how an artist engaged with the full might of the industrial revolution. From the mid-Nineteenth century onwards, however, this reluctance changed. Even works by Monet, Camille Pissaro and van Gogh featured industrial subjects.

Twentieth-century artists have been bold in their representation of industrial processes. Some of the most striking examples are found in the work of Diego Rivera and Graham Sutherland.

The 1932 Detroit Industry Murals by Diego Rivera (1886–1957) were commissioned by Edsel Ford, CEO of the Ford Motor Company, and depict manufacturing processes at the Ford's River Rouge Plant.[10] Controversy and notoriety surrounded these murals, but Rivera and Ford found common ground. The workers are highly productive, and in this case are not alienated. Edsel Ford, who commissioned the work, obviously wanted the Ford motor plant to be shown in a positive light. And Rivera, as a Marxist, was content to acknowledge, as Marx did, the high productivity of capitalism.

Graham Sutherland (1903–1980) was an Official War Artist in the 1939–1945 war, who was commissioned to illustrate how industry supported the war effort. Originally, Sutherland trained as an engineering draughtsman, and this training gave him an understanding of the machinery, and helped him to converse with the labourers about their work. His work depicted steel furnaces, open-cast mining and other industrial landscapes. These are harsh, showing the toil of mining work and the claustrophobic working conditions.

Other artists have made important and memorable paintings of industry, notably L.S. Lowry (1887–1976) and Stanley Spencer (1891–1959). Robert Smithson (1938–1973) took this a step further.[11] His projects were an attempt to build a bridge between industry, ecology, art and society. He recognised that art could mediate between industry and the rest of society. This was, potentially, an extremely important role – though Smithson recognised that the artist-mediator could be 'captured' by industry. His last works were 'land reclamation' projects, where the artist could create art from derelict industrial sites (such as disused quarries). In this chapter, we describe this as common innovation transforming the old industrial site into a work of art. But in Chapter 17 we have already considered a closely related example of how an old industrial site is transformed into a nature reserve.

Art and Economic Research

This example is about the creative use of art forms as a metaphor to help us understand scientific and, indeed, economic ideas.[12] Improbable as it may seem, the central idea of this book – the analytical framework of Chapter 6 – was inspired by a particular detail from the magnificent east window of Lincoln Cathedral in the UK. I was almost tempted to use it as a model for the book. Figure 20.1 is a rough sketch of this detail.

Figure 20.1   Detail from East Window, Lincoln Cathedral

Source: Author's sketch.

Consider the sketch as a whole. It contains seven clusters, one in the centre and six round the sides. Now consider the circle at the centre of this sketch. It also contains seven circles, where the central circle is slightly larger than the others. In that regard, the central cluster is, *roughly speaking*, a reduced version of the whole. This is the idea of self-similarity,[13] so important in the study of fractals (as in Chapter 13). However, the reader will quickly see that this self-similarity does not apply to the six clusters round the outside of the sketch. Each of these contains just five circles – as opposed to seven.

To use this beautiful form to represent the analytical framework for common innovation described in Chapter 6, we need a modified version of this window design. The window for this case would look something like Figure 20.2.

Figure 20.2   A Modified (10*10) Version of Figure 20.1

Source: Author's sketch.

Consider the sketch as a whole. It contains ten clusters, one in the centre and nine round the sides. Now consider the circle at the centre of this sketch. Inside it, we find a 'cluster' of ten circles, where the central circle is slightly larger than the others. Then consider each of the nine circles round the sides of the sketch. Inside each of these, we also find a 'cluster' of ten circles, where the central circle is slightly larger than the others. So in the case of Figure 20.2, self-similarity applies throughout.

How does this relate to our framework? Consider the sketch as a whole. The ten main circles within this can represent the ten categories in my framework. Let R-Wealth be the central circle, and the nine others round the sides can represent the nine other categories. Then take any one of the smaller circles in the interior. Inside any of these there are ten further circles. Once again, let R-Wealth be the central circle, and the nine others round the sides can represent the nine other categories. What the diagram tells us is that any category in our framework is made up of effects coming from every other category. This property applies to every category in turn. In short, everything effects everything else. The criss-cross framework of Figure 6.2, the 10*10 matrix of Figure 6.3, and the 'cathedral window' of Figure 20.2 all tell the same story.

The reader may consider this little detour into Gothic architecture is a bit idiosyncratic, if not plain eccentric. But I emphatically disagree. Economists are too obsessed with algebraic representation and have lost the art of graphical representation. Tufte (1983, 1990) has shown us just how powerful the graphical presentation of data can be. And Szostak (1999) has given us a compelling account of the artistic side of economics, and how important that is to the discipline. Why did I not make more use of this 'window' in Chapter 6? While Figure 20.2 is undoubtedly more elegant than Figures 6.2 and 6.3, I think the last two are slightly easier to explain.

OVERVIEW

Common Innovation that Adds Directly to the Arts

This sub-section is concerned with innovation that comes from within the arts to enhance the arts. The above example of Bartók and Kodály researching folk music fits in this category. And some of the innovation in this category is self-referential.

As an example of that, the pianist Artur Rubinstein recounts some visits to his friend, Pablo Picasso, in Paris. Picasso was painting the same ensemble of bottle, guitar and table, day after day after day, and had completed at least fifty canvasses of the same objects. Rubinstein protested that this was getting boring; why was Picasso not painting anything new? Picasso was clearly irritated by this observation, and responded:[14]

> Every minute I'm a different man, every hour there is a new light, every day I see that bottle with a completely different personality. It is another bottle, another table, another life in another world, and everything is different.

Rubinstein conceded that it was just the same with his music. He was pleased to record the same works (of Chopin) many times because:

> A new recording opens up a new world to me because the music speaks to me in a different language.

We are changed by everyday life, and from our experiences we learn new and better ways to make sense of our world. That is common innovation.

Common Innovation that Exploits other Categories to Enhance the Arts

Our example of how artists made art from depicting industry is a natural starting point. Closely related to that is the way that artists have made art from depicting the natural environment. Obviously, this has been a subject of works of art for centuries, in the form of landscapes and townscapes. I think it is fair to say that early landscapes and townscapes – or at least those that survive in prominent places – tended to concentrate on the picturesque, the charming and the magnificent. Later art, especially in the 20th century, has been bold to include subjects that are not picturesque, but are ugly and are magnificent only in the degree of desecration. Nonetheless, all of this art has helped many people to appreciate the natural environment. In the same way, we can argue that there is a related linkage from the *socio-economic environment* to the arts. An obvious example of this is the interest, from the 19th century onwards, of painting and photographing everyday life – often amongst the poor.

There is, however, a quite different linkage which needs discussion here. This is the potential link from the natural environment to creativity. This is not automatic, but there is no doubt that for some people a pleasant natural environment can be an important stimulus for creativity and innovation in Art. We have already cited the example of Beethoven in Chapter 17, and while it is hardly right to describe Beethoven's work with the adjective 'common', similar processes are also at work for the more modest forms of creativity. In the context of the university, some have argued that the 'beautiful campus' is also a creative campus. This effect can work through two different channels. Perhaps researchers are more creative when placed in a beautiful campus? Or perhaps the university with a beautiful campus attracts better and more creative faculty and students?

Another linkage is the obvious one from education to the arts. The most obvious aspect of this – education in the arts – needs no further comment. But sometimes great artists build on other aspects of their education to enhance their art. One striking example of this was the British potter, Michael Cardew. He could not have achieved his exceptional standards in studio pottery without his expert understanding of the chemistry and geology of clay and glazes (Cardew, 2002). Indeed, the above example could also be described as a link from science to the arts. Scientific knowledge helps the potter to excel in his art. In a similar way, the *pointilliste* innovations of artists Georges Seurat and Paul Signac were based on scientific theories of optics and colour (Rewald, 1978).

In his famous lecture, 'The Two Cultures', C.P. Snow advanced the thesis that most who work in the art and humanities are ignorant of science, and *vice versa*. As just one example, he said that if he were to ask scholars in the arts and humanities what is meant by mass, or acceleration, 'not more than one in ten' would know the answer. And yet, this question, 'is the scientific equivalent of saying, can you read?' He argued that both cultures would benefit from greater mutual understanding, and the net result would be a far greater capacity to solve the world's problems. The reader should bear that in mind if in any doubt about the relevance of these *interaction* innovations to R-wealth creation.

Common Innovation that Exploits the Arts to Enhance other Categories

An obvious place to start (though this is business innovation, rather than common innovation) is with arts and business: companies exploit the arts to improve their products and perhaps their processes. Indeed, as we saw above, that was the mission set for the founders of the V&A Museum: reform of art and design training, so that companies would exploit the arts to improve the quality of domestically-produced goods, and hence increase competitiveness in export markets. Indeed, it has been a continuing theme of British industrial policy – featuring other policy initiatives and institutions such as the Design Council and Design Museum.[15] While some business-people remain sceptical about the commercial value of arts and design in their business, there is no doubt that some of the leading brands of our time owe their massive support in large measure to iconic design – notably Apple (iPhone, iPad), Ferrari, Coca-Cola, Fender (guitars), and so on.

In a similar way, the marketplace has been able to exploit the arts and design to create a more attractive and competitive environment. One example of this is the way some of the leading department stores have attracted customers as much by their environment as by the products they sell (Macy's, Bloomingdale's, Harvey Nicholls, Harrods, and so on). Indeed, an early exhibition at the Design Museum suggested that department stores and museums were become more and more alike. Bayley (1989) observed:

> Shops are becoming more 'cultural', as anybody who has been to Ralph Lauren's Madison Avenue store can testify. Here you find merchandise for sale side-by-side with a permanent exhibition about values and style, set in an environment somewhat reminiscent of the Frick. Meanwhile, a few blocks away in the Metropolitan Museum, the first thing you hear when you cross the threshold is the whirr of cash-registers, evidence of a mighty commercial machine running at considerable speed. Shops and museums have a great deal in common.

Returning to our discussion of consumption in the previous chapter, we can see a wide variety of ways in which the arts can enhance consumption.

Indeed, in the context of the V&A Museum, Henry Cole argued that one essential role of a museum full of objects of art was to create a more enlightened form of consumer. The educated and enlightened consumer has developed a taste for goods and services of superior quality, and is capable of generating far greater R-wealth from these than the ordinary consumer. This argument is relevant to very many of the things we buy: works of art, home decoration, furniture, clothes, books, and many others.

Finally, art (and design) can enhance three more of our categories. First, we noted above the work of Robert Smithson that turns derelict industrial sites into art. We could go a step further and say that Smithson's 'land reclamation' projects used art to enhance the natural environment.

Second, we can also find examples of how art and design can enhance the socio-economic environment. A topical example of this is the use of design to achieve social inclusion, which was recognised as a priority by the Design Council and the Royal Society of Arts (Design Council, 2012).

Third, medical research is finding a large number of ways in which the arts can enhance health care. These include research suggesting that:

- listening to Mozart can reduce the incidence of epilepsy (BBC, 2001);
- participation in art projects can enhance mental health (Guardian, 2008c);
- art and music in the hospital can help patients cope with illnesses (Stanford Medical Center, 1998);
- art therapy can help patients recover from traumatic life experiences (Birch, 1997).

Finally, let us never forget that the arts are an end in themselves. It is quite wrong to argue that arts only contribute to R-wealth through other mechanisms. The arts in themselves contribute more or less directly to our R-wealth. The point is made with great clarity, in the context of urban renewal, by Biggs (1996):

> Let me be clear. Culture is not a means to an end. It is an end in itself. Much research has been undertaken to demonstrate that culture is a peculiarly successful means of furthering renewal or regeneration, but it misses the point if it regards culture as one means to renewal among other economics-driven options. Culture is a successful regenerator because it is an end in itself: the activity is inseparable from the achievement.

This is an essential insight. It captures the Common Innovation philosophy: innovation does not have to work through business to contribute to R-wealth. It can work through other channels or, as here, directly!

CONCLUSION

Does Schumpeter's concept of Creative Destruction apply to the arts? From one perspective, the answer seems to be 'no'. Huxley argued that there is a fundamental difference here: 'Good art survives: Chaucer was not made obsolete by Shakespeare'. By contrast, scientific works that summarise yesterday's thinking 'will go the way of all earlier scientific writings and be forgotten'.[16]

On the other hand, there is no doubt that changes in fashion can mean that artists fall from grace quite rapidly. For example, in the 1920s, the Bloomsbury group were famously dismissive of the Pre-Raphaelites (Barnes, 1998, p. 113):

> The Bloomsbury set laughed at the Pre-Raphaelites. To them it seemed that 'everything of importance in the second half of the 19th Century had happened in France'.

And this attitude was one of the factors leading to a major decline in the value of Pre-Raphaelite paintings from the 1920s, as shown in Figure 20.3.[17] Prices are shown in £ year 2000 – that is, adjusted to year 2000 art prices.

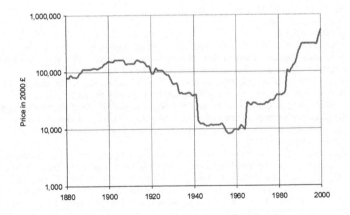

Figure 20.3   A Price Index for the Works of J.E. Millais

Source: Based on data collected by the author.

We could interpret this as 'creative destruction'. Nonetheless, it is clear that the destructive effect was not permanent, for during the 1960s, prices of Millais' work started to rise sharply, and by the 1990s, prices (*in real terms*) were above the peak levels in 1900–1920.

This chapter is important as it shows how many linkages there are between the arts and other categories in my framework. As we shall see in Chapter 25, that is important for R-wealth creation. The simple 'linear model' recognises very few such linkages, and it only recognises a role for the arts in M-wealth and R-wealth creation *if* they can be harnessed by business and business innovation. Here we see that the business exploitation of the arts and design, while potentially important and still underdeveloped, is only one channel amongst many, and probably not the most important.

NOTES

[1] A logical extension of these was the work of Olivier Messiaen. Following advice from his teacher, Paul Dukas, he listened to the birds, recognising that they are great masters (Griffiths, 1985, p. 166), and birdsong had a profound influence on many of his compositions.

[2] Larousse (1971, p. 414).

[3] Wikipedia (2014b).

[4] Larousse (1971, p. 414).

[5] Conforti, M. (n.d.).

[6] Conforti, M. (n.d.).

[7] Conforti, M. (n.d.).

[8] Denis, R.C. (n.d.).

[9] See Smith (1776/1904a, pp. 6–7, note 4).

[10] Wikipedia (2014d).

[11] Smithson (2014).

[12] Many economists believe that science is a more appropriate influence on the study of economics, because economics is aiming to be a science. But in a remarkable book, Szostak (1999) argued that economics is more like art than science.

[13] Self-similarity is a mathematical term, of special relevance in the analysis of fractals. Roughly speaking, an object is self-similar if it is exactly or approximately similar to a part of itself. Or, to put it another way, the object is self-similar if the whole has the same shape as one or more of the parts. In Figure 20.1, the central cluster and the whole are approximately similar, but the outer clusters are not similar to the whole.

[14] Artur Rubinstein (1964).

[15] One complicated factor that is often considered to constrain the use of the arts and design in business is the perceived cultural distinction between arts and business. While business may be comfortable with applied art it is uncomfortable with fine art. But where does the divide lie between these categories? In view of this, Milton Glaser's (1989) suggestion is very interesting: 'I have a modest proposal; why don't we discard the word "art" and replace it with the word "work"?'

[16] Huxley (1963, p. 35).

[17] Another factor in this decline was the characteristic London snobbery towards those who had bought the works of the Pre-Raphaelites (Bell, 1984, p. 16): 'From the very first these painters found their market among those whom contemporaries would have considered an ignorant and philistine clientele, the "self-made" men and manufacturers of the North.'

21. Science

This chapter is concerned with common innovation in and around the sciences. John Stuart Mill's celebrated observation suggests that there could be great scope for common innovation to contribute to science:[1]

> ... the only way in which a human being can make some approach to knowing the whole of a subject, is by hearing what can be said about it by persons of every variety of opinion, and studying all modes in which it can be looked at by every character of mind. No wise man ever acquired his wisdom in any mode but this; nor is it in the nature of human intellect to become wise in any other manner.

As I see it, however, that contribution is currently much smaller than it could be. Certainly I think common innovation from outside the discipline could make a huge and valuable contribution to economics.[2] But of course I may be wrong to draw any general inference from this sample of one. Nonetheless, of all the chapters in Part III, this was the one where it was hardest to choose good examples of common innovation. Again, that may simply reflect on the many gaps in my scientific knowledge.

EXAMPLES

In this chapter, I have chosen just three examples of common innovation in and around science. The first concerns citizen scientists or amateur scientists. The second concerns the key insights that Darwin learnt from reading the work of economist Thomas Malthus. The third considers science fiction.

Citizen-Scientists

Historically speaking, some natural candidates for this section would be people who have made contributions to the advance of science who were not scientists by profession. Five leading examples are Michael Faraday (1791–1867), Mary Anning (1799–1847), Gregor Mendel (1822–1884), Henrietta Swan Leavitt (1868–1921), and William Sealy Gosset (1876–1937).[3] It may seem absurd to include these within a category called 'common innovation' –

for what they did was exceptional and not in the least *common*. But as I have made clear, I use the term 'common innovation' to distinguish it from professional or business innovation – and what follows is not business innovation.

Faraday came from a poor background, and only had a very basic school education.[4] As a teenager, he secured a job as apprentice to a local bookbinder and bookseller and spent most of his spare time educating himself in science. At the end of his apprenticeship, he managed to secure an employment as a secretary, scientific assistant and valet to Humphry Davy of the Royal Institution. Although he did not hold any formal academic post for most of his life, many considered him the best experimental scientist of all time, and his contributions to electromagnetism and electrochemistry were of huge importance.

Mary Anning also came from a poor family. Her father died when she was young, and she struggled financially for much of her life. Her work in collecting fossils was of very great importance, and contributed to fundamental changes in thinking about prehistoric life. As a woman from a poor background, she was not accepted as a 'full member' of the scientific community in her time, but the value and importance of her work is now fully recognised.

Mendel was an Augustinian monk. In 1843, he joined the Abbey of St Thomas in Brünn (now Brno, Czech Republic). He later became a teacher in the Monastery School, and then Abbot. Mendel was very active in the Monastery gardens, and was able to spend much of his time doing experiments with his plants. In 1865, he presented a paper on his path breaking work to the local Natural History Society, and this was published the following year. But his work attracted little interest until 1900, when it was rediscovered by de Vries, Correns and Bateson. By the 1940s, Mendel's work provided the foundations of the new science of genetics.[5]

Leavitt was a graduate of Radcliffe College, and later worked at the Harvard College Observatory as a 'computer'. Her task was fairly menial, and because she was a woman of independent means, she was not paid for her work. But from analysis of her repeated observations and measurements, she noted that brighter stars have longer periods, a principle later called the *period-luminosity relationship*. She did not really receive the recognition she deserved during her lifetime, but her work provided the foundation for Hubble's research into the expanding Universe. Indeed, Hubble himself said that Leavitt deserved the Nobel Prize for her work, though by that time she had died, and the prize is not awarded posthumously.

Gosset is better known amongst statisticians and econometricians by his *nom de plume*, 'Student'. Gosset joined the Guinness Brewery of Dublin, in 1899, and worked in that company for the rest of his career. At that time, use of the normal distribution for testing hypotheses was well known, but these tests were not appropriate for small samples. Gosset's work at the brewery constantly involved small samples, and as he needed a suitable test for that context, he invented the t-distribution and the t-test. The Guinness company had a 'blanket' policy that prohibited employees from publishing papers based on their work, but Gosset was allowed to publish under the *nom de plume*, 'Student'. The t-distribution and t-test became very well-known through the later work of R.A. Fisher. As a mark of his great respect for Gosset, Fisher named it 'Student's distribution', and called Gosset 'the Faraday of statistics'.[6]

When we turn to *contemporary* discussion of citizen scientists, however, most discussion tends to focus on more modest contributions.[7] One definition is this: 'a citizen scientist is a volunteer who collects and/or processes data as part of a scientific enquiry'.[8] Others would allow the citizen scientist a bit more credit, acknowledging that they may also participate in analysis and dissemination. They are often part of a *crowd-sourced*[9] scientific enquiry or project, where the contribution of the 'crowd' is essential. But they are like actors with a small part in a film or play. They are not seen as the intellectual descendants of Faraday, Anning, Mendel, Leavitt or Gosset.

Malthus and Darwin

Reverend Thomas Malthus (1766–1834) needs no introduction to economists. Even the most cursory study of the history of economic thought will feature his work. He is best known for his *Essay on the Principle of Population*. The first edition was published in 1798, but he published several revised editions thereafter. The first edition of book was written while he was a minister in the Church of England, and in view of that, he could also perhaps qualify for the previous section of this chapter! But from 1805, he followed an academic career.

The common innovation I want to consider is not so much what Malthus did, but the link that Charles Darwin made to Malthus's work. In his autobiography, Darwin wrote:[10]

> In October 1838, that is, fifteen months after I had begun my systematic inquiry, I happened to read for amusement Malthus on Population, and being well prepared to appreciate the struggle for existence which everywhere goes on from long-continued observation of the habits of animals and plants, it at once struck me that under these circumstances favourable variations would tend to be preserved, and unfavourable ones to be destroyed. The results of this would be the formation of a new species. Here, then I had at last got a theory by which to work.

Three observations stand out here. The first is his expression, 'to read for amusement'. In this context, it means that he was reading for general interest and not aiming to study the book in detail, as he might study some scientific tome. Some busy scholars might say that they had no time to read 'for amusement', so we may perhaps assume that he did not see reading Malthus as an essential study. The second is that he read this book in 1838, four years after Malthus died (1834), so it seems reasonable to assume that the emergence of this idea did not come from conversation or correspondence with Malthus. The third is his expression, 'I had at last got a theory by which to work'. It suggests that he could find nothing suitable in the usual places that a scientific scholar would look, and only found it when, by chance, he was reading outside his scientific discipline.

This serendipitous cross-fertilisation across traditional discipline boundaries can often be the source of intellectual advance. Dogan and Pahre have written of *creative marginality*[11] – the idea that some of the most interesting advances come from the boundaries between disciplines, and indeed that they must come from there because the core of the discipline becomes like a 'stagnant pool'.

The important common innovation here is the building of a link from a theory in economics to a theory in biology. There have been other linkages from economics to biology. One of the best known is the work of evolutionary biologist John Maynard Smith who played a central role in the application of game theory to evolution. And, indeed, there have been linkages in the other direction. Perhaps the best known is the work of Richard Nelson and Sidney Winter on evolutionary economics,[12] which forged a link from biological theories of evolution to the study of technological and organisational change.

The building of these linkages is an important step in the history of economic thought. Most neoclassical economics models economic science on physics, or perhaps chemistry, but not on biology. Some would say that phase in the development of economics has run its course, and we now know that economics and physics are really very different disciplines. If economics is a science – and I emphasise, *if* – it should perhaps be considered akin to a biological science and not a physical science.

Having said that, when I am asked whether economics is a science, an art or a humanity, I tend to reply that it should really be *all three*. As I see it, economics has three facets. There is an economic science, but it is a soft science compared to the natural sciences. There is an economic art, which involves the design of economic institutions and policies.[13] And last, but certainly not least, the third facet of economics is one of the humanities. This has been the most neglected facet, and we shall not have a *human* or a *humane* economy until we correct that.[14]

Science Fiction

The previous example was about an important fusion between economics and biology. This example is about another important fusion, from science to literature – *science fiction*. Some writers make an important distinction between science fiction proper and science *fantasy*.[15] The former is 'fiction' in the sense that it is about an uncertain future, but it is a story based on a rigorous extrapolation of scientific theories and scientific facts. Science *fantasy*, in contrast, is not based on any such extrapolation, and can deliberately be entirely fanciful.

Here, I am primarily interested in science fiction proper. I believe this performs an important social and economic function within our analytical framework, and does something which scientists, as a profession, seem a bit reluctant to do: to think about the implications and risks of scientific advance, and about dystopian and dysfunctional effects.

Maxwell (1984, 2007) has written extensively about the potential dangers of pursuing scientific knowledge without an equal concern for wisdom. Obviously such scientific knowledge gives us great power to act, but while that can do much good, it can also do much harm. Maxwell's argument is stark: 'all our modern global crises are the outcome of science without wisdom.'[16] Schumacher (1974, p. 26) made a similar observation: 'man is far too clever to be able to survive without wisdom'. This seems crystal clear to me. But while Maxwell's arguments have definitely been gaining ground, his emphasis on *wisdom* is apparently still controversial amongst many scientists and engineers – sufficiently so that Maxwell envisages that a revolution is needed. It would be melodramatic to speak of a 'taboo', but it is an issue some scientists often chose to dismiss.

Indeed, in my dialogue with scientists and engineers about the potentially destructive side-effects of technological innovation, I have encountered a reluctance to face up to such issues. One particular example stands out. I recall one scientist making a bold assertion that fast broadband networks would redistribute economic activity more evenly around the country, and reduce industrial concentration. I told him that in the usual case where industries have scale economies, the economic theory and economic evidence pointed to the opposite outcome: a more uneven distribution of activity, and increased industrial concentration. (The examples in Chapters 9 and 11 are instructive.) But he was evidently unmoved. Some scientists refer to such cases as an instance of their, *Law of Unintended Consequences*. Personally, I find that a frustrating response: it is used as a catch-all excuse for naïve predictions about the socio-economic implications of technological change. It is possible *and essential* that we do better than that.

Science fiction writers, on the other hand, do not shy away from considering the potentially dystopian and dysfunctional implications of science without wisdom. On the contrary, this is exactly the sort of scenario that appeals to many of them. And indeed, while being a scientist is not a necessary condition for being a good science fiction writer, some of the best science fiction writers are, or were, successful scientists.[17] Viewed from the perspective of our common innovation framework of Chapter 6, therefore, science fiction is immensely important. Science fiction does something that scientists and engineers can be reluctant to do. It is not perhaps the sort of 'wisdom' that Maxwell has in mind, but it is an important step in the right direction.

In short, we could say that from the perspective of this book, if science fiction did not exist, we would have to invent it. And some would say that there is another reason why we *have to have* science fiction. As I make the final corrections to this book, I read that film-makers and scientists have recently met at CERN (the European Organisation for Nuclear Research) to discuss ways in which film can make science more compelling.[18] Here it is important to remember that up to the 1960s, at least, science fiction played a very important role in making science more compelling, and in attracting students to study science.[19] It is possible that science fiction can evolve so that it can play this role once again.

OVERVIEW

Common Innovation that Adds Directly to Science

In other chapters, it was relatively easy to locate our examples within the three categories of this 'overview' section. Here it is harder. Some of the exceptional citizen scientists could be classified as offering common innovation from science to science – Faraday and Levitt, especially. The others probably belong in the next category. Moreover, the optimistic economist might classify the influence of Malthus on Darwin as common innovation from one science to another, but I doubt most scientists would see it that way, and most of all I seriously doubt that Darwin and his contemporaries saw it that way.

I suspect that common innovation within science is quite common, though I lack the scientific authority to say so. A striking and popular example is the way that Geim and Novoselov isolated graphene. They used sticky tape to pull off a single layer of graphite!

Common Innovation that Exploits other Categories to Enhance Science

We can place the work of other citizen scientists in this category – especially Anning, Mendel and Gosset. For their work was a common innovation from outside science that mad a major contribution to science. Here also would be the appropriate place for Darwin's common innovation drawing on the work of Malthus. Here moreover belong the more modest contributions of citizen science, and the 'hobby' contributions to science described in Chapter 16 – such as counting birds for a crowd-sourced survey.

Two of our categories are, of course, the scientist's *object of study*: health and natural environment. Four or five are the social scientist's object of study: socio-economic environment, business, marketplace, education and, arguably, health.

Common Innovation that Exploits Science to Enhance other Categories

In this final category we should place science fiction – which is really a common innovation that draws on science to produce literature. In fact, we can broaden this group to include the writings of those who seek to popularise science. This is a common innovation drawing on science to educate and entertain.

And, of course, science can make a substantive and direct impact on health, the natural environment and education, while social science can do the same to the socio-economic environment, business, the marketplace, education and, arguably, health.

CONCLUSION

Maxwell, quoted above, leaves us in little doubt about the potentially destructive effects that can arise when science is harnessed by technology and industry: 'all our modern global crises are the outcome of science without wisdom.' But it is not clear that common innovation in and around science is really implicated in this. Once again, I think it is fair to describe common innovation in this context as a 'gentle and benign breeze'. (Indeed, it would be a very gentle breeze – a pretty low number on the Beaufort scale.) Linus Pauling's famous saying seems to capture the role of common innovation in science:[20]

> If you want to have good ideas you must have many ideas. Most of them will be wrong, and what you have to learn is which ones to throw away.

In particular, common innovation that draws on categories outside science can offer the *rule-breaking* ideas. It can do this because those outside science are not bound by the same conventions as those inside. Mendel's work is one of the greatest examples of this.

NOTES

[1]   J.S. Mill (1859/1929, p. 24).

[2]   I have written about this at length in Swann (2006).

[3]   Some would argue that the early work of Albert Einstein (1879–1955) could be placed in this category. His four groundbreaking papers of 1905 on the photoelectric effect, Brownian motion, special relativity, and the equivalence of mass and energy, were published when he was still working for the Patent Office in Bern. It was not until 1908 that he started a strictly academic career. However, as most of his career was spent as a professional scientist, he does not really fit this category.

[4]   These brief biographies are based on entries in Wikipedia (2014e, 2014f, 2014j, 2014k, 2014u). The entry on Mendel also draws on the biography by Iltis (1932).

[5]   My late father, Michael Meredith Swann (1920–1990) was a biologist and had a great interest in Mendel and his work. His interest was not just in the scientific significance and originality, but also in the way it was ignored for at least 35 years before being rediscovered. He considered it a shining example of how exceptional science sometimes comes from far outside the recognised scientific establishment.

[6]   Some scientists are better known for their contributions outside their home disciplines. For example, William Herschel was a musician and composer by profession, but he is better known today as the scientist who discovered the planet Uranus, and two of its moons. And, ironically, Alexander Borodin was a Professor of Chemistry by profession, but is better known today for his sublime classical music.

[7]   Patrick Moore the citizen astronomer.

[8]   Open Scientist (2011).

[9]   Wikipedia (2014c).

[10] Darwin (1876/1958).

[11] Dogan and Pahre (1990).

[12] Nelson and Winter (1982). We should also mention the work of Kenneth Boulding on evolutionary economics (1981), and note that Veblen (1898) used the same term. Hodgson (1998) describes how Veblen's evolutionary economics has a foundation in Darwinian evolution.

[13] Once again, I remind the reader of Szostak's (1999) book on *Econ-art*.

[14] Carlyle and Ruskin were two of the first authors to assess economics as a humanity.

[15] *Encyclopedia Britannica* (1968, vol. 20, pp. 17–18).

[16] Maxwell, N. (2014).

[17] One of the most memorable pieces of economics I read in my first year as an undergraduate was Jan Pen's (1971) parade of the dwarfs. In a way this can be viewed as a piece of science fiction, because it is based on hard facts, but brings home so memorably just how dysfunctional it is to have such an extremely unequal distribution of income and wealth.

[18] BBC (2014c).

[19] *Encyclopedia Britannica* (1968, vol. 20, pp. 17–18).

[20] Quoted by Francis Crick in his presentation 'The Impact of Linus Pauling on Molecular Biology' (1995). See Wikiquote (2014).

22. Health

I have included health as a category in the analytical framework of Chapter 6, but it is arguably a little different from the others. Common innovation can influence health directly, or can exploit other categories to enhance health. But common innovation linkages from health to other categories seem to be rather limited. True, without health, many human activities would be adversely affected: so, in a way, poor health acts as a constraint on our other categories. But apart from that, I have little to add and, for that reason, this chapter is quite short.

EXAMPLES[1]

Self-monitoring of Blood Pressure

While most of us depend on professional medical advice to deal with some of the health episodes that beset us, many make use of a variety of common innovations to take day-to-day care of their health. At the simplest level, this includes conventional wisdom about a sensible diet, good exercise and avoidance of unhealthy consumption. But common innovation has also found its way into areas where, in the past, we were dependent on professional medical advice. One example is the home-use of blood pressure monitors and self-monitoring of blood pressure.[2]

Now, obviously, this is not all pure common innovation, for it depends on the availability of readily available and cheap electronic blood pressure monitors – and that is business innovation. But given these, the enlightened end-user can make a valuable contribution to the management and diagnosis of hypertension. The common innovation here entails the frequent and intelligent use of this equipment to diagnose under what conditions the individual's blood pressure is raised and which strategies work best to reduce it.

The practice of 'self-measurement' of blood pressure dates back to the 1930s, but it has become much more common in the last 15–20 years with the introduction of cheap electronic blood pressure monitors. McManus et al. (2008) state that almost 10 percent of people in the UK now monitor their own blood pressure. Amongst those with hypertension, the proportion is much higher (about two thirds in the USA).

The traditional manual method of measuring blood pressure is only viable for health professionals as it calls for considerable skill and experience. But now a wide variety of electronic devices are available that meet the standards required by the British Hypertension Society, and equivalent bodies in other countries. Many medical professionals were sceptical about the usefulness of 'self monitoring', and some still are, but McManus et al. (2008) conclude:

- Self monitoring of blood pressure is useful in the diagnosis and management of hypertension.
- Multiple measurements of blood pressure allow a better estimation of 'true' blood pressure.
- Systematic reviews show that blood pressure is lower when self monitored
- Self monitored blood pressure correlates better with risk of stroke than office readings.
- Patient education and clinically validated sphygmomanometers are prerequisites for effective self monitoring.

The interesting observation here is that self-monitoring is not just a cheap and convenient 'second best' to professional monitoring by a doctor. Instead, the conclusion is that regular self-monitoring can be preferable to occasional professional monitoring. This does not deny that the professional may take better individual readings, but self-monitoring can be done frequently, while professional readings are, by definition, infrequent.

There are in fact three sorts of error here. Table 22.1 lists these and their relative importance in the context of professional readings and self-readings:

Table 22.1   Sources of Error in Measuring Blood Pressure

	Doctor's Readings	Self-Monitoring
Measurement error in taking a single reading	Very small	Originally large, but now moderate or small
Uncertain profile from infrequent readings	Moderate	Small
Actual blood pressure biased upwards in surgery	Possible: depends on the patient	Nil

At its simplest, this is a trade-off between measurement errors and sample errors. Professional measurements have lower measurement error, but self-monitoring provides a large number of readings and hence offers an average measure with lower variance. In addition, readings taken at home may be lower than those taken in the surgery, *ceteris paribus*, because some patients are anxious in the waiting room and this increases their blood pressure.

As we said above, the element of common innovation here is the frequent and intelligent use of this equipment to understand a particular individual's problems with blood pressure. Under what conditions is the individual's blood pressure is raised? Which strategies work best to reduce it? This common innovation could also generate data that would – in principle – be of value in medical research. As such, it could become a common innovation that contributes to science.

The Online Help Forum: 2

In Chapter 18, we already encountered one example of the online help forum as a common innovation. This was the sort of forum that aims to help DIY enthusiasts and car mechanics.

The example in this chapter relates to the online help forum aimed at ordinary people who suffer from some of the more unpleasant diseases and medical conditions. A quick search on Google for the words *online help forum* produced links to the following at or near the top of the list.[3] (The table only lists a subset, but it gives a good idea of the field.)

Table 22.2 Some Examples of the Online Help Forum

Alcoholism and Addictions
Alopecia UK (hair loss)
Alzheimer's Society
Asperger and ASD[4] UK
Autism Support
Breast Cancer Care
Cervical Cancer Trust
Dementia
Depression Support Group
GamCare (gambling addiction and problems)
Macmillan Cancer Support
Macular Society (sight loss)
Mental Health
Parkinson's UK
Pregnancy Sickness Support
Prostate Cancer UK
Psoriasis (skin condition)
Terrence Higgins Trust (HIV)

The list is interesting because there are three particular features that many of these conditions have in common.

a) Those who suffer from them may feel that the condition carries a stigma, and would not want their condition to be widely known.
b) The distress caused by these conditions is very specific to the condition, and only those with first-hand experience will really understand what it entails.
c) The incidence of these conditions will be spread quite thinly over a wide geographical area.

The online forum seems well adapted to handle these three features. The anonymity of the online forum, and the fact that no face-to-face interaction is required, make it well suited to handle point (a). And because the forum can connect this very special community even if they are dispersed over a wide geographical area, it is well suited to handle points (b) and (c).

Common sense suggests that the online forum could be very valuable in these cases. What does the evidence suggest? I am of course no expert in this field. But one interesting survey of user attitudes to a mental health forum concluded:[5]

> The respondents ... found forum participation useful for information, and social contact and support. A majority (75 percent) found it easier to discuss personal problems online than face-to-face, and almost half say they discuss problems online that they do not discuss face-to-face. A majority would not have participated had they not had the option of using a pseudonym. Respondents perceive discussion groups as a supplement rather than a replacement of traditional mental health services ... A clear majority want professionals to take an active role in these types of forum. Comments from respondents indicate that forums may have an empowering effect.

This is consistent with the observations above, but also adds two interesting pieces of data. The online discussion group is seen as a supplement, not a replacement, and users want professionals to get involved in the forum. This suggests that the common innovation forum is a valuable addition but may work even better with some professional involvement. This may be a more general property in a variety of contexts: common innovation is not meant to be a substitute for professional or business innovation.

Natural Environment and Health

We all know that there is plenty of scope for common innovation to make use of the natural environment around us to enhance our physiological and mental health. We already touched on this in Chapter 17, and referred there to the New Economics Foundation (2012) report on *Natural Solutions*. This example is so obvious and so well-known that it really needs no further elaboration here.

It is, however, worthwhile to make a few observations around this general point. It is now quite well recognised that living in big cities can, in itself, be bad for health.[6] Equally, it hardly needs saying that living in poverty (a lack of M-wealth) is also bad for health, and most M-wealth is *acquired* [7] in cities. For most people, therefore, healthy living requires a fine balance: access to the city to earn the necessary M-wealth and access to the natural environment for the sort of recreation needed to maintain health.

When we look at any particular city, we see this balance can be achieved in different ways. Most people try to achieve balance by living and working in the city but travelling out for some weekends and holidays. But of course this means living in the 'pressure cooker' of the city. Others try to achieve balance by living out and commuting in – though commuting is hardly a recipe for good health, and is a pretty dysfunctional activity from an environmental point of view.

And when we compare different cities, we again see that the balance is achieved in different ways. Some choose to live in London, despite the noise, pollution and congestion, because they need the sort of M-wealth that can only be acquired in London. Getting out of London to the countryside for recreation is harder and more expensive, but many Londoners can afford that. In contrast, those who live in the cities of the North and Midlands have to accept that they will earn less M-wealth, but find it much easier and cheaper to access the countryside for recreation. One of the striking features of many industrial cities in the north of England is the sheer quality of the natural environment within a short distance of the city. This is in striking contrast to London.

From this point of view, it is good for national health if economic activity is not excessively concentrated in a small area, and if the distribution of economic activity remains reasonably stable. But what we are seeing in the UK (or England at any rate) is an ever-growing concentration of M-wealth in London and the South-East, as it is 'siphoned' out of the rest of the country.[8] This seriously upsets the delicate balance needed to maintain health. London becomes noisier, more congested and more polluted. Living in London becomes more of a health hazard, and it is ever harder to maintain healthy living. By contrast, industrial cities in the North suffer from greater underemployment and poverty, and that makes it increasingly hard to maintain healthy living even if recreation in the countryside is still easily accessible.

I should add one final point of clarification. Much of what we call the natural environment that is such an amenity for recreation is not completely 'natural'. A striking example is the Lake District, in the far North-West of England. As any Cumbrian farmer is quick to point out, this landscape is not 'natural'. It was created by farmers and sheep.[9] Take the farmers and the sheep away, and before long the landscape would look quite different. The implication of this is that human industry on this small scale can have an almost entirely benign effect on the environment. But the quotations from Ruskin in Chapter 17 remind us that 'working the land' is not necessarily benign!

OVERVIEW

Common Innovation that Adds Directly to Health

Our example of intelligent self-monitoring of blood pressure belongs here. The piece of equipment used is a business innovation, but the common innovation arises in the way we use the equipment to monitor health and take evasive action when danger arises. This is probably part of a broader trend, where intelligent self-monitoring of health may help to ensure more efficient allocation of healthcare resources. At present, we make too many type I errors (false positives) and type II errors (false negatives). The false positives are placing huge demands on Accident and Emergency wards at our hospitals, while the false negatives have led to too many deaths because care is offered too late to save the patient.

Common Innovation that Exploits other Categories to Enhance Health

Quite a lot of the common innovation at work here makes use of ideas from the other categories of our analytic framework to enhance health. The most obvious is the way that educated consumers use some basic scientific knowledge to maintain health. This is most obvious with diet, where wise consumers use food composition data and recommended daily amounts to ensure a good and balanced diet. Indeed, wise consumers avoid consuming anything to excess and take account of the malign effects of unwise consumption on all aspects of health – not just physiological, but also mental. This is partly common innovation, in that it reflects the activity of individuals to improve their own health. And it is partly business innovation, as businesses offer innovative new products and services for the health-conscious consumer.

Another obvious example is the way that people exploit a benign natural environment to enhance health. This was one of our examples and we also discussed this in Chapter 17. And our example of the online help forum shows how common innovation can exploit a benign *socio-economic* environment to create a resource that supports those with health problems and may, indeed, improve their health. While the links from socio-economic environment to health are complex, there is widespread belief that living in a safe, harmonious and mutually supportive environment is good for health.

A final example relates to those benign innovations in business and the marketplace which can contribute to health. Examples of these could include flexible working hours, supportive facilities for the workforce, and so on.[10] These could be called business innovations as they are carried out by business, but their immediate objective is a bit different from typical business innovation. The purpose of the business innovation is to increase business performance. By contrast, the immediate purpose of these health-enhancing innovations is different – although the long term effects may also help business performance by keeping a healthy and loyal workforce.

Common Innovation that Exploits Health to Enhance other Categories

I said at the start that this section would be brief. For the most part, the linkages forged by common innovation here are from other categories in our framework to health. But there are some very general effects that operate in the other direction. A healthy consumer is better at creating R-wealth. A healthy worker is a productive worker and a good colleague. A healthy child is easier to teach and a better class-mate. A healthy scientist does better work. By contrast, poor health is a constraint on almost all the categories in our analytical framework.

CONCLUSION

In line with much common innovation, the effects listed in this chapter may be modest, but are potentially quite widespread. Moreover, they are predominantly benign and destructive effects are limited. For an innovation that enhances the health of one person will not usually damage another.[11] There are some exceptions where innovations to benefit the health of one person draw on strictly finite resources, or when resources are subject to congestion costs.[12]

NOTES

[1]　As I mentioned in Footnote 3 of Chapter 1, when the book was in production, Rui Baptista drew my attention to some recent work by Habicht et al. (2012) and Stock et al. (2013) on patient innovation, and the website of *Patient Innovation* (2014). This website provides some very striking examples of common innovation in the context of health care.

[2]　This example draws on Swann (2009b).

[3]　Google search words: *online help forum* (3 April 2014).

[4]　Autism Spectrum Disorder.

[5]　Kummervold et al. (2002).

[6]　*Guardian* (2014a). See also *The Environment and Health Atlas for England and Wales* (2014).

[7]　I must lay great emphasis on the word *acquired*. It hardly needs saying that (in the UK at least), the big salaries are acquired in cities and the biggest salaries of all are acquired in the City of London – i.e. the financial centre. This does not necessarily mean that the greatest M-wealth is *created* in the cities. Bankers get rich through high-frequency trading in the City of London, but I argued in Chapter 13 that this activity makes little contribution to the wealth of nations (plural). If it makes one nation richer, it does so at the expense of others. Or, if it does not do that, then it may make one region of a country (the City) richer at the expense of others. Or, if it does not do that, then it may make a few people richer at the expense of others.

[8]　What disturbs me, especially, is that recent government policy has not sought to compensate for or constrain this trend towards geographic concentration. Indeed, some policies have actually encouraged the process of concentration – whether by accident or design!

[9]　There is hardly any wilderness left in England, though there is still some in the North and West of Scotland.

[10]　Robert Owen's social innovation offered healthcare to his workers. While this was undoubtedly benign, it was also enlightened self-interest (Wikipedia, 2014q). In a similar way, microcredit schemes are often combined with health care, for the simple reason that a healthy debtor is more likely to repay than an unhealthy debtor.

[11]　Competitive sport offers some counter-examples. A healthy team are more likely to beat their opponents, and the opposing team and their supporters may suffer as a result. But the rather contrived nature of this example suggests that we should not be unduly concerned about this sort of effect.

[12]　Rowlandson's drawings of Bath in the early 19th Century offer an amusing example. The attractiveness of this once-fashionable spa resort to a 'genteel' clientele was damaged by the 'gouty cases' that converged on Bath in forlorn hope of cure.

23. Business and the Marketplace

Some readers will immediately be confused by the inclusion of this chapter. How can we have a chapter on common innovation in business and the marketplace? If common innovation is defined as all innovation except business innovation, then how can there be any common innovation in business or the marketplace? Surely this is a contradiction in terms?

In essence, that argument is absolutely right, and once again this means the chapter will be quite a short one. Nonetheless, I believe that there are two types of common innovation that need to be considered in this chapter. One happens 'within the walls' of business, but is not officially business innovation. The other happens 'immediately around' the outside wall of the business, and is strictly common innovation.

I shall give one example of the first type and two of the second type. The first type happens when business organisations give staff some limited discretion to indulge in their own innovative projects during working hours and within the walls of the company. The second type is closer to an informal *joint venture* between the business producer, the consumers that use the products produced by this business, and/or those who live and work in the local economy where the business operates.

EXAMPLES

20 Percent Time

Much has been said about *20 percent time* schemes. Sometimes these are really at most, 15 or 10 percent time schemes. Some of what has been said is perhaps in the realm of myth, but some is certainly reality. The best known is the one that Google operates – or, some would say, *used to* operate.

This is the idea that employees can use up to twenty percent of their working time at the company (one day a week) to pursue their own individual projects. Such an offer would obviously be attractive to the sort of employee who is considering going it alone to pursue his/her own innovation project, but is thus persuaded to stay in the team and work on that project within the walls of the employer. The case *for* calling this common innovation is that the details of the project are decided by the individual employee and are not part of company strategy. It is, on the surface, just as if the employee was working on this in his/her spare time at home. The case *against* calling this common innovation is that the employer may, in effect, be managing an innovation incubator, and the most promising common innovations will, in due course, become part of the company's official business innovation strategy. But in my view, it qualifies as 'common innovation'.

Certainly, many of the projects in Google Labs started life as pieces of common innovation started within the *20 percent time* scheme. The scheme has brought forward some really interesting innovations. But in the last couple of years, several sources have suggested that Google staff are now too busy to take full advantage of this scheme,[1] and even that the scheme is declining because Google doesn't really need it anymore.[2]

This sort of scheme was not invented by Google. Hewlett Packard (HP) and 3M can both claim to have been the pioneers in this sort of scheme. 3M launched their 15 percent program in 1948.[3] This led, amongst other things, to the indispensible *post-it* note. Less has been written about the HP scheme, but it was the source of some important innovations in printer technology.

SMS Texting

It is generally agreed that text messaging was initially envisaged as a tool mainly for telephone engineers. It was not expected that ordinary consumers would use it to any great degree. The first text message by mobile phone was sent in 1992, and for the next five years SMS was not widely used. One issue was the fact that SMS texts were limited to just 160 characters; another issue was pricing.[4]

From 1998, texting became relatively cheap – especially for travellers using text to 'call' home while travelling in foreign countries. And it was at this point that texting started to take off, as users (especially price-sensitive teenagers) created ways of communicating a lot of information in 160 characters. I am referring here to the evolution of 'emoticons', and 'text language', which involves very concise abbreviations. These last are pure pieces of common innovation.

In due course, and against initial expectations, texting became by far the most common reason for using the mobile phone. Indeed, OFCOM research indicates that that text messaging is now more common than phone conversation or face-to-face contact as the method of daily communication between friends and family.[5]

I don't think it is misleading to describe this as an (informal) joint venture between the telecommunications business and users – and hence, a joint venture between business innovation and common innovation. The business innovator produces the mobile phone with SMS added on as something of an afterthought, which might be useful to telephone engineers. Then the user, especially the teenage user, embraces SMS texting and, with some clever common innovations to get around capacity constraints, turns it in into a very important application of the mobile phone.[6] In turn, that piece of common innovation feeds back into the way that handset manufacturers design the next generation of business innovations in mobile phones. And on the back of this common innovation, texting has become big business.

Great Football Clubs

It is also possible to describe the interaction between great football clubs and their supporters as an informal joint venture. These clubs are, of course, very big businesses and have innovative strategies of their own. But without the contribution of un-named supporters over many generations, the club and its games would mean very little.

We could perhaps see this as an extreme case of network effects. But while the consumers that create network effects for ordinary products can be quite passive, football supporters are certainly not passive! To start with, the supporters create the atmosphere in the football stadium, and this can give the home team a considerable home advantage.

Some writers distinguish two sorts of benefits that arise in home advantage. One is the advantage created by the home fans, who usually outnumber visiting supporters, and can make more noise! This encourages the home team, discourages and confuses the opposition, and can (arguably) influence the referee to make decisions favourable to the home side. The other is the convenience of playing at home, with less travel involved and the familiarity of the home stadium.[7]

How much is this worth? As a crude calculation, I have computed the advantage to home sides in the English Premier League 2012–2013 season.

Table 23.1 Home Advantage in Premier League Season 2012–2013

	Pr{win}	Pr{draw}	Pr{lose}	Goals For	Goals Against
Home	44%	28%	28%	1.56	1.24
Away	28%	28%	44%	1.24	1.56
Diff.	16%	0	−16%	0.32	−0.32

Source: Author's calculations using data from BBC website.

Taking the average across all 20 clubs in the Premier League, and across all games played in that season, Table 23.1 shows the difference between performance in home games and performance in away games. The headline figures are that playing at home:

a) increases the probability of winning from 28 percent to 44 percent;
b) increases the expected 'goals for' from 1.24 to 1.56.

How much is that worth over a season of 38 games? Table 23.2 uses the above data to compare the expected performance of an average team that plays all matches at home with one that plays all matches away.

Table 23.2   Expected Value of Home Advantage over Full Season

	Matches Won	Matches Drawn	Matches Lost	Points	Goals For	Goals Against
All Home	16.6	10.8	10.6	60.6	59.2	47.1
All Away	10.6	10.8	16.6	42.6	47.1	59.2
Diff.	6.0	0.0	−6.0	18.0	12.1	−12.1

Source: Author's calculations, based on Table 23.1.

The average team playing all matches at home would expect, over the full season, to:

- win 6 more and lose 6 fewer matches
- earn 18 more points[8]
- score 12 more goals and concede 12 fewer goals

This is a substantial advantage indeed. I don't suggest it is all due to the supporters, but a large proportion must derive from that source.

Moreover, the role of supporters goes beyond chanting for the team on match days! In some ways, the loyal supporter is also what the marketer might call a '*brand ambassador*'. Supporters play an active role in promoting the club, perhaps contributing to the supporters club or the '*fanzine*', and giving the club (and its sponsor) free advertising by 'wearing the shirt'. I would class some of this as common innovation. Few companies enjoy having such enthusiastic *brand ambassadors* as the football clubs!

In law, the shareholders of the club are the owners, but many supporters consider that supporters have some *moral* ownership of the club. In some English football clubs, however, the relationship between supporters and owners has been put under strain because owners have sought to do things that the supporters do not want. Experience suggests that joint ventures are liable to break down in such circumstances.

Some owners are considered to be 'milking', 'fleecing', or 'sweating' the club's brand name.[9] Some have sought to change the name of the club,[10] to change the club colours,[11] or to rename the stadium,[12] and such moves have been met with fierce resistance from supporters. In one instance, a club was relocated from one city to another,[13] and as a result disaffected supporters set up a new club. In another, a club that sought to register its club badge as a trademark faced opposition from citizens who argued that the bird depicted on the badge was a symbol of the city, and it belonged to citizens.[14]

CONCLUSION

At the start, we said that our examples of common innovation in this chapter would be of two sorts. One happens 'within the walls' of business, but is not officially business innovation. The other happens immediately around the outside wall of the business, and is strictly common innovation. The first example (20 percent time) is of the first sort, and the others are of the second sort. But, at a pinch, we can also locate these examples within the three categories used in all the previous chapters of Part III. We can classify the 20 percent time example as common innovation that adds directly to business. And we can classify the other two as informal joint ventures where business innovation and common innovation are – *for a time, at least* – joined in a virtuous circle.

NOTES

1. *Daily Mail* (2013).
2. *Ars Technica* (2013).
3. Fast Co. Design (2011).
4. Wikipedia (2014r).
5. *Guardian* (2012d).
6. Teenagers played a massive role in demonstrating that SMS Texting was credible medium of communication. The 'Emoticon' and 'Abbreviated Text' were not *de novo* innovations, as both have a longer history than that. But teenagers added *so much* new life and new ideas to the emoticon and to text language, that it helped to create a market potential for SMS texting which had not been seen at the start. (Ericsson, 2012).
7. *Daily Telegraph* (2014), *Guardian* (2013), Wikipedia (2014a, 2014g).
8. A win earns three points, a draw earns one point, and a loss earns none.
9. *Guardian* (2014c).
10. BBC (2013b).
11. BBC (2012a).
12. BBC (2011c).
13. Wikipedia (2014p).
14. *Liverpool Echo* (2012).

PART IV

Implications and Hypotheses

24. No Business Monopoly

When I have discussed the ideas in Parts I, II and III with academic colleagues, policy makers and business people, some have asked, 'so what?' A typical response is that these ideas may, perhaps, be interesting *possibilities*, but are, in practice, of minor importance, and the core business of the economics of innovation should carry on as before.

My objective in Part IV, therefore, is to address this, 'so what?' question, and to spell out the implications of Parts I-III. For I believe that these ideas are highly relevant already, and will become more so in future. Moreover, there are several very important implications for the way we should study the economics of innovation in future.

In this chapter, I start by addressing three particular responses to this work which I can paraphrase as follows:

a) Surely, only business creates wealth?
b) Surely, only business innovates?
c) Surely, M-wealth is a greater priority than R-wealth?

In brief, my answer to (a) and (b) is that business has no such monopoly, and my answer to (c) is that we should make no such generalisation.

Only Business Creates Wealth?

First of all, to say that, 'only business creates wealth', simply cannot be accurate when we talk of R-wealth. What of the surgeon working for the National Health Service,[1] who saves a life, who restores someone's sight, or performs other medical miracles? Recall that we defined R-wealth by reference to Ruskin's maxim: 'no wealth but life'. From that perspective, surgeons who save lives or materially enhance quality of life must surely rank as some of the greatest wealth creators of all.

What then of M-wealth? Is it fair to assert that business is the only creator of M-wealth? This remark is, perhaps, closer to the mark, but even so I can't agree with it. For example, surely the committed teacher plays his or her role in the creation of M-wealth? The human capital that is developed by a good education is of value in business, and therefore of value in creating M-wealth, as well as a source of R-wealth.

The 'only business creates wealth' mantra is a convenient one, and arguably a self-serving notion to promote business interests. But it is false, and, as with most monopolies, it is definitely not a good idea to accept that any one sector has a monopoly of wealth creation. Instead, I think it is better to address these two questions:

1) To what extent, and in what circumstances, does wealth creation revolve primarily around business?
2) To what extent, and in what circumstances, does wealth creation take place elsewhere in society?

When we talk about the creation of M-wealth, it is fair to say that in many or most circumstances it revolves primarily around business. This does not mean that other segments of society play no role in creating M-wealth, but this role is usually a supportive one. However, I would stress that in some cases, this supportive role is more important than many in business would acknowledge. And indeed, the number of institutions and actors that play a supportive role is often much larger than many in business would acknowledge.

Using the categories of our analytical framework, such supporting roles may be provided by those in education, the arts and science, or it may be provided by the natural and the socio-economic environment. Of, if we move beyond the confines of my simple analytical framework, we could include other segments and actors – including, for example, parts of the national system of innovation (e.g. standards institutions, metrology institutes, and so on) that support business innovation.

I see a similarity here between the creation of M-wealth and the creation of a Hollywood movie. The stars of the movie and the director receive most of the credit, the limelight and the attention, and are paid the most. But the long list of credits, at the end of the movie, acknowledges in a quiet way the large number of people without whom the film could not have been made.

When we turn to the creation of R-wealth, however, it is wrong to presume that business generally lies at the centre of R-wealth creation. This is not to deny that business is responsible for some of the R-wealth creation, but in this context business is more likely to play a supportive role as opposed to a leading role. Returning to the example of health care, business plays many roles in the National Health Service: building hospitals, producing medical equipment and pharmaceuticals, and so on. But in my view the central roles are played by the surgeons, the consultants and other medical staff.

Moreover, all of the other categories in my framework can directly contribute to the creation of R-wealth, and can play a central role in that. This is true of the artist, the scientist, the teacher, the environmentalist, and others who are not usually a part of business. Part III of the book has tried to give a flavour of some of the many ways in which that can happen.

Only Business Innovates?

My answer to this is essentially the same as my previous answer. To say that only business innovates cannot be right in a setting where there is common innovation. In saying this, I may appear to contradict Schumpeter's definition that innovation happens when an invention is commercially exploited. But I don't think I am really contradicting Schumpeter. The essential distinction in Schumpeter's argument is that innovation happens when invention is *exploited*. His definition refers to commercial exploitation because it was business or commercial innovation that concerned him. But I am not aware of any statement by Schumpeter that *only* business was capable of innovation. I think it would be entirely Schumpeterian in spirit to argue that common innovation happens when inventions are exploited – but this time, *outside* business.

Once again, it is quite likely that business innovation is most relevant to the creation of M-wealth. So if our focus is exclusively on M-wealth, then it is not so far of the mark to claim that only business innovates. But even then, the claim is inaccurate because some common innovation definitely contributes to the creation of M-wealth. And when we turn our attention to the creation of R-wealth, then much of the important innovation that contributes to that end is common innovation – not business innovation.

M-wealth is a Greater Priority than R-wealth?

I cannot accept that M-wealth is always and everywhere more important than R-wealth. Yes, when we speak of those poor in M-wealth – whether they are the poor of a rich country, or those living in a poor country – it may well be correct to say that creation of M-wealth is a greater priority for them than creation of R-wealth. But when we speak of those in M-wealth prosperity, on average and above-average incomes in the UK and other wealthy countries, I suspect that a greater priority for many of these is to learn how to create more R-wealth from what they have, rather than to procure more M-wealth in itself.

As before, it is better to address these two questions:

1) In what circumstances must the creation of M-wealth be a greater priority than the creation of R-wealth?

2) In what circumstances is the creation of R-wealth of comparable or greater importance?

These questions may seem simple, but on closer inspection the answers are not simple. To see why, let us start with a typical answer to the questions, and then show why it won't suffice as a general answer to these questions. Then we can work towards a more satisfactory answer.

A simple initial response to these questions is to claim that M-wealth is a *necessity* while R-wealth is a *luxury*. In common language, this would mean that a certain level of M-wealth is required for survival, and only when that is achieved can we start thinking about R-wealth. And this perspective offers the following answers to our questions: in poverty, M-wealth must be the priority, but in prosperity, R-wealth can be of comparable or greater importance.

This is not a bad answer, but it does not stand up to further scrutiny. Economists use the same distinction between necessity and luxury, and observe that the income elasticity of demand for the necessity is low (between zero and one), while the income elasticity of demand for the luxury is high (greater than one). But is that what we find with regard to M-wealth and R-wealth (respectively)? Consider the two following examples.

First, amongst recently retired people, who have experienced a recent fall in income, it is common to see a flourishing in creation of R-wealth. Instead of paying others to do tasks for them, the recently retired often delight in doing these tasks themselves. Instead of paying for expensive entertainment, they delight in appreciating the natural environment, their socio-economic environment, as well as the easily accessible arts and sciences, in order to create R-wealth.

Second, consider the newly rich. How do they use their riches? As often as not they acquire expensive consumables such as luxury cars, expensive homes, dress expensively and have expensive holidays. Sometimes this is consumption for the pleasure of consumption, but often it is conspicuous consumption. All of these are examples of M-wealth. Do the newly rich also devote equal energies to creating R-wealth? Sometimes they may do so, but often they do not.

In the first example, R-Wealth is *not* an economic luxury. As incomes fall, the newly retired devote more energy, rather than less, to creating R-wealth. And in the second example, M-wealth is the economic luxury. As incomes increase, more M-wealth is devoted to expensive consumption.

I conclude from this that the simple response to these twin questions is misleading. Yes, to escape poverty, a minimum level of M-wealth (food, clothing, shelter, etc) is required. We could call these the *necessities* of M-wealth. But in prosperity, some will spend on the *luxuries* of M-wealth. In short, M-wealth is sometimes a necessity and sometimes a luxury. We simply cannot say that it is always a necessity.

Equally, we simply cannot say that R-wealth is always a luxury. Indeed, if we accept Ruskin's maxim – 'no wealth but life' – then the idea that *life is always a luxury* is an appalling one. Surely every citizen should have a right to the necessities of R-wealth just as they have a right to the necessities of M-wealth? Nonetheless, I recognise that some forms of R-wealth are a luxury in the sense that only a privileged minority have the means to enjoy these. But in contrast to the luxuries of M-wealth which can only be acquired by those of financial means, the means required to create R-wealth are usually not financial but time and capability.[2] In conclusion, just as with M-wealth, we conclude that R-wealth is sometimes a necessity and sometimes a luxury.

Two further points need to be stressed. First, when I say that there are necessities both in M-wealth and R-wealth, I mean that those in M-wealth poverty cannot be adequately compensated by additional R-wealth; 'you can't eat scenery'.[3] Equally, those in R-wealth poverty cannot be compensated by additional M-wealth. The R-wealth poverty of the 'couch potato' is not solved by an even greater diet of take-away food and television.

Second, the question of whether M-wealth and R-wealth are or are not substitutes for each other does not have a simple answer. It follows from the first point that M-wealth and R-wealth are *not* substitutes for each other when citizens are in M-wealth poverty or R-wealth poverty, or both. But when citizens are in M-wealth prosperity and R-wealth prosperity, the two *can* be substitutes for each other.

I conclude this chapter with an essential observation due to Ruskin:[4]

> ... it appears that many of the persons commonly considered wealthy, are in reality no more wealthy than the locks of their own strong boxes ... being inherently and eternally incapable of wealth

As I see it, there is no doubt that some who have much M-wealth are very poor at creating any R-wealth, while others with little M-wealth have a gift for creating much R-wealth from a little M-wealth.

NOTES

[1]   This is the publicly funded health service in the UK.

[2]   Indeed, some of the ingredients of R-wealth are free.

[3]   In the film, *Local Hero* (Forsyth, 1983), Texan oil-man MacIntyre is sent by his company to acquire an idyllic village on the west coast of Scotland, where the company plans to build a large-scale installation. In due course, MacIntyre ('Mac') feels remorse about his

role in encouraging the locals to sell their birthright and in destroying this beautiful place. He shares these thoughts with visiting Russian fisherman, Victor, who replies: 'It's their place, Mac. They have a right to make of it what they can. Besides, you can't eat scenery!'

4   Ruskin (1904, vol. 17, p. 89).

25. Many Routes to Wealth Creation

In this chapter, I turn to a second essential implication of our analytical framework. In Chapter 6, we contrasted two visions of innovation and wealth creation. The first (Figure 6.1) was a framework with *one* main route to wealth creation. The second (Figures 6.2 and 6.4) was a framework where, at least in principle, there are a large number of possible routes to wealth creation. In view of what we have argued in Chapter 6 and seen in Part III, I am interested in the latter.

MANY ROUTES

It is helpful to have another look at Figure 6.4, which I have reproduced below, for convenience.

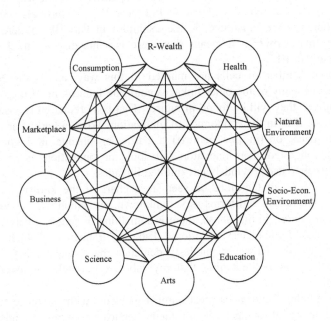

Figure 25.1 Common Innovation

It may help to think of this diagram as a road-map. It contains, on the left hand edge, the 'motorway' from business to marketplace to consumption and M-wealth creation as understood by business, and as shown in Figure 6.1. But it also shows all the many other routes that lead, eventually, to R-wealth creation. These routes may be narrower and more circuitous, but in aggregate, they can be very important – as we shall see later in this chapter. This roadmap metaphor is a useful one. Metaphorically speaking, big business is generally rather preoccupied with the motorway,[1] but the minor routes can also make many important common innovation contributions to the creation of R-wealth.

HOW MANY ROUTES ARE ACTUALLY USED?

At the beginning of my work for this book, I hoped it might be possible to illustrate each linkage in Figure 25.1 with an example. It was not long before I realised this goal would be too ambitious in the present book, and that a collection of 100 such examples would probably be unreadable. Instead, Part III has simply tried to illustrate *some* of these linkages.

While this 'criss-cross' diagram (Figure 25.1) gives a striking idea of the character of common innovation at work, it is easier to work with a matrix representation – as reproduced below. In Figure 25.2, we have also indicated which linkages are illustrated by the examples in Part III. Where a cell contains this arrow↵ , it means that there is some discussion of such a linkage in Part III.[2]

A large number of cells are marked in this way, and I suspect that examples of many of the other linkages could be found – or, if they cannot be found yet, they will be found in future. That last prediction is based on a rather basic idea in the economics of innovation. When a particular area of product space, or (in this context) a particular linkage in Figure 25.2 becomes congested, then innovators will look for innovations in new areas and will seek to use previously unexploited linkages.

Figure 25.2 can therefore be seen as a chart of the known forms of common innovation, and forms as yet unknown, but which will probably be devised in future. In that sense, there is something in common between my framework and Mendeleev's Periodic Table of Elements – which we all learnt at school. However, modesty demands that I make the following disclaimer: I am not claiming that my table is remotely comparable in significance!

The Periodic Table maps the chemical elements with reference to their atomic numbers, their electrons and their chemical properties. Mendeleev's original table included the elements known at the time, but also predicted elements as yet undiscovered that would be expected to fill gaps in his table. Most of his predictions were proved correct when the elements in question were eventually discovered.

		Effect Of:									
		Education	Science	Art	Business	Marketplace	Socio-Econ. Environment	Natural Environment	Consumption	Health	R-Wealth
Effect On:	Education	↵	↵				↵	↵	↵	↵	
	Science	↵	↵		↵		↵		↵		
	Art	↵	↵	↵	↵	↵		↵			
	Business	↵	↵	↵					↵		
	Marketplace	↵	↵	↵			↵				
	Socio-Econ. Envt.	↵	↵	↵	↵		↵	↵	↵		
	Natural Envt.	↵	↵			↵		↵	↵		
	Consumption	↵	↵	↵	↵	↵	↵	↵	↵		
	Health	↵	↵	↵	↵		↵	↵	↵	↵	
	R-Wealth	↵		↵			↵	↵	↵	↵	

Figure 25.2   Common Innovation (Matrix Form)

INSIGHTS FROM THE LEONTIEF FRAMEWORK: 1

In Chapter 6, I stated that all of the variants in my analytical framework could be seen as special cases of a Leontief model. The general form of this Leontief model is (Leontief, 1953):

$$X = C + AX \tag{25.1}$$

where X is a ten-element vector containing the categories used in Chapter 6, C gives the initial values of each element of X, and A describes the linkages that exist between one category and another. As described in Chapter 6, each element A_{ij} describes the *short-run* effect of variable j on variable I, while the *long-run* effect of variable j on variable i (where $i \neq j$) can be written:

$$dX_i / dX_j \;=\; A_{ij} + \sum_{g=0}^{9} A_{ig}A_{gj} + \sum_{g=0}^{9}\sum_{f=0}^{9} A_{ig}A_{gf}A_{fj}$$

$$+ \sum_{g=0}^{9}\sum_{f=0}^{9}\sum_{e=0}^{9} A_{ig}A_{gf}A_{fe}A_{ej} + \ldots \tag{25.2}$$

The frameworks illustrated in Figures 25.1 and 25.2, where anything can influence anything else, are the most general (and least restricted) forms of the Leontief Model. In the case where variable i = 9 (R-wealth), Equation (25.2) reinforces Figures 25.1 and 25.2 in illustrating the multiplicity of routes that lead to wealth creation. The first term describes the direct effect of j on R-wealth. The second term describes the ten 'two-step' effects of j on R-wealth (via g). The third term describes the hundred 'three-step' effects of j on R-wealth (via f and g). And the fourth term describes the thousand 'four-step' effects of j on R-wealth (via e, f and g). In principle, we could add in 'five-step' effects, 'six-step' effects, and so on, but these will typically be quite small.

In this Leontief framework, each time a route is created and added to the picture, it adds to wealth creation. This is especially relevant in the context of common innovation and the creation of R-wealth. Any common innovation that creates greater (positive) interaction between the categories of our framework, and hence develops a new route from one (or more) of our categories to R-wealth, will increase the contribution to R-wealth.

As the repeated summations in Equation (25.2) make clear, there are a very large number of possible routes – even if not all of them are operative. The first term describes just one route, the second term describes ten routes, the third term describes a hundred routes, and the fourth term describes a thousand routes. And, in principle, many of these routes can take a detour via some categories that are very distant from the thing that economists usually think of when they discuss wealth creation.

Some readers may be thinking: there may be many such routes but they are mostly very narrow, so that even in aggregate, they do not matter very much. But this simple intuition may be mistaken. We can get a more precise indication as follows. Let p be the probability that a particular element of A takes a positive (non-zero) value. Let k be the number of categories in our A matrix. And let the typical value of a non-zero element be a. Then it is straightforward to show the following.

The number of possible routes of length s from one variable to another (say, j to i) is $k^{(s-1)}$. The probability that a route of that length is active is the probability that all cells along the route are non-zero, and is given by p^s. The expected number of active routes of length s from j to i is therefore given by $k^{(s-1)}p^s$. And the value of the effect on j on i along a route of length s is given by a^s. So if we add up the effects of j on i along all routes of length s, we get $k^{(s-1)}p^s a^s$.

Table 25.1 shows a typical calculation for $k = 10$, $p = 20$ percent and $a = 0.3$. Each row shows the various steps of the calculation described above. The penultimate row shows the effects of j on i along all routes of length s. And the final row shows the cumulative effects of j on i along all routes of length $\leq s$.

Table 25.1 Long Routes Contribute to R-Wealth Creation

		Length of Route in Steps (s)					
		1	2	3	4	5	6
# Possible Routes	$k^{(s-1)}$	1	10	100	1000	10000	100000
Expected % Active	p^s	30%	9.0%	2.70%	0.81%	0.24%	0.07%
Expected # Active	$k^{(s-1)}p^s$	0.3	0.9	2.7	8.1	24.3	72.9
Typical Route Value	a^s	0.20	0.04	0.008	0.002	0.000	0.000
Contributions	$k^{(s-1)}p^s a^s$	0.06	0.036	0.022	0.013	0.008	0.005
Cumulative Sum		0.06	0.096	0.118	0.131	0.138	0.143

In this example, it is clear that there are many active routes of four or more steps. And even if the typical effect along that route is quite small, the contributions are still of importance. The cumulative effect of all route lengths up to six steps (0.143) is more than double the initial effect (0.06). The main lesson here is that the effects of two step, three step and higher step routes to R-wealth creation can easily outweigh the initial effects in this Leontief model, where a large proportion of the A matrix elements are positive.

INSIGHTS FROM THE LEONTIEF FRAMEWORK: 2

In this final section, we give another numerical example that illustrates the potential importance of common innovation to the creation of R-wealth. The question we are asking here is this. If we have pervasive common innovation spread across the entire A matrix (Figure 25.2), to what extent can that be a substitute for a strong business sector?

We answer the question as follows. We start with a strong business model as illustrated in Figure 6.1. Here wealth is created by a strong link from science to business, a strong link from business to the market place, a strong link from the marketplace to consumption and a strong link from consumption to R-wealth. The value of the relevant cell in A for each of these four strong links is set at 0.9. All other elements of A are set equal to zero. From this strong business model, we find (in an obvious notation) that:

$$\frac{\partial RW}{\partial Sc} = 0.9^4 = 0.656 \tag{25.3}$$

Then we progressively reduce this strong link from 0.9 to 0.8, to 0.7, and so on, and find what value is required for all the other elements of A to ensure that $\partial RW/\partial Sc$ remains at 0.656. Figure 25.3 plots the value of the business link (horizontal axis) and the value of the other links (vertical axis) that achieve the same value of 0.656.

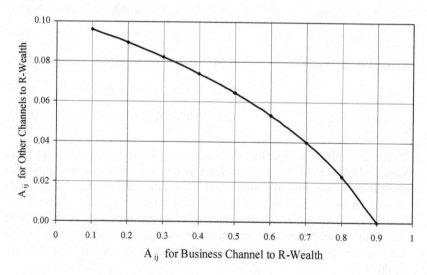

Figure 25.3 An Iso-Wealth Line

What is apparent from Figure 25.3 is that fairly small values for the other A parameters are sufficient to compensate for the reduction in the business link. Obviously, it is hard to take this simple calculation much further because, in this simple example, the variables are not precisely defined, and nor are their units of measurement. Nor indeed do we have any indication of the relative cost of strengthening business links, on the one hand, and all other common innovation links, on the other. But at some level, it seems fair to conclude that pervasive common innovation may be able to compensate for weaker business links.

NOTES

1. Big business is also rather preoccupied with the 'motorway', when we speak geographically, and not just metaphorically.
2. This could be an explicit part of one of the examples, but could also be one of the incidental examples in the 'OVERVIEW' section.

26. C-Innovation and the Future

The last two chapters have been about the *implications* of Parts I–III for the economics of innovation. This final chapter is slightly different, as some of what follows is really *conjecture* rather than a clear implication. I shall advance five hypotheses about common innovation and its role in the future.

C-INNOVATION AND NATIONAL ACCOUNTING

One of the earliest lessons I was taught about national accounting was this: if a man marries his housekeeper, or a woman marries her gardener, then national income, as conventionally measured, will fall. Why is that?

The point here is that, before marriage, the man pays his housekeeper a wage and the woman pays her gardener a wage. National income is usually calculated by one or more of three different methods: income, expenditure and output. In this case, the obvious methods are income and expenditure – because measuring output is often hard in service industries. It is then clear why marriage leads to this accounting change. Before marriage, there are wages to the housekeeper and the gardener, and the householder incurs expenditures in paying these wages. But, after marriage, there are no wages, no income for the housekeeper or gardener, and no expenditures (on wages) for the householders.

Does this really mean that marriage reduces national income? No, it does not. This is just an accounting issue. Suppose the former housekeeper, now wife, and the former gardener, now husband, do all the work they used to do. But now, this is part of a marriage 'contract', rather than a contract between employer and employee. In this case, R-wealth is unchanged. All the housekeeping is still done, and all the gardening is still done. But national income falls – as conventionally measured – because there is no wage, where there used to be a wage.

Accounting for C-Innovation

Exactly the same issues arise when we think about accounting for common innovation. Consider some of the common innovations in the home (as discussed in Chapter 16) or the use of online help forums to aid DIY car maintenance and computer repair (Chapter 18). When the consumer pursues such DIY activities at home, rather than employing a professional to do the job, then we get the same sort of effect on national income – as conventionally measured. With DIY, there is no expenditure on professional work and a reduced income for the professional. So, by the income or expenditure methods, it appears that national income declines. But setting aside any differences in the quality of DIY work and professional work, R-wealth is unchanged. The work is done, but now by the consumer and not by a professional. So the decline in national income is an illusion, not a reality.

Some of the common innovations described in Part III may leave a 'paper trail' (or online trail) from which the extent of their use could be measured. But many will not. Overall, therefore, any growth in the use of common innovation poses something of a challenge for the economic statistician charged with measuring national income and national wealth. On the one hand, conventional methods will miss much of the R-wealth created by common innovation. But, on the other, if economics ignores common innovation, it will make serious errors.

How will that challenge be met? Thus far, I have been dealing with implications. From now on, it is pure hypothesis. It may be that, for the immediate future, we abandon any attempt to *calculate* how common innovation influences R-wealth, but instead simply describe (and if possible, quantify) the elements of the A matrix (as illustrated in Figure 25.2). This would need to be done in considerable detail across a wide variety of sectors and contexts. And what we would obtain will not usually be a measure of how much such common innovations are actually used, but rather a map of *what can be done.*[1]

Such a mapping exercise would be pretty substantial. The examples in Part III are merely a start, but they give a general idea of what we are looking for. I hope that some researchers will rise to this challenge and try to build such a map. If there is sufficient interest, I may post additional examples on my website – please see the *Postscript* for details.

C-INNOVATION AND SUSTAINABILITY

In Part II of the book, I reasserted Schumpeter's well known maxim that business innovation can be likened to a *'perennial gale of creative destruction'*. This maxim is accepted by most serious scholars working on innovation, and yet a surprisingly large number of people are uncomfortable with the idea that innovation has a destructive side. This in itself is quite a paradox.

Moreover, as we saw in Part II, many examples suggest that business innovations can exhibit a variety of destructive effects. The simplest is the capacity to destroy market share of a rival. But there are others, involving damage to several categories in our analytical framework, including socio-economic environment, natural environment, health, education, and so on. Any scholars who are well informed about the fine detail of innovation and its economic effects should be aware of some, at least, of these examples.

We argued there that the main reason these apparently dysfunctional effects happen is because the purpose of business innovation is rarely if ever the maximisation of national wealth (neither M-wealth nor R-wealth). Rather, it is the maximisation of the innovator's interest, usually with little or no regard for any destructive side-effects. Why do we let innovators get away with having so little regard for these destructive effects? The main reason is that these destructive effects are usually thought to be limited to the destruction of a rival's market share. That sort of competitive destruction is accepted as a fair part of business – in the same way that fast accurate bowling is accepted as part of the strategy a cricket team uses to 'destroy' their rivals. But this perspective overlooks the fact that, as we saw in Part II, some of the destructive side of business innovation (e.g. e-waste) is not that sort of competitor destruction. It extends beyond that, and we should care about it.

By comparison, Part III argued that much common innovation – as we currently see it – does not suffer from these destructive effects. Why should that be? The main reason is that common innovation is generally, if not invariably, directed at improving the R-wealth and wellbeing of the innovators or their kin – *and just that*! Another way of putting this is, using the ideas of Chapter 4, is that common innovation is usually close to *oikonomia*, while business innovation is often quite remote from *oikonomia*.

These observations lead us back to Maxwell's observations about the dangers of science and engineering without wisdom (see Chapter 21). As I see it, many scientists and engineers (and many economists too!) consider that the challenge of innovation for sustainability involves finding a solution to random exogenous factors that threaten sustainability. This overlooks the unfortunate reality that earlier innovation is itself often one of the main challenges to sustainability – for example, consider again the case of software and e-waste (Chapter 10).

I can summarise my second hypothesis thus. When we properly compare the 'perennial gale of creative destruction' associated with business innovation and the 'gentle and benign breeze' of common innovation, I believe that the latter will become a more appropriate pattern for sustainable innovation in a finite world. In saying that, I don't imply that common innovation will solve all issues of sustainability. But I do mean that the 'gentle and benign breeze' is consistent with sustainability where the perennial gale is not.

C-INNOVATION MORE IMPORTANT IN FUTURE

My third hypothesis is that common innovation will become more important for a large number of people as a source of R-wealth, especially in a macroeconomic environment dominated by 'planned austerity' and an ever more unequal distribution of income and M-wealth.

Why do I say this? In brief outline, my argument is this. We have learnt much about 'late capitalism' since the Crash of 2007 onwards. We can now see it as a system that:

a) admirably serves the interests of an elite, who enjoy steady and rapid increases in their M-wealth;
b) does much less for the majority, some of whom struggle in 'planned austerity';
c) stands by and does nothing much to help the poorest.

In the face of these shortcomings, we might expect our elected governments to do more to correct these inequities. But in fact, they seem preoccupied with meeting the insatiable demands of the elite, who they pamper to excess, while washing their hands of the majority and the poorest.

If the future is an 'Unbalanced Economy' (to quote Driver and Temple, 2012), and I fear it seems to be, then increasing numbers of people will need to abandon any ambitions to afford business innovations, and depend instead on common innovation to create R-wealth.[2] In saying that, I repeat what I have said above: R-wealth cannot always be a substitute for M-wealth. For some in M-wealth poverty, increased R-wealth will not alleviate that poverty. But in the absence of a solution to M-wealth poverty, people will have to settle for the best option within reach.

Planning for this sort of future started some time ago. The pioneering 'green economist', Douthwaite (1996) described many examples of currency, banking, energy and food production systems which communities could use to strengthen themselves in the face an increasingly unstable world economy. If my hypothesis is right, a lot more planning is needed.

DECLINING SOCIAL VALUE OF B-INNOVATION?

My fourth hypothesis is, in a sense, the 'flip side' of the third. While common innovation becomes more important to many people, I believe that business innovation will exhibit declining social value. Why do I say that?

Part of the reason was already mentioned in the previous section. If the macroeconomic scenario described there is accurate, then increasing numbers of people will abandon ambitions to purchase the latest product innovations from business. I am referring especially to expensive new products, or products that replace something that still works and 'will do'.

And if this happens, it will reinforce a trend that is already apparent. It appears that much business innovation is already becoming ever more remote from *oikonomia* and is located further into the 'outer economy'. I am referring here to innovations in ownership, governance, supply chains and so on, which are important to the company but of little or no importance to the end consumer – who may, indeed, be completely unaware of such innovations. As I argued in Chapter 5, the result of this is that the ratio of the social value of an innovation to the value captured by the innovator declines with remoteness from *oikonomia*.

That is my justification for the hypothesis that the social value of business innovation will decline over time. For the sake of clarity, I should emphasise that this prediction applies to the 'average' business innovation, and will not necessarily apply to all.

A COUNTER-BALANCE TO BUSINESS INNOVATION

My final hypothesis is, in a way, a compendium of all the others. Common innovation will increasingly become an antidote to business innovation, and even to some features of business itself. These may sound like harsh words: what is my justification for ending on this note? Just this. For 200 years or so, various criticisms have been levelled at big business, and business innovations, and it is arguable that none of these have ever really gone away. A very selective list is as follows.

In the 1820s, William Cobbett travelled the country on his *Rural Rides* (1830) and ranted at length about how the 'Great Wen' (London) has devoured the wealth of distant villages and impoverished their agricultural workers. As he saw it, London's wealth was gained by, 'the beggaring of the parts of the country distant from the vortex of the funds'.[3] It seems to me that something very similar is happening today.

Thomas Carlyle was an early and loud critic of the 'new science' of economics, which he called, 'the dismal science'. In particular, he was adamant that (Carlyle, 1843, Chapter 6):

... 'Laissez-faire,' 'Supply-and-demand,' 'Cash-payment for the sole nexus,' and so forth, were not, are not, and will never be, a practicable Law of Union for a Society of Men.

Many would still agree – though not necessarily many economists. Ruskin was an equally loud critic of big business and economics, as we have already seen in Chapters 2, 8 and 17. And J.S. Mill, though an influential figure in the development of economics, was blunt in raising some essential concerns about the effects of business innovation:[4]

> Hitherto [1848] it is questionable if all the mechanical inventions yet made have lightened the day's toil of any human being. They have enabled a greater population to live the same life of drudgery and imprisonment, and an increased number of manufacturers and others to make fortunes.

In this respect, if not in others, Mill's view is not so far away from Marx's view (1867). A similar take on this was offered by Huxley (1937, p.8):

> Technological advance is rapid. But without progress in charity, technological advance is useless. Indeed, it is worse than useless. Technological progress has merely provided us with more efficient means for going backwards.

We have already seen William Morris's memorably scathing attack on the division of labour and capitalism, but it bears repetition:[5]

> the division of labour, once the servant, and now the master of competitive commerce, itself once the servant, and now the master of civilization.

This last observation is my own favourite way of describing what is dysfunctional about late capitalism: business is now, firmly, the master.

Matthews and Shallcross (1935) went even further in the title of their book, *Partners in Plunder: The Cost of Business Dictatorship*. They applied this term to big business, not to small business, but even so, the expression, 'business dictatorship', is strong stuff indeed! Some contemporary writers, George Monbiot (2000), have also written of the 'captive state' and the 'corporate takeover of Britain'.

And I could cite more: this is just a sample. This is not the place to assess all these criticisms. I leave it to the reader to decide which of these (s)he accepts and which (s)he does not. But the fact that this stream of criticisms keeps coming endorses what I said before: none of the criticisms have really gone away.

Big business has taken much of our society away from the rest of us. Common innovation is one of the things we have left. Business innovation has undermined the art of common innovation, but we can recover that art. It is our antidote to big business innovation – and even, big business itself. Let us use it as well as we can.

NOTES

[1] Referring again to the concept of 'harmonious society' (see Chapter 3, footnote 5), a good indication of a harmonious society is one in which the A matrix only contains positive elements. This means that all of the categories in our framework work to reinforce each other.

[2] Because of this, it seems likely that common innovation will be counter-cyclical, because it is used especially when business innovations are unaffordable. Mensch (1979) argued that some important innovations were counter-cyclical and played an important role in overcoming depression. The econometric evidence (based on econometric studies of the larger business innovations) has tended to contradict Mensch, as it finds that innovation and patenting are pro-cyclical (see Geroski and Walters, 1995). But Mensch's prediction seems exactly right in the context of common innovation, and there are good reasons to expect that the pattern for business innovation and common innovation will be different.

[3] Cobbett (1830/2001 p. 36).

[4] Mill (1848/1923, p. 751).

[5] Morris (1879/1966, p. 82).

Postscript

As the title says, common innovation is about how *we*, ordinary people, create the wealth of nations. Business has no monopoly of innovation or of wealth creation. While common innovation may not have the raw power of business innovation, it is in some ways better suited to our needs. The 'gentle and benign breeze' is generally preferable to the 'perennial gale'.

This book is no more than an introduction to the basic story of common innovation. To avoid overwhelming the reader, I have given just a few examples of common innovation at work, and just a few examples of the destructive side of business innovation. While writing the book, however, I have considered many other examples and, if there is sufficient interest, some of this additional material and other relevant papers may be placed on the following site:

www.commoninnovation.org.uk

The reader may wish to follow this link. Most of all, however, I shall be interested to see how other scholars can develop our understanding and analysis of common innovation.

Appendix

This appendix derives the results relevant for our analytical frameworks, as used in Chapters 6 and 25. Each of the frameworks illustrated in Chapter 6 can be described as a Leontief model (Leontief, 1953):

$$X = C + AX \qquad (A.1)$$

Here, X is a ten-element vector containing the categories used in Chapter 6:

$$X = \begin{bmatrix} X_0 \text{ (Education)} \\ X_1 \text{ (Science)} \\ X_2 \text{ (Arts)} \\ X_3 \text{ (Socio-Economic Environment)} \\ X_4 \text{ (Natural Environment)} \\ X_5 \text{ (Health)} \\ X_6 \text{ (Business)} \\ X_7 \text{ (Marketplace)} \\ X_8 \text{ (Consumption)} \\ X_9 \text{ (R-Wealth)} \end{bmatrix} \qquad (A.2)$$

C gives the initial values of each element of X, and A describes the linkages that exist between one category and another:

$$A_{ij} = \partial X_i / \partial X_j \qquad (A.3)$$

This describes how a change in one category enhances another. In this model, innovation (whether business innovation or common innovation) involves a change in the linkage from j to i: that is, a change in A_{ij}. In principle, the model can also cater for innovations that are wholly contained within one category; these would be changes in the main diagonal elements of the matrix A (i.e. A_{ij}).

To describe the dynamics, it is useful to give each X a time superscript:

Appendix

$$X_{t+1} = C + AX_t \tag{A.4}$$

A change in the initial values (C) will have a short run effect on X_{t+1}, but that in turn will lead to further effect on X_{t+2}, and so on. The long run effect is computed in the usual way, by using the Leontief Inverse:

$$X = [I - A]^{-1}C \tag{A.5}$$

The long run effects of changes in C on X are given by the set of derivatives:

$$\frac{dX_i}{dX_j} = [I - A]_{ij}^{-1} \tag{A.6}$$

If the matrix A were of small dimension (3*3, say) we could derive an explicit solution for these derivatives. But the matrix A here is of dimension 10*10, so that is not possible. Instead we have to make do with an approximation:

$$[I - A]^{-1} = I + A + AA + AAA + AAAA + ... \tag{A.7}$$

Any specific element of the Leontief Inverse can be approximated as follows (ignoring terms of fifth order and above):

$$[I - A]_{ij}^{-1} = \delta_{ij} + A_{ij} + \sum_{g=0}^{9} A_{ig}A_{gj} + \sum_{g=0}^{9}\sum_{f=0}^{9} A_{ig}A_{gf}A_{fj}$$

$$+ \sum_{g=0}^{9}\sum_{f=0}^{9}\sum_{e=0}^{9} A_{ig}A_{gf}A_{fe}A_{ej} + ... \tag{A.8}$$

where:

$$\delta_{ij} = \begin{cases} 1 & \text{if } i = j \\ 0 & \text{otherwise} \end{cases} \tag{A.9}$$

Equation (A.8) illustrates the way that the existence of multiple linkages between the different categories in our framework serves to 'amplify' the long term effect of one variable on another.[1]

As indicated above, an innovation in this model is represented by a change in the linkage from one category (say k) to another (say h): that is, a change in A_{hk}. We can compute the effects of this innovation by calculating the derivative of Equation (A.8) with respect to A_{hk}. Depending on the indices h and k, there are four cases.

Case 1 is the derivative with respect to A_{ij}, where $i \neq j$. This draws on 1st, 2nd and 3rd order terms, but not the 4th order term in Equation (A.8).

$$\frac{\partial[I-A]_{ij}^{-1}}{\partial A_{ij}} = (1+A_{ii})(1+A_{jj}) + \sum_{g=0}^{9} A_{ig}A_{gi} + \sum_{g=0}^{9} A_{jg}A_{gj} + ... \qquad (A.10)$$

Case 2 is the derivative with respect to A_{ik}, where $i \neq j$ and $k \neq j$. This draws on 1st, 2nd and 3rd order terms, but not the 4th order term in Equation (A.8).

$$\frac{\partial[I-A]_{ij}^{-1}}{\partial A_{ik}} = (1+A_{ii})A_{kj} + \sum_{g=0}^{9} A_{kg}A_{gj} + ... \qquad (A.11)$$

Case 3 is the derivative with respect to A_{hj}, where $i \neq j$ and $h \neq i$. This draws on 1st, 2nd and 3rd order terms, but not the 4th order term in Equation (A.8).

$$\frac{\partial[I-A]_{ij}^{-1}}{\partial A_{hj}} = (1+A_{jj})A_{ih} + \sum_{g=0}^{9} A_{ig}A_{gh} + ... \qquad (A.12)$$

And finally, Case 4 is the derivative with respect to A_{hk}, where $i \neq j$, $h \neq i$ and $k \neq j$. This draws on 1st, 2nd, 3rd and 4th order terms in Equation (A.8).

$$\frac{\partial[I-A]_{ij}^{-1}}{\partial A_{hk}} = A_{ih}A_{kj} + \sum_{g=0}^{9} A_{ig}A_{gh}A_{kj} + \sum_{g=0}^{9} A_{ih}A_{kg}A_{gj} + ... \qquad (A.13)$$

As illustrated above, all of these expressions allow for the full range of parameters.

It is worth mentioning that the above equations could be simplified somewhat in the case of a recursive model. A recursive model is one where the endogenous variables (and equations) can be placed in order, so that the jth equation determines the value of the jth endogenous variable as a function of variables 1 to j-1. In a recursive model, therefore, there is no feedback from variable j to variable i, when $j > i$.

In short, the matrix A is lower triangular, so $A_{ij} = 0$ for $i < j$. This reduces the number of non-zero parameters in Equations (A.8), (A.10), (A.11), (A.12) and (A.13). However, although this is a theoretical possibility, it is our belief that common innovation is so pervasive that the models describing the effects of common innovation will generally not be recursive.

Finally, we can compare the results above with the crude Linear Model noted in Chapter 6. In the linear model, there is only one route to R-wealth creation and, moreover, there is an exact result instead of the approximation in Equation (A.8). Considering the effect of education (variable 0) on R-wealth creation (variable 9), the result is:

$$\frac{\mathrm{d}X_9}{\mathrm{d}C_0} = A_{98}A_{87}A_{76}A_{60} \tag{A.14}$$

There are no indirect effects or feedback effects in this simple linear model. Compare this to the effect of education on R-wealth in the general Leontief model:

$$\frac{\mathrm{d}X_9}{\mathrm{d}C_0} = A_{90} + \sum_{g=0}^{9} A_{9g}A_{g0} + \sum_{g=0}^{9} \sum_{f=0}^{9} A_{9g}A_{gf}A_{f0}$$

$$+ \sum_{g=0}^{9} \sum_{f=0}^{9} \sum_{e=0}^{9} A_{9g}A_{gf}A_{fe}A_{e0} + \ldots \tag{A.15}$$

We can quickly see why the linear model gives such a restricted view of how innovation creates R-wealth, and why it will usually lead to an underestimate of the relevant effects. The right hand side of the linear model (Equation A.14) is *just one* of the terms in the triple summation in Equation (A.15) – where $g = 8$, $f = 7$ and $e = 6$.

SOME CALCULATIONS WITH THE MODEL

Does this difference between the simple linear model and the more complex model matter in practice? Yes, it does! We can show that neglecting even quite small interaction effects A_{ij} can have a substantial effect on the computed derivatives. To see this, consider the following estimates of the effect of education on R-wealth creation – as in Equations (A.14) and (A.15). In the calculations that follow, we split the A parameters into four groups:

a) those in the linear model: A_{60}, A_{76}, A_{87} and A_{98}
b) those on the principal diagonal: $A_{00} \ldots A_{99}$
c) those in the upper triangle: A_{ij} where $j > i$

d) the rest of those in the lower triangle: A_{ij} where $i > j$, excluding those in group (a).

In the linear model calculations, we assume that the parameters in groups (b), (c) and (d) are set at zero. Table A.1 shows how the computations for dX_9/dC_0 depend on the assumed parameter values for group (a).

Table A.1 Linear Model Calculations

Parameter Values for Group (a)				
40%	50%	60%	70%	80%
0.03	0.06	0.13	0.24	0.41

In the recursive model calculations, we assume that the parameters in groups (b) and (c) are set at zero. Table A.2 shows how the computations for dX_9/dC_0 depend on the assumed parameter values for groups (a) and (d).

Table A.2 Recursive Model Calculations

		Parameter Values for Group (a)				
		40%	50%	60%	70%	80%
	0%	0.03	0.06	0.13	0.24	0.41
Parameter Values for Group (d)	1%	0.05	0.09	0.16	0.28	0.46
	2%	0.08	0.12	0.20	0.32	0.51
	3%	0.10	0.16	0.24	0.37	0.56
	4%	0.13	0.19	0.28	0.42	0.62
	5%	0.17	0.23	0.33	0.47	0.68

In the full interdependent model calculations, we assume that the parameters in group (b) *only* are set at zero. Table A.3 shows how the computations for dX_9/dC_0 depend on the assumed parameter values for groups (a), (c) and (d).

The first rows in Tables A.2 and A.3 are simply the linear model results. As we look down each column in these tables, we can see the effects of quite modest innovations that increase the values of the parameters in groups (c) and (d) by a few percentage points. It is apparent that even such modest innovations can have a marked effect on R-wealth creation. The effects are especially pronounced in the case of the full interdependent model.

Appendix

Table A.3 Full Interdependent Model Calculations

		Parameter Values for Group (a)				
		40%	50%	60%	70%	80%
Parameter Values for Group (d)	0%	0.03	0.06	0.13	0.24	0.41
	1%	0.05	0.10	0.17	0.30	0.49
	2%	0.08	0.14	0.23	0.38	0.61
	3%	0.12	0.19	0.30	0.49	0.79
	4%	0.17	0.26	0.41	0.66	1.07
	5%	0.24	0.36	0.57	0.94	1.62

In short, it is clear that the simple linear model can seriously underestimate the effects of innovation on R-wealth creation – as defined in this book. These results also illustrate the powerful effects of ubiquitous common innovation. The reason for these results is clear from Equation (A.15): there are a huge number of effects in this model besides the simple linear model effect. When we take account of a large number of interaction effects, we can expect these to make a large difference – even if individually they are small.

There is an important corollary here. If a government is concerned to encourage innovation to increase R-wealth creation, what route should they follow? Should they concentrate mainly on enhancing the linkages in the linear model (i.e. business innovation)? Or should they have a more diffuse objective to grow all the linkages in the model (i.e. common innovation)? A perusal of Table A.3, especially, suggests it may be better to do the latter. This would be the case especially if, as we have suggested in the main part of the book, that the traditional linear model – creating R-wealth exclusively through business innovation – is running into diminishing returns.

One final observation: the frameworks here can also be used to explore the significance of the destructive side of innovation: that is, the negative effects of innovation on the natural environment, the socio-economic environment, on education and sometimes on the arts as described in Part II of the book. Do these negatives matter? Are they not a small price to pay for the beneficial effects of innovation on productivity, consumption and hence R-wealth creation? It is hard to distil a simple answer as it all depends on how exactly the negatives show up in the A matrix. But in some exploratory calculations, I have found examples where the negatives can be very important, and can undo much of the good done by innovation.

NOTE

[1] This framework can also be applied in the context of policy innovations, and the concept of 'amplification' is also important there. Frenz and Lambert (2013) give a striking example of that in the context of accreditation. The interested reader can find a short paper about this on the website: www.commoninnovation.org.uk.

References

Abe Books (2012), http://www.abebooks.com/

Allen, R.C. (1983), 'Collective Invention', *Journal of Economic Behavior and Organization*, **4**, 1–24

Antonelli, C. (1995), *The Economics of Localized Technological Change and Industrial Dynamics*, Dordrecht: Kluwer Academic Publishers

Antonelli, C. (2008), *Localised Technological Change: Towards the Economics of Complexity*, London: Routledge

Ars Technica (2013), *Google's 20 percent time is 'as good as dead' because it doesn't need it anymore*, August 17, http://arstechnica.com/business/2013/08/googles-20-percent-time-is-as-good-as-dead-because-it-doesnt-need-it-anymore/

Ashcraft, M.H. (1989), *Human Memory and Cognition*, Glenview, US: Scott, Foresman and Company

Atkinson, A.B. and J.E. Stiglitz (1969), 'A New View of Technological Change', *Economic Journal*, **79**, 573–8

Attenborough Nature Centre (2012a), *Attenborough Nature Reserve*, http://www.attenboroughnaturecentre.co.uk/about/attenborough-nature-reserve/

Attenborough Nature Centre (2012b), *Attenborough Nature Reserve: Nature Trails and Map*, http://www.attenboroughnaturecentre.co.uk/docs/Map-for-website.jpg

Babbage, C. (1835), *On the Economy of Machinery and Manufactures*, 4th edn, London: Charles Knight

Barnes, R. (1998), *The Pre-Raphaelites and Their World*, London: Tate Gallery

Barthes, R. (1957/1972), *Mythologies*, London: Paladin

Bartók, B. (1931/1976), 'The Influence of Peasant Music on Modern Music (1931)', in B. Suchoff (ed.), *Béla Bartók Essays*, London: Faber & Faber, pp. 340–44

Baumol, W.J. (2002), *The Free-Market Innovation Machine: Analyzing the Growth Miracle of Capitalism*, Princeton, NJ: Princeton University Press

Bayley, S. (1989), 'Foreword', in Design Museum, *Commerce and Culture*, Tunbridge Wells: Penshurst Press Ltd

BBC (2001), *Mozart 'can cut epilepsy'*, April 2, http://news.bbc.co.uk/1/hi/health/1251839.stm

BBC (2002), *Computer dumping polluting Asia*, February 25, http://news. bbc.co.uk/1/hi/sci/tech/1839997.stm

BBC (2003), *Buffett warns on investment time bomb*, March 4, http://news. bbc.co.uk/1/hi/2817995.stm

BBC (2006), *Dealing with Toxic Computer Waste*, December 27, http://news.bbc.co.uk/1/hi/business/6110018.stm

BBC (2010), *Big increase in brewery numbers in UK, says CAMRA*, September 16, http://www.bbc.co.uk/news/uk-11323119

BBC (2011a), *Decline in High Street bookshops continues in 2011*, October 4, http://www.bbc.co.uk/news/entertainment-arts-15149546

BBC (2011b), *Buy British: Why isn't there a new campaign?*, November 8, http://www.bbc.co.uk/news/magazine-15551818

BBC (2011c), *Newcastle rename St James' Park the Sports Direct Arena*, November 9, http://www.bbc.co.uk/sport/0/football/15668207

BBC (2011d), *Thatcher urged 'let Liverpool decline' after 1981 riots*, December 30, http://www.bbc.co.uk/news/uk-16361170

BBC (2012a), *Cardiff City FC confirm rebranding with new red shirts*, June 6, http://www.bbc.co.uk/news/uk-wales-south-east-wales-18337392

BBC (2012b), *World's first 'tax' on Microsoft's Internet Explorer 7*, June 14, http://www.bbc.co.uk/news/technology-18440979

BBC (2012c), *Asia's fastest data cable links Tokyo to Singapore*, August 20, http://www.bbc.co.uk/news/technology-19275490

BBC (2012d), *UK Internet 'to be fastest in Europe by 2015*, August 20, http://www.bbc.co.uk/news/technology-19316824

BBC (2012e), *Autism: Traffic pollution linked, study suggests*, November 27, http://www.bbc.co.uk/news/health-20493360

BBC (2013a), *Wonga row: Archbishop of Canterbury 'embarrassed' over Church funds*, July 26, http://www.bbc.co.uk/news/business-23459932

BBC (2013b), *Hull City: Hull Tigers name change submitted to FA*, December 11, http://www.bbc.co.uk/sport/0/football/25341248

BBC (2014a), *My quest to fix a broken iPad*, February 16, http://www. bbc.co.uk/news/technology-26197229

BBC (2014b), *New York seeks curbs on high-frequency trading*, March 18, http://www.bbc.co.uk/news/business-26637465

BBC (2014c), *Film-makers challenged to make science compelling*, April 11, http://www.bbc.co.uk/news/technology-26938150

BBC Wildlife Magazine (2006), 'Top 10 Eco-Destinations', *BBC Wildlife Magazine*, **24** (13), 80–81

Becher, J.T. (1812), *Letter to Home Office*, http://ludditebicentenary. blogspot.co.uk/2012/02/11th-february-1812-reverend-j-t-becher.html

Becker, G.S. (1965), 'A Theory of the Allocation of Time', *Economic Journal*, **75**, 493–517

Becker, G.S. (1996), *Accounting for Tastes*, Cambridge, US: Harvard University Press

Beckett, J. (2012), *Luddites*, http://www.nottsheritagegateway.org.uk/people/luddites.htm

Beethoven, L. van (2009), *Beethoven: the Man and the Artist*, Project Gutenberg, http://www.gutenberg.org/files/3528/3528-h/3528-h.htm

Bell, Q. (1984), 'The Pre-Raphaelites and their Critics', in L. Parris (ed.) *Pre-Raphaelite Papers*, London: Tate Gallery, pp. 11–22

Bianchi, M. (ed. 1998), *The Active Consumer: Novelty and Surprise in Consumer Choice*, London: Routledge

Biggs, L. (1996), 'Museums and Welfare: Shared Space', in P. Lorente (ed.) *The Role of Museums and the Arts in the Urban Regeneration of Liverpool*, Working Paper 9, Centre for Urban History, University of Leicester

Binfield, K. (ed. 2004), *Writings of the Luddites*, Baltimore: The Johns Hopkins University Press

Birch, M.A. (1997), *The Health Benefits of Art Therapy Following Traumatic Life Experiences*, Alameda: California School of Professional Psychology

Bookseller (2009), *Indies predict 'golden age' for bookselling*, http://www.thebookseller.com/news/97925-indies-predict-golden-age-for-bookselling.html

Booksellers Association (n.d.), *Bookshops in the Cultural Life of a Nation*, http://www.booksellers.org.uk/BookSellers/media/SiteMediaLibrary/AboutTheBA/Bookshops-in-the-Cultural-Life-of-a-Nation.pdf

Booksellers Association (2011), *The Proposed Acquisition of The Book Depository by Amazon: Submission from the Booksellers Association to the Office of Fair Trading*, http://www.booksellers.org.uk/BookSellers/media/SiteMediaLibrary/AboutTheBA/The-Proposed-Acquisition-of-The-Book-Depository-by-Amazon-BA-Submission-to-The-Office-of-Fair-Trading.pdf

Bourdieu, P. (1984), *Distinction: A Social Critique of the Judgment of Taste*, London: Routledge & Kegan Paul

Boulding, K.E. (1981), *Evolutionary Economics*, London: Sage Publications

Braun, C.F. von (1997), *The Innovation War*, Prentice Hall

Brewery History Society (2005), *A Century of British Brewers 1890–2004*, Longfield, Kent: Brewery History Society

Broxtowe (2012), *Attenborough Officially Britain's 2nd Favourite Nature Reserve*, http://www.broxtowe.gov.uk/index.aspx?articleid=11168

Byron, Lord (1812), *Speech to the House of Lords*, http://www.luddites200.org.uk/LordByronspeech.html

Cardew, M. (2002), *Pioneer Pottery*, London: A&C Black Publishers Ltd

Carlyle, T. (1843/1899), *Past and Present*, London: Chapman and Hall

Cemex (2012), *Nottinghamshire – Attenborough Quarry*, http://www.cemex. co.uk/su/su_Nottinghamshire.asp

Chesborough, H. (2003), *Open Innovation: The New Imperative for Creating and Profiting from Technology*, Boston, MA: Harvard Business School Press

Chick, V. (2013), 'Economics and the Good Life: Keynes and Schumacher', *Economic Thought*, **2** (2), http://et.worldeconomicsassociation.org/papers/ economics-and-the-good-life-keynes-and-schumacher/

Church, J. and N. Gandal (1992), 'Network Effects, Software Provision and Standardization', *Journal of Industrial Economics*, **40**, 85–103

Cobbett, W. (1830/2001), *Rural Rides*, London: Penguin Books

Conforti, M. (n.d.), 'The Idealist Enterprise and the Applied Arts', in *A Grand Design: A History of the Victoria and Albert Museum*, http://www. vam.ac.uk/vastatic/microsites/1159_grand_design/essay-the-idealist-enterprise_new.html

Countryfile (2012), *Countryfile Magazine Awards: The Results 2012*, http:// www.countryfile.com/countryside/countryfile-magazine-awards-results-2012

Crich (2012), *Framework Wreckers in Crich*, http://www.crichparish.co.uk/ webpages/framewreckers.html

Cusumano, M.A. and R. Selby (1996), *Microsoft Secrets*, London: HarperCollins

Dalle, J.M. and P.A. David (2007), *It Takes All Kinds: A Simulation Modelling Perspective on Motivation and Coordination in Libre Software Development Projects*, SIEPR Discussion Paper No. 07–24, Stanford Institute for Economic Policy Research

Daily Mail (2008), *Liverpool's Fernando Torres and Gunners star Fábregas 'too English' for Spain*, June 10, http://www.dailymail.co.uk/ sport/football/article-1025416/Liverpools-Fernando-Torres-Gunners-star-Fabregas-English-Spain.html

Daily Mail (2013), *Google's staff now too busy for 20% time off perk, claim former employees*, August 29, http://www.dailymail.co.uk/news/article-2405301/Googles-20-time-policy-gives-employees-day-week-work-projects-effectively-abolished-claim-employees.html

Daily Telegraph (2011a), *Every bookshop closure creates a hole in our communities*, August 25, http://www.telegraph.co.uk/culture/books/ booknews/8722710/Every-bookshop-closure-creates-a-hole-in-our-communities.html

Daily Telegraph (2011b), *Internet and supermarkets kill off 2000 bookshops*, September 2, http://www.telegraph.co.uk/culture/books/booknews/8738701/ Internet-and-supermarkets-kill-off-2000-bookshops.html

Daily Telegraph (2013), *Barcelona's Xavi completes the perfect passing game against PSG*, April 11, http://www.telegraph.co.uk/sport/football/teams/barcelona/9986677/Barcelonas-Xavi-completes-the-perfect-passing-game-against-PSG.html

Daily Telegraph (2014), *Arsenal supporters need to cheer up, they are not doing enough to help their team in title race*, February 13, http://www.telegraph.co.uk/sport/football/teams/arsenal/10636262/Arsenal-supporters-need-to-cheer-up-they-are-not-doing-enough-to-help-their-team-in-title-race.html

Darwin, C. (1876/1958), *The Autobiography of Charles Darwin, 1809–1882*, ed. N. Barlow, London: Collins, http://darwin-online.org.uk/content/frameset?itemID=F1497&viewtype=text&pageseq=1

Davies, R. (2013), *Alternative Currency Systems*, http://projects.exeter.ac.uk/RDavies/arian/local.html

Denis, R.C. (n.d.), 'Teaching by Example', in *A Grand Design: A History of the Victoria and Albert Museum*, http://www.vam.ac.uk/vastatic/microsites/1159_grand_design/essay-teaching-by-example_new.html

Derbyshire (n.d.), *High Peak and Tissington Trails*, http://www.peakdistrict.gov.uk/__data/assets/pdf_file/0009/90486/hptisstrails.pdf

Design Council (2012), *RSA Design Directions: Design for Social Inclusion*, http://www.designcouncil.org.uk/our-work/challenges/communities/dott-cornwall1/rsa-design-directions/

Dogan, M. and R. Pahre (1990), *Creative Marginality: Innovation at the Intersection of Social Sciences*, Boulder, US: Westview Press

Douglas, M. (1983), 'Identity: Personal and Socio-Cultural', *Uppsala Studies in Cultural Anthropology*, **5**, 35–46

Douthwaite, R. (1996), *Short Circuit: Practical New Approach to Building More Self-Reliant Communities*, Totnes: Green Books

Douthwaite, R. (1999a), *The Growth Illusion: How Economic Growth has Enriched the Few, Impoverished the Many and Endangered the Planet*, revised edn, Totnes: Green Books

Douthwaite, R. (1999b), *The Ecology of Money*, Totnes: Green Books

Driver, C. and P. Temple (2012), *The Unbalanced Economy: A Policy Appraisal*, Basingstoke: Palgrave Macmillan

Durkheim, E. (1893/1984), *The Division of Labour in Society*, translated by W.D. Halls, New York: Free Press

Easterlin, R.A. (1973), 'Does money buy happiness?', *The Public Interest*, **30** (Winter), 3–10

Easterlin, R.A. (1995), 'Will raising the incomes of all increase the happiness of all?', *Journal of Economic Behavior and Organization*, **27**, 35–47

Economist (2000), 'Internet Economics: A Thinker's Guide', *Economist*, March 30

Eden Project (2013), http://www.edenproject.com/

Encyclopedia Britannica (1968), 'Science Fiction', *Encyclopedia Britannica*, **20**, pp. 17–18

Engelbrecht, H.-J. (2014), 'A General Model of the Innovation – Subjective Well-being Nexus', *Journal of Evolutionary Economics*, **24**, 377–97

Ericsson (2012), *Twenty years of Short Message Service (SMS): how text messaging helped to change the world*, November 30, http://www.ericsson.com/news/121130-twenty-years-of-short-message-service_244159017_c

Eureka (2013), http://www.eureka.org.uk/

Fagan, B.M. (ed. 2004), *The Seventy Great Inventions of the Ancient World*, London: Thames and Hudson

Fast Co. Design (2011), *How 3M Gave Everyone Days Off and Created an Innovation Dynamo*, February 1, http://www.fastcodesign.com/1663137/how-3m-gave-everyone-days-off-and-created-an-innovation-dynamo

Forsyth, B. (1983), *Local Hero*, Warner Brothers / 20th Century Fox

Foster, R.N. (1986), *Innovation: The Attackers Advantage*, London: Guild Publishing

Frenz, M. and R. Lambert (2013), *The Economics of Accreditation*, http://www.ukas.com/Library/Media-Centre/News/News-Archive/2013/Economics of Accreditation Final Report.pdf

Frey, B.S., M. Benz and A. Stutzer (2004), 'Introducing Procedural Utility: Not Only What, but Also How Matters', *Journal of Institutional and Theoretical Economics*, **160**, 377–401

Fromm, E. (1976/1997), *To Have or To Be?*, New York and London: Continuum

Gagliardi, G. (2006), *Business Warrior: Strategy for Entrepreneurs*, Seattle: Clearbridge Publishing

Galbraith, J.K. (1958), *The Affluent Society*, Boston, MA: Houghton Mifflin

Geddes, P. (1884), *John Ruskin: Economist*, Edinburgh: William Brown

Geroski, P.A. and C.F. Walters (1995), 'Innovative Activity Over the Business Cycle', *Economic Journal*, **105**, 916–28

Glaser, M. (1989), 'Commercial Art', in Design Museum, *Commerce and Culture*, Tunbridge Wells: Penshurst Press Ltd

Gorman, W.M. (1959), 'Separable Utility and Aggregation', *Econometrica*, **27**, 469–81

Gourvish, T.R. and R.G. Wilson (1994), *The British Brewing Industry 1830–1980*, Cambridge: Cambridge University Press

Greenpeace (2008), *Toxic Tech – Not in Our Back Yard: Uncovering the Hidden Flows of e-Waste*, http://www.greenpeace.org/international/en/publications/reports/not-in-our-backyard-summary/

Griffiths, P. (1985), *Olivier Messiaen and the Music of Time*, Ithaca, US: Cornell University Press

Grindley, P. (1995), *Standards, Strategy, and Policy: A Casebook*, Oxford: Oxford University Press

Guardian (2008a), *Fábregas takes positive view, from the bench*, June 10, http://www.theguardian.com/football/2008/jun/10/euro2008.euro2008groupd

Guardian (2008b), *Have you forgotten how to 'deep read'?*, July 21, http://www.theguardian.com/books/booksblog/2008/jul/21/haveyouforgottenho wtodeep

Guardian (2008c), *Mental health and art*, September 24, http://www.guardian.co.uk/society/gallery/2008/sep/24/mental.health.art

Guardian (2011), *Pro bono cannot plug the gap left by legal aid cuts*, December 7, http://www.theguardian.com/law/2011/dec/07/pro-bono-cannot-plug-gap

Guardian (2012a), *Frugal innovation: learning from social entrepreneurs in India*, March 20, http://www.guardian.co.uk/public-leaders-network/blog/2012/mar/20/frugal-innovation-social-entrepreneurs-india

Guardian (2012b), *Archbishop of Canterbury's Farewell Book Blasts at March of Consumerism*, June 23, http://www.guardian.co.uk/uk/2012/jun/23/archbishop-canterbury-rowan-williams-book

Guardian (2012c), *Vince Cable tells shareholders: throw out bank cheats*, June 30, http://www.guardian.co.uk/business/2012/jun/30/vince-cable-shareholders-bank-cheats

Guardian (2012d), *Text messaging turns 20*, December 1, http://www.theguardian.com/technology/2012/dec/01/text-messaging-20-years

Guardian (2013), *Atmosphere and fans' role in Premier League games becoming a concern*, November 16, http://www.theguardian.com/football/2013/nov/16/premier-league-fans-atmosphere-concern

Guardian (2014a), *Sick cities: why urban living can be bad for your mental health*, February 25, http://www.theguardian.com/cities/2014/feb/25/city-stress-mental-health-rural-kind

Guardian (2014b), *Legal aid cuts: six lawyers on why they will damage our justice system*, April 1, http://www.theguardian.com/law/2014/apr/01/legal-aid-six-lawyers-damage-legal-system

Guardian (2014c), *Manchester United: how did they get into this mess?*, April 8, http://www.theguardian.com/football/2014/apr/08/manchester-united-how-got-into-crisis-alex-ferguson-glazer

Habicht, H., P. Oliveira and V. Shcherbatiuk (2012), *User Innovators: When Patients Set Out to Help Themselves and End Up Helping Many*, August 27, available at SSRN: http://ssrn.com/abstract=2144325

Hall, G.C. (1979), 'The Effects of Mergers on the Product–mix Offered by the Brewing Industry', *Applied Economics*, **11**, 21–34

Hare, D. (2011), *Rowan Williams: God's Boxer*, http://www.archbishopof canterbury.org/articles.php/2123/david-hare-interviews-archbishop

Hawkins, K.H. and C.L. Pass (1979), *The Brewing Industry, A Study in Industrial Organisation and Public Policy*, London: Heinemann Educational

Hayek, F. (1945), 'The Use of Knowledge in Society', *American Economic Review*, **35**, 519–30

Hayne, T. (1812), *Letter to Home Office*, http://ludditebicentenary. blogspot.co.uk/2012/02/12th-february-1812-thomas-hayne-lace.html

Henderson, R.M. and K.B. Clark (1990), 'Architectural Innovation: The Reconfiguration of Existing Product Technologies and the Failure of Established Firms', *Administrative Science Quarterly*, **35**, 9–30

Hippel, E.A. von (1988), *The Sources of Innovation*, Oxford: Oxford University Press

Hippel, E.A. von (2005), *Democratizing Innovation*, Cambridge, MA: MIT Press

Hirsch, F. (1977), *The Social Limits to Growth*, London: Routledge & Kegan Paul

HM Treasury (2000), *Productivity in the UK: The Evidence and the Government's Approach*, November

Hodgson, G.M. (1998), 'On the Evolution of Thorstein Veblen's Evolutionary Economics', *Cambridge Journal of Economics*, **22**, 415–31

Hornsey, I.S. (2003), *A History of Beer and Brewing*, Cambridge: The Royal Society of Chemistry

Hu Jichuang. (2009), *A Concise Economic History of Chinese Economic Thought*, Beijing: Foreign Languages Press

Huxley, A. (1937), *Ends and Means*, London: Chatto and Windus

Huxley, A. (1963), *Literature and Science*, London: Chatto and Windus

IFixit (2014), http://www.ifixit.com/

Ilich, I. (1982), 'Vernacular Values', in S. Kumar (ed.), *The Schumacher Lectures*, London: Abacus/Sphere Books Limited, pp. 70–79

Iltis, H. (1932), *The Life of Mendel*, translated from the German by E. and C. Paul, London: George Allen and Unwin

Intel (n.d.), 'Moore's Law', http://www.intel.com/technology/mooreslaw/ index.htm

Jenkins, D. (2000), Market Whys and Human Wherefores, London: Cassell

Jones T., D. McCormack and C. Dewing (eds, 2012), *Growth Champions: The Battle for Sustained Innovation Leadership*, Chichester: John Wiley & Sons

Kay, J. (2010), *Obliquity*, London: Profile Books

Kay, J. (2012), *The Kay Review of UK Equity Markets and Long-Term Decision Making*, Final Report, Department for Business, Innovation and Skills (BIS), July, http://www.bis.gov.uk/assets/biscore/business-law/ docs/k/12-917-kay-review-of-equity-markets-final-report.pdf

Kitchen, J.M.W. (1885 / 2010), *Consumption: Its Nature, Causes, Prevention, and Cure*, New York: G.P. Putnam's & Sons

Krugman, P.R. (1980), 'Scale Economies, Product Differentiation, and the Pattern of Trade', *American Economic Review*, **70**, 950–59

Krugman, P.R. (1991), 'Increasing Returns and Economic Geography', *Journal of Political Economy*, **99**, 483–99

Krugman, P.R. (1992), *Geography and Trade*, Cambridge, Mass: MIT Press

Kummervold, P.E., D. Gammon, S. Bergvik, J.A. Johnsen, T. Hasvold, J.H. Rosenvinge (2002), 'Social support in a wired world: use of online mental health forums in Norway', *Nordic Journal of Psychiatry*, **56**, 59–65 http://www.ncbi.nlm.nih.gov/pubmed/11869468

Landes, D. (2003), *The Unbound Prometheus: Technological Change and Industrial Development in Western Europe from 1750 to the Present*, 2nd edn, Cambridge, UK: Cambridge University Press

Langlois, R.N. (1992), 'External Economies and Economic Progress: The Case of the Microcomputer Industry', *Business History Review*, **66**, 1–50

Larousse (1971), *Larousse Encyclopedia of Music*, London: Hamlyn Publishing Group

LawWorks (2014), http://www.lawworks.org.uk/

Layard, R. (2005), *Happiness: Lessons from a New Science*, London: Penguin Books

Leontief, W.W. (1947), 'Introduction to a Theory of the Internal Structure of Functional Relationships', *Econometrica*, **15**, 361–73

Leontief, W.W. (ed. 1953), *Studies in the Structure of the American Economy: Theoretical and Empirical Explorations in Input–Output Analysis*, New York: Oxford University Press

Lewis, P. (1986), 'William Lee's Stocking Frame: Technical Evolution and Economic Viability 1589–1750', *Textile History*, **2**, 129–47

Liverpool Echo (2012), 'Liverpool FC wins fight to keep Liver Bird copyright', December 14, http://www.liverpoolecho.co.uk/news/liverpool-news/liverpool-fc-wins-fight-keep-3327437

McDaid, E. (2005), *The Nottinghamshire Wildlife Trust and Attenborough Nature Reserve*, http://web.archive.org/web/20100114231557/http://www.bna-naturalists.org/mags/sprg-summ04/atten.html

McManus R.J., P. Glasziou, A. Hayen, J. Mant, P. Padfield, J. Potter, E.P. Bray and D. Mant (2008), 'Blood pressure self monitoring: questions and answers from a national conference', *British Medical Journal*, 337:a2732, http://www.bmj.com/cgi/content/extract/337/dec22_1/a2732

Malthus, T.R. (1798/1926), *First Essay on Population*, London: Macmillan and Co

Mandelbrot B.B. (1967), 'How Long Is the Coast of Britain? Statistical Self-Similarity and Fractional Dimension', *Science*, New Series, **156** (3775),

636–8

Mandelbrot, B.B. (1982), *The Fractal Geometry of Nature*, revised edn, San Francisco: W.H. Freeman

Mandelbrot, B.B. (1997), *Fractals and Scaling in Finance: Discontinuity, Concentration, Risk*, Berlin: Springer

Mark, J. (1985), 'Changes in the British Brewing Industry in the 20th Century', in D.J. Oddy and D.S. Miller (eds), *Diet and Health in Modern Britain*, London: Croom Helm

Marx, K. (1844), 'Wages of Labour', in *Economic and Philosophic Manuscripts of 1844*, http://www.marxists.org/archive/marx/works/1844/manuscripts/wages.htm

Marx, K. (1857), *Grundrisse: Outlines of the Critique of Political Economy*, http://www.marxists.org/archive/marx/works/1857/grundrisse/index.htm

Marx, K. (1867/1974), *Capital: A Critical Analysis of Capitalist Production*, vol. I, London: Lawrence and Wishart. [I have also used this edition, which provides a translation of the Latin passage on p. 59 of this book: http://www.marxists.org/archive/marx/works/1867-c1/ch15.htm]

Marx, K. and F. Engels (1848), *Manifesto of the Communist Party*, http://www.marxists.org/archive/marx/works/1848/communist-manifesto/index.htm

Matthews, J.B. and R.E. Shallcross (1935), *Partners in Plunder: The Cost of Business Dictatorship*, New York: Covici, Friede

Maxwell, N. (1984), *From Knowledge to Wisdom*, Oxford: Blackwell

Maxwell, N. (2007), *From Knowledge to Wisdom,* 2nd edn, London: Pentire Press

Maxwell, N. (2014), *From Knowledge to Wisdom: We Need a Revolution*, http://www.ucl.ac.uk/from-knowledge-to-wisdom

Mensch, G. (1979), *Stalemate in Technology: Innovations Overcome the Depression*, Cambridge, MA: Ballinger

Microsoft (n.d), *Support Lifecycle Index*, http://support.microsoft.com/gp/lifeselectindex

Mill, J.S. (1848/1923), *Principles of Political Economy*, London: Longmans and Co

Mill, J.S. (1859/1929), *On Liberty*, London: Watts and Co

Millns, T. (1998), 'The British Brewing Industry, 1945–1995', in R.G. Wilson and T.R. Gourvish (eds), *The Dynamics of the International Brewing Industry since 1800*, London: Routledge

Mises, L. von (1951), *Socialism: An Economic and Sociological Analysis*, New Haven: Yale University Press

Mitchell, L.E. (2010), *Financialism: A (Very) Brief History*, Case Western Reserve University School of Law, http://ssrn.com/abstract=1655739

Mitchell, W.C. (1912), 'The Backward Art of Spending Money', *American*

Economic Review, **2**, 269–81

Monbiot, G. (2000), *Captive State: The Corporate Takeover of Britain*, London: Macmillan

Moore, G.E. (1965), 'Cramming more components onto integrated circuits', *Electronics*, **38** (8), April 19, 114–17

Morris, W. (1879/1966), 'Making the Best of It: Paper Read Before the Trades' Guild of Learning and the Birmingham Society of Artists', in *The Collected Works of William Morris*, vol. XXII, New York: Russell and Russell

Moulaert, F., D. MacCallum, A. Mehmood, and A. Hamdouch (2013), *The International Handbook On Social Innovation: Collective Action, Social Learning and Transdisciplinary Research*, Cheltenham: Edward Elgar Publishing

Mulgan, G. (2007), *Social innovation: what it is, why it matters & how it can be accelerated*, http://www.sbs.ox.ac.uk/ideas-impact/skoll/research/social-innovation-reports-resources/social-innovation-what-it-why-it-matters-how-it-can-be-accelerated

Nelson, R.R. and S.G. Winter (1982), *An Evolutionary Theory of Economic Change*, Cambridge, MA: The Belknap Press of Harvard University

Network to Supplies (n.d.), *WEEE Recycling*, http://n2s.co.uk/project/weee-recycling/

New Economics Foundation (2012), *The natural solutions to our economic problems*, November 19, http://www.neweconomics.org/blog/entry/the-natural-solutions-to-our-economic-problems

New Economics Foundation (2013), *Why Europe needs community currencies*, http://www.neweconomics.org/blog/entry/why-europe-needs-community-currencies

NewStart (2012), *Do Local Currencies Work?*, November 27, http://newstartmag.co.uk/features/do-local-currencies-work/2/

Nussbaum, M.C. (1986), *The Fragility of Goodness: Luck and Ethics in Greek Tragedy and Philosophy*, New York: Cambridge University Press

Nussbaum, M. and A. Sen (eds, 1993), *The Quality of Life*, Oxford: Clarendon Press

Observer (2012), *Rowan Williams Pours Scorn on David Cameron's 'Big Society'*, http://www.guardian.co.uk/uk/2012/jun/23/rowan-williams-big-society-cameron

Office of Government Commerce (2004), *Open Source Software Trials in Government*, http://www.ogc.gov.uk/documents/CP0041OpenSource SoftwareTrialReport.pdf

Ontkush, M. (2007), 'Linux Prevents Obsolescence: Could Reduce E-Waste by Millions of Tons of per Year', February 27, http://www.ecogeek.org/content/view/459/

Open Scientist (2011), *Finalizing a Definition of 'Citizen Science' and 'Citizen Scientists'*, September 3, http://www.openscientist.org/2011/09/finalizing-definition-of-citizen.html

Open Source Initiative (2014), http://www.opensource.org/

Oware Society (2014), http://www.oware.org/

Oxford Dictionary of Phrase, Saying and Quotation (1997), Oxford: Oxford University Press

Oxford Dictionary of Quotations (1979), 3rd edn, Oxford: Oxford University Press

Oxford English Dictionary (2013), http://www.oxforddictionaries.com/

Patient Innovation (2014), https://patient-innovation.com/

Pen, J. (1971), *Income Distribution*, Harmondsworth: Penguin Books

Pomerantz, H. (1997), *The Role of Calculators in Math Education*, Urban Systemic Initiative: Comprehensive Partnership for Mathematics and Science Achievement, http://education.ti.com/sites/US/downloads/pdf/therole.pdf

Protz, R. (1978), *Pulling a Fast One*: *What the Brewers Have Done to Your Beer*, London: Pluto Press

Quill and Quire (2012), *World's Biggest Bookstore in Toronto up for rent*, http://www.quillandquire.com/blog/index.php/2012/06/20/worlds-biggest-bookstore-in-toronto-up-for-rent/

Radjou, N., J. Prabhu and S. Ahuja (2012), *Jugaad Innovation: Think Frugal, Be Flexible, Generate Breakthrough Growth*, San Francisco: Jossey Bass

Reinert, H. and E.S. Reinert (2006), 'Creative Destruction in Economics: Nietzsche, Sombart, Schumpeter', in J.G. Backhaus and W. Drechsler (eds), *Friedrich Nietzsche (1844–1900): Economy and Society*, New York: Springer, pp. 55–86

Restart Project (2014), http://therestartproject.org/

Rewald, J. (1978), *Post-Impressionism: From van Gogh to Gauguin*, New York: The Museum of Modern Art

Ries, A. and J. Trout (2001), *Positioning: The Battle for Your Mind*, 2nd edn, McGraw-Hill Professional

Rodrik, D. (2004), *Industrial Policy for the 21st Century*, http://www.hks.harvard.edu/fs/drodrik/Research papers/UNIDOSep.pdf

Rohlfs, J.H., *Bandwagon Effects in High-Technology Industries*, MIT Press, Cambridge MA, 2001

Rosenberg, N., R. Landau and D.C. Mowery (1992), *Technology and the Wealth of Nations*, Stanford, CA: Stanford University Press

Round Table (2014), http://www.roundtable.co.uk/

Rubinstein, A. (1964), *Chopin Waltzes*, New York: RCA Victor Records

Ruskin, J. (1904/1996), *The Works of John Ruskin* (edited by T. Cook and A.

Wedderburn), CD-ROM edn, Cambridge: Cambridge University Press

Salzman, L.F. (1923/1970), *English Industries of the Middle Ages*, London: H. Pordes

Scholes, P.A. (1970), *The Oxford Companion to Music*, 10th edn, Oxford: Oxford University Press

School Trips (2014), www.ukschooltrips.co.uk

Schumacher, E. (1974), *Small is Beautiful*, London: Abacus/Sphere Books

Schumpeter, J.A. (1942), *Capitalism, Socialism and Democracy*, New York/London: Harper

Schumpeter, J.A. (1946), *Kapitalismus, Sozialismus und Demokratie*, translated from English by Dr. Susanne Preiswerk, Bern: Francke

Scitovsky, T. (1976), *The Joyless Economy: An Enquiry into Human Satisfaction and Consumer Dissatisfaction*, Oxford: Oxford University Press

Sen, A.K. (1999), *Commodities and Capabilities*, Delhi: Oxford University Press

Smit, T. (2002), *Eden*, London: Corgi Books

Smith, A. (1776/1904a), *An Inquiry into the Nature and Causes of the Wealth of Nations*, vol. I, London: Methuen

Smith, A. (1776/1904b), *An Inquiry into the Nature and Causes of the Wealth of Nations*, vol. II, London: Methuen

Smithson, R. (2014), http://www.robertsmithson.com/index_.htm

Snow, C.P. (1959), *The Two Cultures*, London: Cambridge University Press

Stanford Medical Center (1998), *Conference Explores Benefits of Art, Music in Health Care*, http://med.stanford.edu/shs/update/archives/mar98/confrnce.html

Stern, N. (2006), *Review on the Economics of Climate Change*, October 30, http://www.occ.gov.uk/activities/stern.htm

Stock, R.M., P. Oliveira and E.A. von Hippel (2013), *Impacts of Hedonic and Utilitarian User Motives on the Innovativeness of User-Developed Solutions*, May 3, available at: http://ssrn.com/abstract=2260436

Stoneman, P. (2010), *Soft Innovation: Economics, Product Aesthetics and the Creative Industries*, Oxford: Oxford University Press

Strotz, R.H. (1957), 'The Empirical Implications of A Utility Tree', *Econometrica*, **25**, 269–80

Swann, G.M.P. (1999), 'Marshall's Consumer as an Innovator' in S. Dow and P. Earl (eds), *Economic Organisation and Economic Knowledge: Essays in Honour of Brian Loasby*, Cheltenham: Edward Elgar Publishing

Swann, G.M.P. (2001a), 'The Demand for Distinction and the Evolution of the Prestige Car', *Journal of Evolutionary Economics*, **11**, 59–75

Swann, G.M.P. (2001b), 'No Wealth But Life: When Does Conventional Wealth Create Ruskinian Wealth', *European Research Studies*, **4**, 5–18

Swann, G.M.P. (2006), *Putting Econometrics in its Place: A New Direction in Applied Economics*, Cheltenham: Edward Elgar Publishing

Swann, G.M.P. (2009a), *The Economics of Innovation: An Introduction*, Cheltenham: Edward Elgar Publishing

Swann, G.M.P. (2009b), *The Economics of Metrology and Measurement*, Report for National Measurement Office and Department for Business, Innovation and Skills, October 14, http://www.bis.gov.uk/assets/nmo/docs/nms/prof-swann-report-econ-measurement-revisited-oct-09.pdf

Swann, G.M.P. (2009c), *Three Perspectives on an Innovation; Thirty years of PC operating systems software*, https://sites.google.com/site/gmpswann/home/cv/recent-papers-unpublished/three-perspectives-on-an-innovation

Swann, G.M.P. (2009d), *Software Marketing and e-Waste*, https://sites.google.com/site/gmpswann/home/cv/recent-papers-unpublished/software-marketing-and-e-waste

Swann, G.M.P. (2010), *The Fall and Rise of the Local Brew*, https://sites.google.com/site/gmpswann/home/cv/recent-papers-unpublished/the-fall-and-rise-of-the-local-brew

Swann, G.M.P. (2012), 'Innovation and the Division of Labour', in T.S. Pitsis, A. Simpson and E. Dehlin (eds), *Handbook Of Organizational And Managerial Innovation*, Cheltenham: Edward Elgar Publishing

Szostak, R. (1999), *Econ-Art: Divorcing Art from Science in Modern Economics*, London: Pluto Press

Taproot Foundation (2014), http://www.taprootfoundation.org/

The Environment and Health Atlas for England and Wales (2014), available at: http://www.envhealthatlas.co.uk/homepage/

Thomis, M.I. (1970), *The Luddites: Machine Breaking in Regency England*, New York: Schocken Books

Thomis, M.I. (ed. 1972), *Luddism in Nottinghamshire*, Thoroton Society Record Series vol. XXVI, London: Phillimore

Tufte, E.R. (1983), *The Visual Display of Quantitative Information*, Cheshire CT: Graphics Press

Tufte, E.R. (1990), *Envisioning Information*, Cheshire CT: Graphics Press

Vaizey, J. (1960), The Brewing Industry 1886–1951: An Economic Study, London: Pitman

Valdez-Cepeda, R.D. and E. Solano-Herrera (1999), 'Self-Affinity of Records of Financial Indexes', *Fractals: Complex Geometry, Patterns, and Scaling in Nature and Society*, **7**, 427–32

Valerio, N. (1988), *Mangiare Italiano: I piatti ricchi della cucina povera*, Milan: Arnoldo Mondadori Editore

Veblen, T. (1898), 'Why is Economics Not an Evolutionary Science', *Quarterly Journal of Economics*, **12**, 373–97

Veblen, T. (1899), *The Theory of the Leisure Class: An Economic Study of*

Institutions, New York: Macmillan

Veblen, T. (1914), *The Instinct of Workmanship: And the State of Industrial Arts*, New York: Macmillan

Victor, P.A. (2008), *Managing without Growth: Slower By Design, Not Disaster*, Cheltenham: Edward Elgar Publishing

Victorian Web (2005), *Rev. William Lee, inventor of the Stocking Frame*, http://www.victorianweb.org/technology/inventors/lee.html

Wall Street Journal (2009), *Paul Volcker: Think More Boldly*, December 14, http://online.wsj.com/news/articles/SB10001424052748704825504574586330960597134

Wikiquote (2014), *Linus Pauling*, http://en.wikiquote.org/wiki/Linus_Pauling

Wikipedia (2013a), *Amazon*, http://en.wikipedia.org/wiki/Amazon.com

Wikipedia (2013b), *Big Society*, http://en.wikipedia.org/wiki/Big_Society

Wikipedia (2013c), *Eudaimonia*, http://en.wikipedia.org/wiki/Eudaimonia

Wikipedia (2013d), *Home Economics*, http://en.wikipedia.org/wiki/Home_economics

Wikipedia (2014a), *Association football culture*, http://en.wikipedia.org/wiki/Association_football_culture

Wikipedia (2014b), *Bartok*, http://en.wikipedia.org/wiki/Bartok

Wikipedia (2014c), *Citizen Science*, http://en.wikipedia.org/wiki/Citizen_science

Wikipedia (2014d), *Detroit Industry Murals*, http://en.wikipedia.org/wiki/Detroit_Industry_Murals

Wikipedia (2014e), *Gregor Mendel*, http://en.wikipedia.org/wiki/Gregor_Mendel

Wikipedia (2014f), *Henrietta Swan Leavitt*, http://en.wikipedia.org/wiki/Henrietta_Swan_Leavitt

Wikipedia (2014g), *Home Advantage*, http://en.wikipedia.org/wiki/Home_advantage

Wikipedia (2014h), *Ithaca Hours*, http://en.wikipedia.org/wiki/Ithaca_Hours

Wikipedia (2014i), *Local Currency*, http://en.wikipedia.org/wiki/Local_currency

Wikipedia (2014j), *Mary Anning*, http://en.wikipedia.org/wiki/Mary_Anning

Wikipedia (2014k), *Michael Faraday*, http://en.wikipedia.org/wiki/Michael_Faraday

Wikipedia (2014m), *Monopoly (game)*, http://en.wikipedia.org/wiki/Monopoly_(game)

Wikipedia (2014n), *Pro Bono*, http://en.wikipedia.org/wiki/Pro_bono

Wikipedia (2014p), *Relocation of Wimbledon F.C. to Milton Keynes*, http://en.wikipedia.org/wiki/Relocation_of_Wimbledon_F.C._to_Milton_Keynes

256   *References*

Wikipedia (2014q), *Robert Owen*, http://en.wikipedia.org/wiki/Robert_Owen
Wikipedia (2014r), *SMS language*, http://en.wikipedia.org/wiki/SMS_language
Wikipedia (2014s), *Syms Corporation*, http://en.wikipedia.org/wiki/Syms_Corporation
Wikipedia (2014t), *Tiki-Taka*, http://en.wikipedia.org/wiki/Tiki-taka
Wikipedia (2014u), *William Sealy Gosset*, http://en.wikipedia.org/wiki/William_Sealy_Gosset
Williams, R. (2000), *Lost Icons: Reflections on Cultural Bereavement*, London: T&T Clark
Williams, R. (2009), *Human Well-Being and Economic Decision-Making*, A Keynote Address at TUC Economics Conference, November 16, http://rowanwilliams.archbishopofcanterbury.org/articles.php/767/human-well-being-and-economic-decision-making
Williams, R. (2012), *Faith in the Public Square*, London: Bloomsbury
Young, T. (2007), 'Vista poses environmental dangers: 10 million PCs could be discarded over the next two years', *Computing*, February 8, http://www.computing.co.uk/computing/news/2174400/vista-poses-environmental
Youngner, R.C. (2006), *Industry in Art: Pittsburgh, 1812 to 1920*, University of Pittsburgh Press
Yunnus, M. (1998), *Banker to the Poor*, London: Aurum Press
Zheng, Y. and S.K. Tok (2007), *'Harmonious Society' and 'Harmonious World': China's Policy Discourse Under Hu Jintao*, China Policy Institute Briefing Series, 26, China Policy Institute, University of Nottingham

Index